MARKET FORCES IN PLANNED ECONOMIES

Market Forces in Planned Economies

Proceedings of a Conference Held by the
International Economic Association in Moscow,
USSR

Edited by

Oleg T. Bogomolov

NEW YORK UNIVERSITY PRESS
Washington Square, New York

First published in the U.S.A. in 1990 by
NEW YORK UNIVERSITY PRESS
Washington Square
New York, N.Y. 10003

Library of Congress Cataloging-in-Publication Data
Market forces in planned economies : proceedings of a conference
    held by the International Economic Association at Moscow,
    USSR/edited by Oleg T. Bogomolov.
        p.   cm.
    Includes bibliographical references.
    ISBN 0–8147–1148–0
    1. Economic policy—Congresses.   2. Mixed economy—Congresses.
3. Central planning—Congresses.   I. Bogomolov, Oleg Timofeevich.
II. International Economic Association.
HB73.M246   1990
338.9—dc20   89–49638
                                                                  CIP

Printed in Hong Kong

Contents

The International Economic Association

A non-profit organisation with purely scientific aims, the International Economic Association (IEA) was founded in 1950. It is in fact a federation of national economic associations and presently includes fifty-eight such professional organisations from all parts of the world. Its basic purpose is the development of economics as an intellectual discipline. Its approach recognises a diversity of problems, systems and values in the world and also takes note of methodological diversities.

The IEA has, since its creation, tried to fulfil that purpose by promoting mutual understanding of economists from the West and the East as well as from the North and the South through the organisation of scientific meetings and common research programmes and by means of publications on problems of current importance. During its thirty-seven years of existence, it has organised seventy-nine round-table conferences for specialists on topics ranging from fundamental theories to methods and tools of analysis and major problems of the present-day world. Eight triennial World Congresses have also been held, which have regularly attracted the participation of a great many economists from all over the world.

The Association is governed by a Council, composed of representatives of all member associations, and by a fifteen-member Executive Committee which is elected by the Council. The present Executive Committee (1986–89) is composed as follows:

President:	Professor Amartya Sen, India
Vice-President:	Professor Béla Csikós-Nagy, Hungary
Treasurer:	Professor Luis Angel Rojo, Spain
Past President:	Professor Kenneth J. Arrow, USA

Other members:	Professor Edmar Lisboa Bacha, Brazil
	Professor Ragnar Bentzel, Sweden
	Professor Oleg T. Bogomolov, USSR
	Professor Silvio Borner, Switzerland
	Professor P. R. Brahmananda, India
	Professor Phyllis Deane, United Kingdom

Professor Luo Yuanzheng, China
Professor Edmond Malinvaud, France
Professor Luigi Pasinetti, Italy
Professor Don Patinkin, Israel
Professor Takashi Shiraishi, Japan
Professor Tigran S. Khachaturov, USSR
(deceased 1989)

Adviser: Professor Mohammed Germouni, Morocco
Secretary-General: Professor Jean-Paul Fitoussi, France
General Editor: Mr Michael Kaser, United Kingdom
Adviser to General Editor: Professor Sir Austin Robinson, United
                            Kingdom
Conference Editor: Dr Patricia M. Hillebrandt, United Kingdom

The Association has also been fortunate in having secured the following outstanding economists to serve as President: Gottfried Haberler (1950–53), Howard S. Ellis (1953–56), Erik Lindahl (1956–59), E. A. G. Robinson (1959–62), G, Ugo Papi (1962–65), Paul A. Samuelson (1965–68), Erik Lundberg (1968–71), Fritz Machlup (1971–74), Edmond Malinvaud (1974–77), Shigeto Tsuru (1977–80), Victor L. Urquidi (1980–83), Kenneth J. Arrow (1983–86).

The activities of the Association are mainly funded from the subscriptions of members and grants from a number of organisations, including continuing support from UNESCO.

Acknowledgements

The conference was organised for the International Economic Association by the Institute of Economics of the World Socialist System of the USSR Academy of Sciences and the Soviet Committee for European Security and Cooperation with financial support from the *Financial Times East European Markets* (UK), the Soros Foundation (USA) and *Yomiuri* newspaper (Japan). It was held in the conference facilities of the Council for Mutual Economic Assistance, Moscow, by kind permission of the Executive Secretary, Mr Vycheslav Sychev, who welcomed participants at the opening session.

The International Economic Association wishes to thank all those who enabled the conference to take place.

Thanks are also expressed to the International Social Science Council under whose auspices the publication programme is carried out and to UNESCO for its financial support.[*]

Programme Committee:

Oleg Bogomolov ⎱
Sukhamoy Chakravarty ⎰ co-Chairmen
Pawel Bozyk
László Csaba
Gerhard Fink
Ed Hewett
Michael Kaser
Marie Lavigne
Luo Yuanzheng

[*] Grant number 1988–89/DG/7.7.2/SUB.16 (SHS).

List of Participants

Academician Leonid I. Abalkin, Institute of Economics, USSR Academy of Sciences, Moscow, USSR.

Academician Abel G. Aganbegyan, Social Sciences Department, USSR Academy of Sciences, Moscow, USSR.

Academician Oleg T. Bogomolov, Institute of Economics of the World Socialist System, USSR Academy of Sciences, Moscow, USSR.

Professor Morris Bornstein, University of Michigan, USA.

Professor Włodzimierz Brus, University of Oxford, UK.

Dr A Bykov, Institute of Economics of the World Socialist System, USSR Academy of Sciences, Moscow, USSR.

Professor Sukhamoy Chakravarty, Delhi School of Economics, University of Delhi, India.

Professor Ante Čičin-Šain, Institute of Economics, Zagreb, Yugoslavia.

Dr László Csaba, Institute for Economic Informatics and Market Research, Budapest, Hungary.

Professor Béla Csikós-Nagy, Economic Advisory Board, Government of Hungary.

Professor Dong Fureng, Institute of Economics, Chinese Academy of Social Sciences, Beijing, China.

Dr Ruben Evstigneev, Institute of Economics of the World Socialist System, USSR Academy of Sciences, Moscow, USSR.

Dr Karel Dyba, Institute for Forecasting, Czechoslovak Academy of Sciences, Prague, Czechoslovakia.

Professor Mohammed Germouni, University of Casablanca, Morocco.

Dr John P. Hardt, Library of Congress, Washington DC, USA.

Professor Karl-Hans Hartwig, Westfälische Wilhelms-Universität, Münster, FRG

Dr Patricia M. Hillebrandt, University of Reading, UK.

Ing. Miroslav Hrnčiř, Institute of Economics of the Czechoslovak Academy of Sciences.

Mr Taniguchi Ichiro, *Yomiuri*, Japan.

Mr Michael Kaser, Institute of Russian, Soviet and East European Studies, University of Oxford, UK.

Academician Tigran S. Khachaturov, Adviser to IEA Executive Committee, Moscow, USSR.

Professor Peter Knirsch, Free University of Berlin, FRG.

Academician Janós Kornai, Hungarian Academy of Sciences, Budapest, Hungary and Harvard University, USA.

Dr Karel Kouba, Institute for Forecasting, Czechoslovak Academy of Sciences, Prague, Czechoslovakia.

Professor Kazimierz Laski, University of Linz and Vienna Institute of Comparative Economic Studies, Austria.

Professor Marie Lavigne, Centre d'Economie Internationale des Pays Socialistes and University of Paris I, Panthéon-Sorbonne, Paris, France.

Dr Edwin Lim, World Bank Representative in China.

Mr Cyril Lin, St Antony's College, Oxford, UK.

Ms Margie Lindsay, *East European Markets, Financial Times*, UK.

Professor Luo Yuanzheng, Beijing College of Economics, China.

Professor Carl McMillan, Carleton University, Ottawa, Canada.

Professor Alec Nove, Centre for Development Studies, University of Glasgow, UK.

Professor Mario Nuti, European University Institute, Florence, Italy.

Professor Gur Ofer, Brookings Institution, Washington DC, USA and Hebrew University of Jerusalem, Israel.

Professor S. Ohtsu, Ryukohu University, Kyoto, Japan.

Professor Don Patinkin, Hebrew University of Jerusalem, Israel.

Professor Nikolay Ya. Petrakov, Central Economic-Mathematical Institute, USSR Academy of Sciences, Moscow, USSR.

Dr Urszula Płowiec, Foreign Trade Research Institute, Warsaw, Poland.

Professor Sir Austin Robinson, University of Cambridge, UK.

Professor Zdzisław Sadowski, University of Warsaw, Poland.

Professor Tsuneaki Sato, Faculty of Economics, Nihon University, Tokyo, Japan.

Professor Hans Schilar, Central Institute of Economic Research, GDR Academy of Sciences, Berlin, GDR.

Professor Nikolay P. Shmelev, Institute of USA and Canada, USSR Academy of Sciences, Moscow, USSR.

Professor Gleb V. Smirnov, Institute of Africa, USSR Academy of Sciences, Moscow, USSR.

Dr Pekka Sutela, Department of Economics, University of Helsinki, Finland.

Dr Márton Tardos, Financial Research Ltd., Budapest, Hungary.

Professor Aleksander Vacić, Division for Economic Analysis and Projections, United Nations Economic Commission for Europe, Geneva, Switzerland.

Professor Dragomir Vojnić, Institute of Economics, Zagreb, Yugoslavia.

Dr Thomas Wolf, International Monetary Fund, Washington DC, USA.

Dr Leon Z. Zevin, Institute of Economics of World Socialist Systems, USSR Academy of Sciences, Moscow, USSR.

Abbreviations and Acronyms

CMEA	Council for Mutual Economic Assistance
CMS	Constant market share
CoCom	Coordination Committee for Multilateral Export Controls
CCP	Chinese Communist Party
CPE	Centrally planned economy
CPSU	Communist Party of the Soviet Union
CRCE	Centre for Research in Communist Economies (UK)
CREES	Centre for Russian and East European Studies (University of Burmingham, UK)
DCC	Differentiated currency coefficients
ECE	Economic Commission for Europe
EEC	European Economic Community
FRG	Federal Republic of Germany
FTO	Foreign trade organisation
GATT	General Agreement on Tariffs and Trade
GDP	Gross Domestic Product
GDR	German Democratic Republic
HCB	Hungarian Credit Bank
HNB	Hungarian National Bank
HSWP CC	Hungarian Socialist Worker's Party Central Committee
IMF	International Monetary Fund
LDC	Less-developed country
MCP	Modified central planning
NCCB	National Commercial and Credit Bank (Hungary)
NIC	Newly industrialised country
NEM	New Economic Mechanism (Hungary)
NEP	New Economic Policy (USSR)
NIE	Newly industrialised economy
OECD	Organisation for Economic Cooperation and Development
R & D	Research and development
RE	Reformed economy

RMB	Renminbi (Chinese currency)
RSE	Reformed socialist economy
SFR	Socialist Federal Republic (of Yugoslavia)
TCP	Traditional central planning
TES	Traditional economic system (of socialism)
WIDER	World Institute for Development and Economic Research

Introduction

Oleg Bogomolov

A radically new understanding of the role of market forces in the economy and their interaction with central planning is gaining momentum in the Soviet Union and other countries of Eastern Europe. For a number of reasons the economists of these countries were in the past deprived of the opportunity to carry out fundamental research into such issues as markets, competition, equilibrium prices and inflation. Today favourable conditions have been created for such studies and there is accordingly, a growing desire to become familiar with the latest developments in Western economic thought on the theory of markets. In this connection, the International Economic Association (IEA) convened a round-table conference in Moscow (28–30 March 1989) at which well-known economists from different countries discussed various theoretical and practical aspects of this problem.

I commend to the attention of readers the papers presented at the conference, as well as the comments on them by discussants. They demonstrate the complexity of the transition from a command-administrative economy to one of the market type and the consequent necessity to elaborate conceptually how to achieve such a transition.

The conference started with consideration of the theory of markets in planned economies. Academician Leonid Abalkin (USSR) (Chapter 1 in this volume) drew attention to the fact that modern socialism did not reject the economic forms which had taken shape during preceding stages, but rather inherited their best characteristics. In this context he stressed that market relations were not alien to socialism, but were immanent features of its economic system. The indispensible role of the market resided, in his opinion, in that it alone ensured a feedback mechanism without which there was no stability or efficiency of any organic economic system. Realisation of the laws of the market brought elements of competition into the system of economic relations; it orientated production towards the satisfaction of actual public needs and minimisation of costs; it also formed an economic basis for a subsequent democratisation of social life. At the same time, Abalkin contended that a market can have a socialist nature as determined by the 'socialist type of ownership' for the means of production. In conclusion he noted that the process of the formation of such a market in the USSR would be long and difficult: there were problems associated with the transition itself but also a general unpreparedness for a market system because people lacked a developed commercial culture.

Professors Brus (UK) and Laski (Austria) dealt with the interrelationship between the commodity market and the capital market in the context of the economic reform in Hungary (Chapter 2). In particular, they drew attention to the presence of a direct link between the exclusion of a capital market and weakening of the commodity market. In their opinion, the Hungarian experience had revealed the vulnerability of any reform concept which limited the controllable market to commodities. From the standpoint of the efficiency of the new economic system, Brus and Laski went on to pose interesting questions on conditions for the creation of a labour market in the reformed economies: the central issue was the dominance of a single employer in the economy, which could hinder the regulatory function of wages in changing demand and supply in the labour market. Their conclusion was unambiguous: as changes in ownership take place a sound self-regulating economy inevitably requires distribution on the basis of market criteria, not only of goods, but also of capital and manpower.

Academician Kornai (Hungary) referred to the discontinuous and even somewhat random character of the ongoing economic reforms which was inevitably reflected in their result (Chapter 3). Having described the evolution of the private sector in the reformed economies, he stressed that the 'explosion' of the activity of this sector in China, Hungary and Poland could be regarded as the most tangible result of the reforms. At the same time, it revealed serious contradictions in the behaviour of private firms which was not always socially positive and which, in turn, was a response to the uncertain prospects for their own development. Kornai also analysed the essence and methods of resistance of bureaucratic forces to the various socio-economic transformations and the forms of a social coordination which become a counterweight to purely market or purely administrative mechanisms.

Professor Sadowski (Poland) and Michael Kaser (UK) formulated for the conference a new role for planning which had to be qualitatively different when decentralised decision making was expanded in the economic sphere.

Sadowski (Chapter 4) noted that the transition from an economic system based on central planning to one based primarily on the play of market forces, as envisaged by the reform, necessitated the solution of problems which were very complicated from both a scientific and a practical point of view. Central planning in its traditional form proved to be incapable of producing an optimal distribution of resources which, in his opinion, could not but cause doubts as to the necessity of having central planning in any of its forms at all. He rejected that conclusion on the grounds that the very meaning of the reforms carried out at the present time was a search for a new qualitative shape for a system which should remain socialist in its basic orientation towards objectives of social justice. Although the definition of the latter presents certain difficulties, they should be considered obligatory only for the government and would be implemented by planned influence on certain market variables, without interference with the behaviour of individual production entities. Having described in detail the difficulties of the transition period (from one system to the other), Sadowski called for a pragmatic approach to overcome them. The movement along a difficult and narrow route away from a shortage economy was for him more important for a successful realisation of the new concept of planning than an *a priori* detailed understanding of it.

Mr Kaser (Chapter 5) devoted his presentation to a number of particular problems, whose solution defines the success of the implementation of market mechanisms in socialist countries. Drawing upon the well-known article by J. Drewnowski[1] and the current state of the reforms in these countries, Kaser analysed these problems of transition within a concept of duality where certain economic activities were subordinated both to central planning and to market forces. He illustrates his idea by examples from the practice of several socialist countries, the dualism of the situation of enterprises subject simultaneously to centrally imposed tasks (such as obligatory state contracts) and to profit maximisation by marketing of output in excess of the plan-contracted level according to market forces. Bearing in mind this dualism, Kaser put interesting questions on the optimisation of production programmes and perspective proportions between fixed and flexible prices, both of which would long have to coexist at least in the USSR. In particular, he noted that "everywhere the persistence of the industrial ministry system and the protection from foreign competition still exercised allows monopoly power which in turn wards the government away from price decontrol".

The problem of price formation in the light of economic reforms was one of the most vividly debated topics at the conference. All the discussants on this issue were of the same opinion – namely, that the spirit of the reforms required decentralised price formation according to market criteria.

Professor Csikós-Nagy (Hungary) presented a profound analysis of the evolution of the socialist theory of prices (Chapter 7), which at present is essentially a search for an optimal combination of the spheres of action of market prices and centrally-controlled prices in accordance with the democratically determined social priorities.

Professor Bornstein (USA) (Chapter 6), having presented a review of the Soviet price system, was sceptical of the feasibility of the initial official version of the price reform in the USSR: it was merely a centralised revision of their present levels and relativities bearing no relationship to market criteria.

Professor Petrakov (USSR) defended the alternative version of the price reform, as a phased departure from centralised price formation which retained state control over prices in key sectors of the economy and of the production of consumer goods and services of a high social significance.

The round table also discussed the role of financial institutions in money creation in the course of the reforms. Professor Čičin-Šain (Yugoslavia) stated (Chapter 8) that the main functions of central and commercial banks in the socialist market economy should be similar to those of the corresponding institutions of a developed capitalist economy. Having described the intrinsic features of the reform of the banking system in Yugoslavia, he drew attention to the grave difficulties of its banks in efficient intermediation role. Until recently most of the banks could grant inexpensive credits without taking into consideration the real structure and price of bank deposits. The bank activities of the banking system were assumed to be backed by society as a whole, which in practice means the government. The Yugoslav situation was changing; it is expected that the introduction of the share-holding form of ownership will result in a more efficient management of the activities of the banks and in a greater responsibility for the allocation of money resources. Dr Tardos (Hungary) illustrated the Hungarian experience in the formation of a banking system adequate for the market-type organisation of the economy (Chapter 9). He notably assessed of the experience of two years of functioning of the new banking system in Hungary, as well as proposals for its improvement.

Dealing with the interrelationship between the progress of domestic economic transformations and the ability of the reformed economies to increase efficiency in external economic relations, Dr Wolf (IMF) (Chapter 10) produced a detailed analysis of the expansion of the autonomy of enterprises in the foreign trade sphere. His report provided a full picture of the results attained and difficulties in this area, especially in the regulation of monetary relations and the interaction of domestic and foreign-trade prices. Wolf showed clearly, and it was the principal conclusion of his paper, that the efficiency of foreign trade reform in socialist countries and their integration into the world economic environment depended in the final analysis on the success of the whole complex of their internal reforms.

Professor Shmelev (USSR) spoke in this respect about prospects for 'opening up' the Soviet economy, for which a number of preconditions would have to be created. In his opinion, such preconditions are now either lacking or only in a formative stage. He sought to distinguish between current problems and long-term objectives. To resolve the current problems (among which he singled out the disequilibrium of the domestic consumer market, the threat of inflation and the high budget deficit), in addition to the utilisation of domestic resources, believed it necessary to combine fuller use of the opportunities of international credit with measures to rationalise imports. Shmelev also offered a prescription of practical measures (first of all the introduction of the wholesale trade and a partial convertibility of the rouble) which, if realised, could ensure the 'openness' of the Soviet economy in the long term.

Lively debates took place at the conference on the problems of plan and market in their application to the experience of developing countries.

Professor Chakravarty (India) (Chapter 11), referring to Indian experience, defended the thesis of a basic compatibility of planning and market forces. In his opinion, the former was frequently improperly understood as an excessive centralisation. At the same time, a mere market organisation of the economy was far from ideal. In any case, the process of market accommodation cannot fully replace an appropriate form of planning. He thinks that for India, for example, planning was necessary for the protection of the environment, for the rapid promotion of education, science and technology, as well as for the implementation of innovations enabling the effective employ-ment of the labour force.

Professor Dong Fureng (China) (Chapter 12) discussed the issue of the compatibility of public ownership with the market mechanism. The incorporation of the latter into the Chinese economy had caused certain difficulties but it was the problem of ownership which re-mained the most difficult problem for any socialist country undertak-ing economic reform. He actively supported the need for a plurality of forms of property, in which public property represented by cooperative and state forms would occupy the dominating position but not excluding enterprises belonging to private owners.

Great interest was shown in the discussion of the last topic of the Moscow Round Table – the international consequences of the re-forms going on in socialist countries. In Academician Bogomolov's paper, attention was focused on *perestroika* in the Soviet economy and its influence on East–West relations (Chapter 13). The problems of the shift from a command-administrative system to the planned-market type under conditions of the economy in a state of crisis and the chronic shortage of many goods were vividly debated. The transition could be facilitated by an expansion of East–West econ-omic relations. The participants in the discussion came to the conclu-sion that good prospects could be opened up by industrial co-operation and the establishment of joint ventures, as well as the organisation in Soviet territory of special tax-free zones of joint entrepreneurship with preferential legal and economic conditions. Enterprises operating in these zones could have the opportunity of making transactions in freely convertible currencies and at prices operating in Western markets, thereby bypassing the continuing problem of incompatibility with the domestic economic mechanism. On the subject of the activation of economic partnership with the West, conversion of military industry to civilian production was mentioned as conducive to the reduction of constraints on the import opportunities of the USSR. Finding a balance of interest in inter-national politics was today a major factor in the intensification of business cooperation. In turn, expansion and deepening of the latter enhanced the desirability of political détente.

Professor Lavigne (France) discussed in her paper (Chapter 14) the conditions and problems of the incorporation of the socialist countries into the world economy. Having listed these conditions, she noted that there was still insufficient preparedness in these countries for active involvement in world economic processes. For their part

Western governments and business were sceptical on the prospects for reform in socialist countries. Pointing to the centrifugal tendencies among CMEA membership in Europe, Lavigne rejected the view that these were of any benefit to the West. In her opinion, a strong socialist community with a market orientation would serve the interests of the West to a greater extent than the disintegrating of the present system. Lavigne also raised the question of the introduction of convertibility of their currencies as a prerequisite for participation in the world economic system. She believed that internal convertibility (for residents) should be introduced as soon as possible, whereas external convertibility was less urgent because it depended on the commodity convertibility of the national currency. In principle, she supported the idea of special economic zones, having noted, though, that outside competition would yield results only where competitive relations were rooted in the domestic market.

An active part in the discussion and a valuable contribution to the high scholarly level of the conference was made by such well-known specialists as A. Nove and Sir Austin Robinson (UK), J. Hardt (USA), M. Nuti (Italy), D. Patinkin and G. Ofer (Israel), P. Sutela (Finland), T. Sato (Japan), C. Lin (Philippines), P. Knirsch and K-H. Hartwig (FRG), E. Lim (World Bank), Luo Yuanzheng (China), M. Germouni (Morocco), L. Csaba (Hungary), A. Vacić (ECE), K. Dyba and K. Kouba (Czechoslovakia), H. Schilar (GDR), U. Płowiec (Poland), D. Vojnić (Yugoslavia), the late Academician T. Khachaturov, L. Zevin, G. Smirnov and A. Bykov (USSR).

The papers of the conference published in this book enable the reader to obtain a remarkably full impression of the entire spectrum of the problems now facing the economies of the USSR, Hungary, Poland, China and those of some other countries which are taking the road towards the use of markets forces while retaining certain forms of state control over them. Up to now a successful and relatively painless way to dismantle the command system of management and stimulate the market mechanisms of self-regulation has not been found. However, as the conference has shown, a growing number of prerequisites for achieving this goal are being identified both in theory and in practice through the accumulation of experience in carrying out the economic reforms.

Note

1. Professor Shmelev's paper does not appear in the present volume but is published in Fink, G. (ed.), *The Impact of Governments on East–West Economic Relations* (London: Macmillan, 1990).

Reference

Drewnowski, J. (1961) 'Economic Theory of Socialism: A Suggestion for Reconsideration', *Journal of Political Economy* (August) pp. 341-54

Part I

The Theory of Markets in a Planned Economy

1 The Market in the Socialist Economic System

Leonid Abalkin
INSTITUTE OF ECONOMICS, USSR ACADEMY OF
SCIENCES, MOSCOW

1 INTRODUCTION

The last decades of the twentieth century are marked by profound
qualitative changes in world-wide social progress. Among the most
important processes today the renewal of socialism should be singled
out. Socialism has been confronted by historic challenge, the core of
which is the testing of socialism for its renewal capacity, its capability
to create a system combining the highest production efficiency with
social values and ideals, a flexible system, ready to adopt achievements of scientific and technological progress and to meet constantly
changing social needs and requirements.

The renewal of socialism is a global though uneven process. Reconstruction of the soviet society is an integral link of this complex
and multidifferentiated process. It demands radical rethinking and
renewal of theory and politics, drastic transformations in all spheres
of public life, the economy, social and spiritual aspects.

Economic reforms, carried out in socialist countries, cover the
problem of commodity production, that of value and of the market
are among the key issues today. But it would be incorrect to identify
the whole set of problems within the transformation process of the
socialist economic system as a mere transition to market methods of
economic regulation. The model of economic system we are planning
to create as a result of *perestroika*, is to combine:

- the highest production efficiency with humanitarian goals

3

- deeper differentiation in remuneration of labour, depending on final results of production performance, with sophisticated systems of social guarantees
- freeing labour power surplus from the production sphere with full and efficient employment;
- revival of the cooperative movement and large-scale development of the cooperative basis with consolidation and renewal of general public sector in our economy
- creation of a socialist market, its growing influence on production work perfecting the methods of centralised planned management.

The process of creation and development of the socialist market should be viewed within the framework of this model, as its integral part.

2 THE RENEWAL OF THEORETICAL CONCEPTS

Reconstruction of the society requires radical renewal of theoretical notions about socialism and further development, particularisation and correction of the concepts of the Marxist–Leninist economic theory. We are working out (and to a certain extent have achieved some progress in this connection) a number of theoretical ideas and tenets, qualitatively disclosing the new face of socialism. These theoretical concepts take into consideration the realities of the modern world and incorporate revision of previously formed concepts about theoretical dogmas. Naturally, formation of new concepts about socialism is accompanied by hot debate, discussion and struggle between new and old, in the course of which new economic thinking is being shaped.

Modern approaches to the economic structure of socialism are based on critical analysis of historical experience, on studying the positive results of the early stage of the New Economic Policy (NEP) as well as the experience of other socialist countries. In this connection Lenin's theoretical heritage, especially his last works, where he comes to the conclusion about the necessity 'to accept fundamental change in our whole concept of socialism', plays a great role in working out modern ideas and approaches in the field of socialist economy.

As a result we can form some important conclusions. First, it is necessary to acknowledge that socialism accepts and inherits the best previous historical forms rather than blankly rejecting all of them, because the element of continuity, heritage of rational experience, accumulated by human civilisation, is a distinguishing feature of social progress. It's quite significant, that this inheritance applies not only to the sphere of material culture, but to the use of economic forms, proved and tested by multicultural experience (such as market, cooperatives, leasing, etc.) including democratic institutions and moral norms.

With this approach to the problem it becomes evident that the market is not a pure capitalist economy phenomenon but is common to very different stages of social progress. Strictly speaking, such a conclusion is not unexpected for Marxism. It is well known, for example, that Marx proved that 'commodity production and commodity turnover are phenomena characteristic to different models of production, though with varied output volumes and significance'. From this derives the conclusion that commodity forms, including the market, exist in various social systems and enjoy common general basic features as well as manifesting their own differences and particularities connected with the nature of concrete social structure or the level of social development.

On this theoretical basis another no less major conclusion was reached. Commodity relations, including the market, are far from being alien to socialism. On the contrary, they constitute immanent features of socialist economic structure. Absence of at least fairly well-shaped commodity relations means that either it is developing under extreme conditions or its immanent economic relations are deformed. Normal natural development of the socialist economic system assumes strengthening, expansion and concrete manifestation of common features and symptoms of commodity production in general, including the market.

Certainly, these common features and signs function and reveal themselves in specific socialist forms, thus putting before science and practice quite a complicated task to separate them from each other and distinguish these two moments – namely general content and specific concrete forms of commodity production and market.

Clear understanding of the fact that enterprises of both public and cooperative sectors in our economy are commodity producers of a socialist nature, plays the prime role for elaboration of the whole set of the problems under consideration in this paper. Each of those enterprises and sectors represents quite an autonomous link in the economic system and should perform on the basis of business relations, self-efficiency and self-financing. As a result of this move-ment, social product and its components follow the law of the market with all the consequences stemming from it.

On the whole, recognition of commodity models and immanence of the market in socialism is indivisibly connected with the analysis of the system of relations of socialist property, economic interests, their complex, contradictory structure and the functioning of these interests as incentives for the economic activity of individuals.

Lately we have also been witnessing an elaboration of notions about the complex, multiform system of economic ties and relations in the structure of the national economy. Alongside the traditional forms of state and cooperative enterprises, new types of cooper-atives, enterprises and farms on lease, share-based forms of pro-duction units, banks and other offices have been created. This process is at the very starting point, but even now analysis of these trends encourages us to forecast further considerable sophistication and spread of the economic structure of socialism, thus enriching our concepts about the structure and directions of development of the socialist market.

3   THE SOCIALIST MARKET AND ITS FUNCTIONS

In contemporary scientific literature, political and scientific materials there are different meanings of the term 'market'. Sometimes these meanings are very broad, describing types of economic relations which do not correspond to the strict traditional determination of the market as an economic category. According to traditional under-standing, which we use here in this paper, the market is viewed as a certain form or type of economic relations and ties, characterised by direct relations between producers and consumers, free and volun-tary choice of business partners, and economic competition among producers. In this sense 'market' means rejection of a system based on rigid, command control over the development of economic re-lations and so-to-say 'follow the order' management of national economy.

This consideration must be taken into account both from a theor-etical and practical approach. Considering the market as a certain type of economic relations, it is necessary to underline that today the market is not equal to the traditional classical free market which existed at the beginning of the capitalist era.

The free classical market of the nineteenth century does not exist in any country now. So mechanical opposition of the market to the planned economy can be handy for teaching purposes, but this comparison cannot reveal all the complexity and contradictory character of the present world.

The scale of modern production, the crucial developments in the technical basis of production, the high level of socialisation both in national and world economies are transforming the place, role and functions of the market. John K. Galbraith was probably right when he insisted that 'the cost and associated risk can be greatly reduced if the state pays for more exalted technical development or guarantees a market for the technically advanced product' (Galbraith, 1967, p. 5).

Recent reanimation of monetarism does not contradict this presumption. Present processes, going on in western countries, are modifying forms, methods and goals of the state regulation of the economy but are not diminishing the economic role of the state.

While analysing the problems of the socialist market it is necessary to identify its social specifics – that is, the features that determine its socialist nature. This issue is the subject for numerous discussions, but this does not exclude the possibility of outlining some of the most important features which reveal the socialist nature of the market – and one should note that all of them are determined by its incorporation into the economic system of socialism rather than by market itself.

Among these features are:

- the functioning of enterprises and other economic bodies without hired labour while workers or work collectives are real masters of the means of production
- the system of social guarantees and social protection of the worker or work collectives; so, development of the market does not create conditions under which the human being or the collective are defenceless against the market forces
- the combination of the socialist market mechanisms with the developed system of planning regulation of the national economy based mainly on economic methods of such regulation.

The presence of certain features listed above, not only in socialist but in western countries as well, is not a significant argument for the exclusion of these features as *characteristic peculiarities, immanent to the socialist market*. Here, as well as in this paper in general, mechanical opposition of different social types is considered unacceptable.

The outstanding leading role of the market in development of the economic system of socialism is determined by its essential functions. The market provides the feedback system, and today it has been theoretically proved that this feedback mechanism is an integral part of any organic system, including the socialist economy, developing on the basis of objective laws. This is supported by historical experience as well, showing that attempts to substitute the feedback system with a command-administrative layout leads to disproportions in the economic system of socialism, deficits and loss of economic incentives.

With the development of the socialist market, elements of competition and emulation must be introduced into the system of economic ties. Only their active development can orient production towards the fulfilment of public needs and the minimisation of costs which is proved by practice. In the circumstances of economic competition, production is oriented towards meeting customers' demands, renovation and high quality. Economic competition, developing on the basis of the socialist market, stimulates individual cost reduction by the producers towards a lower level than that which is determined by the market.

Lastly, the emphasis must be put on close interconnection between the socialist market and the economic basis, which is vitally important for continuing economic life and the implementation of principles of independence and freedom of economic units as well as the democratisation of society. The laws of the market are strict, but they are incompatible with any administrative attempts to interfere with the economic functioning of enterprises. These laws are stimulating initiative and socialist enterpreneurship – that is, the qualities without which it is impossible to create a highly efficient economy.

In the conditions of a developed market, a consumer (an individual or enterprise) is free to choose how to dispose of his or her income, and without this it is impossible fully to realise the qualitatively changed position of individuals engaged in socialist production. This freedom of choice excludes any command-administrative control over distribution and creates an economic basis for real freedom of personality. Surely, the socialist nature of the market is determined by the socialist character of ownership of the means of production. At the same time the existence of the market is a necessary condition for the successful functioning of the socialist property, the realisation of the potential and advantages of this property.

4 THE STRUCTURE OF THE MARKET AND METHODS OF ITS REGULATION

The structure of the contemporary market consists of various components, including organic interaction between domestic and world markets. The commodity market serves as a basis of this structure including markets of means of production, consumer goods and, besides, various paid services.

Certain theoretical problems also exist in this sphere, demanding distinct discrimination between market and non-market forms of economic relations and the movement of inner elements of social production. It should be stressed that not every type of exchange means market relations. Even the movement of products through the process of buying and selling does not sufficiently prove the existence of a market. Thus, under a rationing system of foodstuff supply or material and technical resource allocation, when all suppliers and consumers, the volume and list of articles to be delivered are known in advance, money payments have a purely formalised character. In this case, strictly speaking, we have no market; regulation of economic relations is non-market, highly administrative.

The transition to the market economy means establishing relations with no preliminary rationing allocation of products. This does not mean, of course, that the wholesale trade will cease to exist, but it will play its role in the next necessary condition: it will be a trade mediator, an agent of selling and buying, not an element of the allocation system. Only in this case the realisation of the value of a given good, which takes place in exchange, becomes a condition and prerequisite of the realisation of its use value, which occurs in consumption (personal or productive).

Currently an active formation of consumer goods market is being carried out, first steps are made in order to create a real market of the means of production. Various kinds of services are becoming still more deeply involved in the system of market relations.

Now we can speak about first steps in the direction of creating a market for securities and investment resources. In this case we also face a lot of complex questions both in theory and in the practical establishment of such a market. Still it seems quite obvious that we have no theoretical grounds for the denial of the existence of this market under socialism. Surely this market will be very specific, strongly state-regulated with the help of financial, interest rates and taxation methods. Financial resources should be easily moveable and flexible because of the irregularity of their creation and needs in them the dynamism of modern production and structural change, connected with curtailing of traditional industries and emergent new ones. The mobilisation and reallocation of financial resources with the help of various kinds of securities becomes a necessary condition for the successful and effective functioning of the economy. And there are no grounds for denying the expediency of the use of market methods in the regulation of the movement these resources.

The question of resources of income, created as a result of securities movement (interest, dividend, etc.) should be thought out on an entirely new basis. All these forms cannot be identified with the exploitation of other persons' labour. The receipt of income on means invested in securities acts as a form of participation according to one's share in the increase of the economic effect which is created with the help of additional financial resources used in production. The primary labour basis of the creation of these resources using the personal savings of the population as well as income of the socialist enterprises which do not use hired labour, determines eventually the socially just labour character of receiving income on securities.

No less complex theoretical problems arise in connection with the discussion of the problem of establishing a socialist labour force market. The principal peculiarity of this market consists in the fact that, firstly, it is created under conditions of full and effective employment of the population; secondly, it excludes the use of hired labour as a means of making private proprietors rich. The establishment of a labour force market does not mean the admission of the existence of alienation of the worker from the social means of production. The idea is different: the practical ties of a worker with social, collective or individual means of production takes place in a rather flexible form and is based on a free choice by every person of the sphere of allocation of his labour and a contract agreement as to the size of payments.

From this, it is necessary both in theory and in practice to analyse carefully the creation of demand for labour, labour supply in different branches and regions, determination of sufficient conditions of salaries and wages, which are essential for the real inclusion of the worker in the process of social production. The peculiarity of the socialist labour force market suggests creating a developed and well-functioning system of reallocation, retraining and finding jobs for workers. This is one of the qualitative characteristics of the socialist labour market, which suggests the existence of a well-developed all-union system of regulation, control and information on these problems.

The modern highly socialised production market is not and cannot be the only all-embracing system which regulates proportions of production. On the macroeconomic level, the realisation of major research and development, social and economic programmes, the creation and functioning of production and social infrastructure are the objects of planned state regulation. It is clear that scientific – mainly economic – methods should be used in this case. But they are qualitatively and radically different from methods of market regulation.

Planned regulation influences to a certain degree the microeconomic level, too.

The creation, with the help of centralised methods, of a healthy atmosphere on the market, establishing the necessary conditions for free economic competition among its agents in order to remove all kinds of monopolisation becomes increasingly essential. Planned regulation influences different aspects of the market: supply, demand and prices. The state directly influences the volume and structure of supply by using planned formation of social production structure and proportions, allocation of state orders for strategic and social priority products. Simultaneously it regulates the volume and structure of demand, because state order is one of its most important forms. Indirect methods of regulation, which are connected with prices, taxes, interest rates and so on, also influence supply of goods.

Regulation, with the help of the banking system, of the volume of money in circulation and money incomes of enterprises and population is the main means of influencing the volume and structure of demand. Profit allocation normatives and the tax system, direct determination of money income of the population in the form of pensions, stipends, winnings on loans and lotteries, also influence the structure of aggregate demand. If regulation of the macroproportions of supply and demand is reliable, a solid foundation is laid for active usage of market methods in regulating the microproportions of social production.

There are also different methods and forms of state price regulation, shares of which, on the basis of their volume, character and direction, can be quite different, taking into consideration actual situation in the economy and emerging tendencies of its development.

5 DIFFICULT PROBLEMS OF MAKING A SOCIALIST MARKET

A socialist market in its developed form cannot be made by means of a decree, or appear within one day. It is a long and laborious process, which requires time and struggle between old and new forces. Both the objective hardships of the present period and stereotypes inherited from the past play a significant role here. Success is being prevented by the fact that this issue has often been tackled, not from the point of view of science and objective logic of life, but from an emotional stand and ideological prejudices. It is quite appropriate to recall here Lenin's warning about the danger of finding oneself in the power of 'socialism of emotions', to subordinate oneself to 'Old-russian, semi-grand, semi-muzhik, patriarchal spirit, which is characterised by instinctive neglect of trade'.

In contemporary conditions, the process of making and developing a market cannot be an autonomous one. It is a part of a single programme of measures, which presupposes solving a number of complex issues. These measures include primarily: a programme of financial improvement of the economy, elimination of budget deficits, abolishing disproportions in production and imbalance in the sphere of circulation.

Only under such circumstances can one speak about real restoration of money not only as the means of accounting method, but also as a real meaning of the total equivalent which can be freely, without any limits, exchanged for any consumer value. Any developed market is bound to fail without real money of full value. This is linked with a question of a gradual shift to a convertible national currency of socialist countries (first of all the rouble) not only inside the country, but also on the world market.

It is equally clear that the creation of the present-day market, oriented at meeting consumer needs and lowering social expenditures, presupposes overcoming monopolism in all its forms and types. They are:

– monopoly of ministries and bank agencies
– monopoly of large enterprises, which are sometimes the only manufacturers of certain types of products
– monopoly of scientific and research institutions, which keep their R & D outside the system of competition based selection and choice

and so on.

The mere listing of these problems shows how complex and time-consuming the process of creation of a modern developed socialist market is.

The problem of pricing reform should be solved along with the above-mentioned issues. The reform does not imply a single act of price change but a process of transition to a qualitatively new model of price formation. Price reform as well as other changes are not an autonomous process. It is organically linked by tens and hundreds of ties with the other related transformations. Therefore, it should be expected that the transition to a new model of price formation in the USSR would mean a process requiring time and interaction with the programme of financial improvement, the elimination of budgetary deficit and the overcoming of monopolistic tendencies.

We should also consider the need for the simultaneous creation of the whole system of anti-inflationary measures, the introduction of stabilising systems, calling for the protection of the population from being affected by growing prices. This primarily concerns people and families with fixed incomes. A variety of measures is to be used here. One of them is the introduction of an income index, which will permit balancing the real incomes of the population with the dynamics of sale prices for goods and services.

But even with this one cannot expect 100 per cent transition to free market prices. In modern economic systems (and this practice is common not only in socialist countries but also in western societies) the state exercises different measures of control over price formation. This control should provide a variety of important social guarantees by levers of price regulation for goods of mass general demand as well as subsidising food production and infrastructure. This must be done to maintain the socially acceptable level of prices for consumer goods and services. The forms, methods and limits of control over price dynamics should be flexible and must reflect the present situation in the economy and its shifts.

All these issues require thorough consideration and experimental testing. It would have been a mistake to tie oneself in advance by certain decisions which might need correction later.

Development of the socialist market entails the question of a possible bankruptcy of socialist enterprises. We should acknowledge first of all that the existence of unprofitable enterprises (with the exception, probably, of some social spheres) contradicts the nature and principles of a socialist economy. Artificial support of such enterprises is the result of the domination of the administrative system, dooming the socialist economy to low efficiency.

We have to understand the need and necessity to close down such units, though forms and methods of such actions might prove to be diverse and very specific. For example, the first steps of tough application of cost-accounting methods of economic regulation in the USSR brought into life such a peculiar form of abolishing state enterprises as their transformation into cooperatives or leasing them to work collectives. Enterprises can be shut down, liquidated, their property can be sold to other socialist enterprises, cooperatives or individual producers. The state, of course, guarantees social protection of our people, including employment, training for a new profession and making up previous income for a certain period.

One of the most complex problems on the way of the socialist market development is the need for personnel trained in commercial activity. Decades of supervision by the command-administrative system have resulted in the loss of traditions, experience and professional skill. We are to train our managerial staff practically anew and to raise professionals who will acquire knowledge of methods of marketing, banking policy, tax system, fund institutions, etc.

At the same time we have to create a general commercial culture, the habit of thinking within the framework of new notions and images. This concerns not only those employed in the economic sphere but practically all strata of our population.

The process of forming the present-day developed system of a socialist market is expected to be a hard and long one. The road will not be free of zigzags, shifting of accents and even reverse movements. This is caused by the fact that we are not prepared to solve all very complicated problems at once. There can be situations of possible aggravation of economic situation and other unpredictable factors.

But this, however, should not intimidate us. Social progress has never been a straightforward movement and evidently will never be so in future. Its movement is always contradictory and uncertain. Of prime importance here is the main general direction of development. This direction is quite clear and is targeted at the formation of a qualitatively new economic system of socialism. An effectively functioning socialist market will become an integral part of this system.

Reference

Galbraith, J. K. (1967) *The New Industrial State* (London: Hamish Hamilton).

2 Product Market and Capital Market in the Light of the Experience of the Hungarian New Economic Mechanism

Włodzimierz Brus
UNIVERSITY OF OXFORD, UK

and

Kazimierz Laski
UNIVERSITY OF LINZ AND VIENNA INSTITUTE OF
COMPARATIVE ECONOMIC STUDIES, AUSTRIA

1   THE THEORETICAL INFLUENCES

Economists are seldom – many would say never – lucky enough to have their theoretical propositions tested empirically in a way sufficient to pronounce on the validity of the theories. The *ceteris paribus* clause is usually the main culprit: 'other things' are simply not equal . . . We cannot pretend therefore that the experience of the Hungarian New Economic Mechanism (NEM) provides us with the decisive proof of the virtual impossibility of expecting product markets to operate properly without simultaneously opening up these markets for factors of production, especially the capital market. Nevertheless, the fact that most analysts of the experience of the Hungarian NEM point to this flaw in the 1968 blueprint as the major reason for the new system falling short of expectations has to be taken as an important point of departure both for practical thinking on reform and for theoretical considerations (or reconsiderations, as in our case).

It should be stressed at the outset that whatever the interpretations of the general attitude to the market under socialism in Marxist theory, there can hardly be doubts with regard to its outright and uncompromising rejection of the capital market. This is understandable enough and not merely on doctrinal grounds (the capital market, even limited to non-private participants, denies labour the alleged role of the ultimately single factor of production and the only legitimate, non-exploitative source of income), but also because socialisation of capital – its allocation on behalf and in the interests of the community as a whole – represents the mainstay of the postulated economic superiority of socialism over capitalism. Unfettered development of productive forces, elimination of fluctuations and of the absurdity of having side by side excess capital, excess labour and unsatisfied needs – all this has been closely linked in Marxist theory with direct social responsibility for the accumulation and distribution of resources taken out of current consumption for the purpose of expanded reproduction. There is thus no reliance on individual savings as a determinant of accumulation, and no place for the market in deciding how accumulation should be used, as Engels emphasised reacting angrily to Dühring's idea of leaving the rate of saving to individual decisions: the most important progressive function of society, accumulation, is to be taken from society and put into the hands, placed at the arbitrary discretion of individuals.

When the concept of 'market socialism' was expounded in the 1930s, Engels's stand that accumulation in a socialist economy must be a public concern was firmly upheld. Lange had no doubt that the rate of capital accumulation would be determined 'corporately', that is by the Central Planning Board, which would impose its own, and not the consumer's, valuation of the 'optimum time-shape of the income stream'. Lange called this type of decision arbitrary and acknowledged the argument that it might involve diminution of the consumer's welfare, but the alternative – leaving all accumulation to the saving of individuals – was 'scarcely compatible with the organization of a socialist society'. So, the loss of the right to determine the rate of capital accumulation should be regarded as a price paid by the individual for living in a socialist society, the benefits of which richly exceed this particular cost; among the benefits Lange lists the overcoming of capitalism's inability to secure full utilisation of resources, especially full employment (Lange, 1938). A similar view is taken by Lerner as far as the collectivist (socialist) model is concerned, although his position becomes different with regard to the 'mixed but controlled economy' (Lerner, 1944). All this means is that among other things an integral feature of a socialist economy must be an incomes policy on a macro-scale that is determination of the overall ratio of the aggregate value of incomes of the population (net of individual savings) to the total value of consumer goods and services in the given period (net of changes in stocks) – or, in simplified form, the relation of wages to prices and taxes. Thus, elimination of the market from the sphere of determination of the rate of capital accumulation spills over in some sense to the labour market because it establishes limits beyond which no bargaining should move; (perhaps it is this implicit link which prompted in Hungary in the 1980s the activation of debate on the labour market simultaneously with that on the capital market).

The 'arbitrariness' of the determination of the overall rate of accumulation notwithstanding, Lange's model contains a capital market (or simulation of a capital market) for the purposes of allocation of investment between various sectors and projects: the allocating mechanism operates through the price of capital – the rate of interest – 'simply determined by the condition that the demand for capital is equal to the amount available' (Lange, 1938). However, the rationality of using this kind of mechanism for investment allocation met with sharp criticism by Dobb who argued that the method proposed would either let in capitalist-type fluctuations or require very complex and cumbersome countercyclical measures (Dobb, 1939). Besides, both Dobb and other opponents of the idea of allocating investment through the market mechanism (for instance, Paul Baran, 1952) insisted on the superiority of direct central planning of investment through time in view of wider information available to the central planner compared with individual managers as to the future development trends of the economy as a whole, and because there is no need to guess the future reactions of these managers to the (again guessed) future prices.

Scepticism with regard to the use of the rate of interest in a socialist economy was strengthened by the implications of Keynesian economics, and particularly by the firmness of Kalecki's statement that 'the rate of interest cannot be determined by the demand for and supply of new capital because investment "finances itself" regardless of the level of the rate of interest' (Kalecki, 1965). At a later stage Kalecki was emphatic in maintaining that in a centrally-planned economy the calculation of investment efficiency with the help of a surrogate rate of interest ('marginal recoupment period') can serve only the choice of techniques for the achievement of given productive targets and the pattern of foreign trade, but not the choice of the directions of change in the general structure of the economy (Kalecki, 1972).

The theoretical argument against subjecting allocation of investment to the market mechanism fitted well with the concepts of economic reform gradually emerging in communist countries after the death of Stalin. The reformist Marxists were profoundly affected by the inefficiencies of the command system, but they – the present writers included – ascribed failures not to central planning as such but to excessive centralisation which clearly put burdens on the planners which exceeded their capacity to collect and to process the flow of information. This seemed to be the result of the attempt to cover by detailed obligatory target planning and physical allocation of resources all aspects of current operations of state enterprises: size of output and its composition, labour and material inputs, sources of supply and directions of sales, prices, financial outcome etc.; decisions of this kind could and should therefore be left to the enterprises themselves, horizontal relations of which would be coordinated by a regulated market. However, unlike current decisions, not only the possibility of major investment decisions being taken rationally by the centre remained unquestioned: on the contrary, it was the market which was considered incapable of ensuring efficient allocation by long-term social criteria. Again, negative past experience in the field of investment was attributed to over-burdening of the central plan with details of current operations, a defect which would be removed by leaving them to the regulated market coordination. Needless to say, the ingrained ideology of socialist central planning and of socialist property relations which were interpreted as giving to the state the exclusive right to create new productive capacities and determine the future structure of the economy must have played a role in the tendency to limit the scope of change. The reformers (even those who were branded as 'revisionists') were prepared to move only some way from the old positions of absolute all-embracing planning. But, whatever the role of ideological (and political) factors, substantive considerations – conviction that central choices between major economic alternatives can bring better results than market mechanism – were, in our opinion, decisive for the virtual exclusion of the capital market from the reform blueprints which began to appear in communist countries from the mid-1950s onwards.[1]

A number of attempts to provide a theoretical foundation for the exclusion of a capital market were undertaken in the course of economic debates in connection with the search for an appropriate reform concept. Some of them, like that by the distinguished Chinese economist Sun Yefang (1979), based themselves on the Marxian distinction between the simple and expanded reproduction as the guidance on how to draw the line between the sphere of autonomous activity of an enterprise and that reserved for the centre. Some went beyond this distinction, arguing in favour of giving to the enterprise also the opportunity to expand and to modernise productive capacities, but still within its prescribed sector of activity, thus preserving the predominance of the vertical mechanism of redistribution of investment funds, and leaving the centre as the decisive force in determining both the rate of accumulation and the shape of structural change in the economy through sectoral and spatial allocation. To the latter category belongs also Brus's 'model of a planned economy with a built-in market mechanism' which is sometimes mentioned among the sources of inspiration for the actual Hungarian 1968 reform.[2]

One should never exaggerate the impact of a theoretical construction on practical solutions, especially in the case of systemic reform which must usually contain elements of political compromise as well. Nevertheless, it can be said that by and large the blueprint of the Hungarian NEM followed the distinctions indicated above, albeit in the less rigid version.

2 THE HUNGARIAN NEW ECONOMIC MECHANISM

The relation of the Hungarian NEM to theory comes out very clearly in an authoritative presentation of the main features of the reformed system published just after the introduction of NEM (Friss, 1969).

Starting from the premise that 'the growth rates and major proportions characterising the main processes of economic development can be best assessed and planned in the central planning organisations' (Friss, 1969, p. 73), the role of the centre in allocation of investment was to be predominant. As Friss, the editor of the publication, puts it, 'In the new system a considerable and increasing part of investments will be realised on the grounds of autonomous enterprise decisions. In this field the state will assert its own points of view of investment policy mainly through the means of credit policy. But, in addition, the state has also other means of influencing decisively the main tendencies of development, namely by the centrally-taken decisions regarding the largest investment products, by the determination of a set of lump sums, each of which will be used for investments serving a special purpose and, finally, by financing certain investments out of the state budget' (Friss, 1969, pp. 19–20). Mention of bank credits in connection with enterprises' autonomous investment may suggest opening up an embryonic capital market (without using the term), but the qualification that 'also the credit policy of the banks is, in its main features, prescribed by the government and thus becomes another tool of planned economic control' (Friss, 1969, p. 20) undermines this impression. Moreover, in view of the frequently insufficient amount of enterprise's own development fund (out of profits) for starting an investment, state directed bank credits become indispensable, which extends the planner's control even over the use of decentralised accumulation. This is one of the reasons why the statistical picture of the shares of central and decentralised investment activity in the Hungarian state sector does not reflect properly the respective scope of administrative coordination on the one hand, and market coordination on the other.

The determination of capital market combined with the unequivocal interpretation of public property rights as exercised by the state administration was reflected in the NEM blueprint in the provisions concerning the foundation and liquidation of enterprises. The quotation from Friss is rather lengthy but instructive: 'Evidently, *the considerable increase of enterprise autonomy* and the wider competence of enterprise executives *do not interfere with their dependence on the state as the owner of the enterprises*' [original italics]. The autonomy is expressed, among others, in the right of disposition of the enterprises over their assets (within the limits set by legal rules); . . . On the other hand, their dependence on the state is reflected in the principles ruling that enterprises can be founded only by a minister or leader of a national authority or by the executive committee of a local council, and that the founder has the right to determine the sphere of activity of the enterprise, as well as to appoint and discharge its director and deputy director(s). Moreover, the founder may liquidate the enterprise if its activity is no longer needed by the national economy, if its profitable operations cannot be continued, or if the activity in question can be pursued more economically by another enterprise. Exceptionally, when national economic interests make it necessary, the founder may also order the reorganization of an enterprise. The founder may join up several enterprises into a trust. . . . The founder has also the right and obligation critically to evaluate the activities of the enterprise as a whole and the work performed by the manager and his deputies, as well as to take decisions regarding their salaries and premia' (p. 17). Quite consistent with this position is the shift of what may be called entrepreneurial risk connected with new technology to the economic administration: 'Economic and technical conceptions are elaborated for the development tasks of various scope and importance, at corresponding higher or lower levels of various organizations. Such conceptions must then be brought into relation between themselves and coordinated accordingly. Conceptions related to a branch of national economy must, in general, be elaborated by the competent ministry or another national authority; conceptions of national importance and those covering several branches belong to the competence of the National Board of Technical Development' (p. 16).

2.1 Implications of Rejection of Capital Market

What interests us most are the implications of the virtual exclusion of capital market from the design of NEM for those elements of market coordination which were supposed to operate and enhance the efficiency of the new system compared with the old. As in other matters, the separation of the impact of this particular factor alone is difficult, and one must be wary not to overstate its significance in relation to other factors likely to act in the same direction – to curtail the scope of market coordination in the economy. Nevertheless, we think – in the light of the Hungarian literature and our own analysis – that some valid links between the exclusion of capital market and weakening of the product market can be established.

The first, and obvious, corollary from the principles presented above is the need to retain a strong centre of economic administration ('bureaucratic coordination' in Kornai's terms). Any sort of economic dynamics requires a mechanism of inter-sectoral and spatial reallocation of resources for capital investment, and if the channels of horizontal reallocation are blocked, the function must be taken over by the centre which collects and redistributes funds through vertical channels. This might have been the straightforward intention in theoretical models like that of Brus mentioned above and in the blueprint of NEM – without, however, apparently taking into account the inherent tendency of a body powerful in one field to spread its influence into other areas as well. The experience of all reform attempts in communist countries leaves no doubt as to the strength with which this tendency manifests itself in resurrecting the real control over supposedly decentralised economic activities by the central decision makers. Furthermore, the blockage of horizontal flows of capital – except for the very minor role of the banks as genuine intermediaries, and not as 'another tool of planned economic control' (Friss, 1969) – creates a peculiar centralising feedback: enterprises deprived of the right to use their development fund outside the prescribed sphere of activity tend to invest as much as possible internally, which may lead to inefficient allocation; in order to prevent this, higher administrative organs, having a wider purview of opportunities, react with restrictions on freedom of enterprise decisions.

The second implication of the elimination of capital market concerns the role of the centre in the distribution of national income. A macroeconomic incomes policy which effectively allows adjustment of the overall ratios of investment and consumption in the broad sense is an indispensable element of a planned economy in pursuance of the objective of avoiding demand-determined fluctuations and to secure full employment and a high level of capacity utilisation. This, as indicated earlier, requires control over prices and wages, but in the absence of a capital market, which would in part open the game between current and future benefits also to enterprises and even to households (as lenders), the full burden of such control falls on the shoulders of the centre. Inevitably it becomes more rigid and more detailed – as witnessed, for instance, by the most elaborate scheme of division of enterprise profits into the sharing and development funds in the very design of NEM. The same has been true of the rules of wage regulation, particularly after the initial general ones (control of average wage with punitive taxation in case of excess) have proved inadequate and subjected to rather frequent changes as well as differentiation by industries; needless to say, the degree of arbitrariness and dependence of enterprises' wage policy on their administrative superiors must have increased. All this must bear on the operation of the labour market (see below).

The third issue which ought to be discussed in connection with the attempt to use the market mechanism without a capital market is competition. The negative experience of the command system has taught the reformers that competition has its benefits, and both in the theoretical model-building and in most of the blueprints of the new system of functioning of the economy the role of competition has been linked to the rejection of the Stalinist claim that excess demand under socialism spurs production; market clearing prices have been firmly postulated as an indispensable means to overcoming the endemic shortages, as well as a generator of signals for adjustment in product-mix and input composition. Short of proposing abolition of controls over foreign economic relations, the familiar form of 'state monopoly of foreign trade', with its 'price equalisation mechanism' isolating the domestic from the foreign market, has been expected to give way, at least gradually, to interaction between those two via 'transaction prices' (prices paid or received in foreign markets converted into domestic prices by a single exchange rate) modified by a normal system of tariffs and duties; this should create a competitive alternative both for the producers and for the consumers.

The expectations with regard to the external pro-competitive factor proved over-optimistic for reasons of balance of payments constraints which in turn reflected a combination of external shocks and insufficient adaptive ability of the economy. This side apart, however, the good intentions to promote competitive behaviour generally have not been properly tested against other, sometimes fundamental, features of the aimed-at reformed socialist edifice, either in theoretical writings or in the reform blueprints. To begin with, this has been the case in respect of one of the main planks of the claim to socialism's superior economic rationality – the capacity fully to employ human and material resources: how does this affect the conditions, the scope and directions of competitive behaviour? The answers to this question have been rather vague – ranging from acceptance of the need of 'some' excess supply (including 'some' unemployment) to the insistence that aggregate correspondence between demand and supply at full employment level can never mean partial equilibria everywhere, hence the room and incentives for competition. The reference to unavoidable partial disequilibria is certainly correct, but if the capital market is excluded, there is no reason to expect competition for a place in the developing sectors because the boundaries between sectors cannot be crossed on enterprises' own investment initiative; at the most, competition may emerge within the limited framework of shifts in the markets for goods which it is possible to produce within the existing production lines. Even less likely under the circumstances is the kind of competition generated by the entrepreneurial spirit of 'creative destruction' (Schumpeter), the essence of which consists not of adjustment leading to restoration of equilibrium but of upsetting the existing equilibrium by opening up new opportunities; without access to venture capital and new spheres of activity there is no room for such processes. This in itself does not mean that disequilibria cannot be countered and new opportunities sought but this would occur not through the mechanism of competition but through appropriate administrative regulation which is a different proposition, even regardless of how the comparative efficiency of the two allocation mechanisms may be evaluated. As for combating monopolistic behaviour, the obvious requirement is that of free entry into the sectors and areas involved, which is clearly connected with the possibility of horizontal flows of capital. Theoretically, as in Lange's model, free entry can be simulated by an appropriate rule; in practice, it is again the centre which may act accordingly, treating the maintenance of competitive conditions as one of the criteria of capital allocation, establishment of new enterprises, etc. However, the likelihood of the latter course of action is small because it runs against the interests of effective central control (a small number of larger units is easier to control than a large number of small ones), not to mention the exaggerated perceptions of the economies of scale, rather characteristic of economic bureaucrats. All in all, the idea of having competition in product markets, or within the sphere of current economic decisions (terms of Brus's model) without opening up some sort of capital market, has hardly proved itself.

Finally, the fourth element of the implications of the bar on capital market in the design of NEM and its theoretical antecedents: the impact on the disciplinary function of the market, or – to revert to the widely-accepted Kornai terminology – on the hardness of the budget constraint for state enterprises. This is connected (but not identical) with the problem of competition discussed above; after all, one can have strict financial and other norms imposed on sub-units inside a larger organisation without putting them into mutually competitive relations – as practised, for instance, in quite a number of multi-divisional capitalist corporations. It is in the subjection of state enterprises to the discipline of the market which would enforce the heeding of the correct signals on what and how to produce that the main contribution of the economic reform is expected. The essence of the concept of central planning with regulated market mechanism has been to make the enterprises profit-orientated through the appropriate incentive scheme and to confront them with 'parameters of choice', that is, with monetary magnitudes – prices in general sense – independent of their volition and applied in a uniform way to all. These parameters were to reflect the macroeconomic priorities of the central plan and to translate them into binding guides for action on the micro-level; they could include subsidies in cases of special preferences, but fixed in advance and product-specific, not differentiated by enterprises and following their balance sheet. And yet the 'parametric system' of managing the economy has failed to materialise properly in Hungary where, to use Granick's formulation, 'financial tutelage was substituted for the earlier physical planning'. This failure is linked particularly strongly to the lack of capital market by several Hungarian economists, especially so by Tardos (1986).

As far as investment activity is concerned, the 'softening' of the budget constraint becomes an unintended effect of the high degree of concentration of decisions in the hands of administrative authorities, particularly at the centre. This means, on the one hand, that investment demand of enterprises is not constrained by the test of the market-place, and their success in obtaining funds depends on their ability of convince the bureaucracy of the relevance of the project; the problem here is thus that of information – the capacity of the centre independently to assess the project in question and to compare it with the range of alternatives available. On the other hand, contrary to implicit or even explicit model assumptions of the centre as a homogenous representation of societal interest, in reality it may more often than not seek a compromise between various partial interests, and hence become susceptible to pressure; the problem here is that of motivation – the capacity of the centre to withstand particularisms for the well-perceived sake of the whole. Taking into account that under the circumstances the centre is almost the only barrier to investment demand, the likely inadequacy of its information and motivation structures must have highly damaging effects not only for macroeconomic equilibrium, but also – in the context of our discussion – for the financial discipline of enterprises. A frequent secondary consequence appears as well: when completed defective projects are put on stream they give rise to *sui generis* legitimate claims for support from the administration, and so become a source of breaks in financial discipline of current operations as well.

However, the implications of the lack of capital market for softening the budget constraint in current operations are not limited to the aspect just mentioned. The most serious implications, as emphasised by Hungarian economists, consist of engendering conditions which make it extremely difficult, if not outright impossible, to expose underperforming enterprises to the threat of forced curtailment of their activities, and ultimately of bankruptcy. If a currently unsuccessful enterprise is prevented from attempting to raise capital in the market in order to restructure its operations, including branching out into other more promising fields, or cannot be taken over by a more dynamic firm which sees latent opportunities, strict application of the market rules of the game would actually lead to gross inefficiencies:

not only enterprises unable to recover would go out of business, but also those with good prospects although in temporary difficulties. Under the circumstances, in the absence of the evaluating mechanism of the capital market, the administration must step in, which again opens the gates to arbitrary breaks of financial discipline. Tardos summarises this side of the experience of NEM in the following way: 'At present the new economic mechanism is unable to apply financial pressure successfully as an adjustment method not only because without central interventions the generally introduced rules would push an unduly large number of enterprises into bankruptcy, but also because, in a market system, bankruptcies infer the existence of free [capital] ready to take over the ruined enterprises. Such free [capital is] lacking [in Hungary] not as a consequence of capital scarcity, but of the centralization of incomes and of the fact that, if at all, only so much is left with the enterprises as [is] necessary for the economic objectives agreed with the centre. Thus the government could not allow a general hardening of the financial constraint. During the last almost twenty years the central organs have been continuously forced to use not only the methods of intervention declared to be normative . . . but also openly differentiated interventions of varying intensity, and different for each enterprise . . . Central organs often approved increases in producers' prices and were compelled to grant individual tax exceptions, subsidies and preferential credits' (Tardos, 1986, p. 83). This amounts to an unequivocal proposition that the roots of the softness of budget constraint for the economic units cannot be reduced to paternalistic policies in general and to the principle of microeconomic job-security in particular, but should be traced to the flaws in the design of the system; even explicit abandonment of such policies would not be sufficiently effective against the inherent systemic tendencies.

On the whole, the case for the capital market seems strong in the light of the Hungarian experience which has revealed the inconsistencies of reform concepts limiting 'the regulated market mechanism' to product markets alone. Another question is the scope and shape of the capital market, its relationship to the economic role of the state, and particularly its viability in the framework of socialist ownership.

2.2 Consequences of Absence of Labour Market

Less clear, as far as we can judge, is the criticism frequently voiced in Hungarian economic literature as to the lack of provision for a labour market in the design of NEM. One should expect a labour market actually to emerge whenever there is freedom of choice of occupation and place of work, in other words when people are not assigned to jobs by order of the authority. In so far as the practice of administrative and penal (forced labour in the strict sense) assignments diminishes, we can speak of a labour market even under a command system. Admittedly, within the dominant state sector this is a most peculiar market – with a single general employer who himself establishes the rules which cannot be openly challenged (the bar to the challenge is very much a consequence of the political system). Nonetheless, relative prices of labour (wage differentials) have to be used in the process of allocation, and the necessity to adjust wages (and/or other forms of remuneration) to the changing conditions of supply and demand has to be recognised in one way or another, quite often in breach of the regulations from above. The switch from a command system to NEM has undoubtedly broadened the sphere of operation of the labour market along with the enhanced autonomy of enterprises less constricted by obligatory targets and physical distribution of producer goods, and particularly under the influence of increased activity outside the state sector. Of course, taking into account what has been said above about the true overall relationship between administrative and market coordination under NEM, the labour market must also have failed expectations, especially as certain traditional provisions for protection of employees' rights (for instance, legal obligation of the management to present specific personal reasons for every dismissal) continued to affect labour mobility.

However, behind the not very clearly spelt out demands to 'introduce' a labour market in the new stage of economic reform in Hungary seems to lie a real major problem: how to create conditions which would allow the fundamentals of the process of wage determination to be brought out of the administrative sphere into that of market coordination. We have stressed several times already the importance of income distribution (price/wage relationship) for macropolicy objectives, as well as the link between the lack of capital market and the scope of state regulation in this field. But there is more to it: the absence of market-type opposition of interests between the 'buyers' and 'sellers' as far as labour is concerned presents a formidable obstacle to arrive at a market ('rational') price of labour, and by itself throws the door open to bureaucratic coordination. The managers of state enterprises are not intrinsically motivated to limit wage payments; they will try to do so under outside pressure only, and if there is no (or insufficient) 'budget constraint' generated by the market this means pressure from above, that is of an administrative nature. Hence the perennial struggle in all reform attempts to find a replacement for the wage control of the command system, the main instrument of which is the linkage be-tween the *planned* wage bill and *planned* output (corrected for over- or under-fulfilment by a normative coefficient again fixed from above). Since the introduction of NEM in 1968 several methods have been tried with very mixed success, leading to the rather plain message that the more effective the control the less efficient becomes the allocation of labour by market criteria.

Therefore, if the criticism of the lack of the labour market leads to the conclusion that both the managers and the workforce of state enterprises should be subjected to the discipline and allocative mech-anism of the market – it would make sense (which, of course, is not the same as providing easy solutions). To some extent the activation of the labour market depends on the consistency of operation of other elements of the market mechanism, as well as on more resolute macroeconomic policies. But in many respects it depends on the possibility of regenerating a true bargaining process, and this in turn – needless to say – touches upon fundamental aspects of the essence of socialism.

CONCLUSION

To sum up: flaws in the very concept of 'central planning with regulated market mechanism' which underlie the design of NEM have to be regarded as not the only, but evidently as a very serious and perhaps even the main, substantive reason for the failure to subject the Hungarian state economy to market coordination. The elimination of the capital market from the blueprint is apparently to be blamed in the first place for the fact that the role of market-type institutions within the state sector has been reduced mostly to that of a new form of bureaucratic coordination. Instead of interacting with the plan on a macroscale, market-type institutions have been used by and large as instruments of the plan, different from the previous (command) ones, but ultimately serving a similar purpose and pro-ducing roughly similar effects. The experience of the NEM in this respect has shown that even such important measures as the abolition of obligatory output targets and of rationing of producer goods, which for a long time have been hard fought for by the reformers (in most countries unsuccessfully), can fail in bringing about a major change in substance when necessary complementary factors are missing. The significance of this lesson in the need to distinguish between form and substance ought not to be overlooked in assessing other aspects of the reform process in countries of 'real socialism' as well.

The demands to institute a capital market, as well as to widen the labour market followed by tentative practical steps – in Hungary, in China, in Poland, even in the USSR at the end of the 1980s – reflected to some extent conclusions similar to those presented here.

Notes

1. An examination of east European economic reforms *inter alia* from this point of view can be found in Kaser (1986), vol. III, Chapters 25 and 26.
2. This is the model developed in Brus (1972).

References

Baran, Paul (1952) 'National Economic Planning', in Haley, B. (ed.), *A Survey of Contemporary Economics, Vol. 2*, (Homewood Ill.: Irwin).

Brus. W. (1972) 'Ogólne problemy funkcjonowania gospodarki socjalistycznej' (Warsaw, 1961) and published in English as *The Market in a Socialist Economy* (London: Routledge & Kegan Paul, 1972).

Dobb, Maurice (1939) 'A Note on Savings and Investment in a Socialist Economy', *Economic Journal* (December).

Friss, Istvan (ed.) (1969) 'Reform of the Economic Mechanism in Hungary' (Budapest: Akadémiai Kiadó – Publishing House of the Hungarian Academy of Sciences).

Kalecki, M. (1965) *Theory of Economic Dynamics* (London: Allen & Unwin) 2nd edn; published in the USA by Monthly Review Press (1968).

Kalecki, M. (1972) 'The Scope of the Evaluation of the Efficiency of Investment in a Socialist Economy', in Kalecki, M., *Selected Essays on the Economic Growth of the Socialist and the Mixed Economy* (Cambridge: Cambridge University Press).

Kaser, M. C. (ed.) (1986) *The Economic History of Eastern Europe 1919–75*, 3 vols. (Oxford: Oxford University Press).

Lange, Oskar (1938) 'On the Economic Theory of a Socialist Economy', in Lange, O. and Taylor, F. M., *On the Economic Theory of Socialism* (Minneapolis: University of Minnesota Press).

Lerner, Abba P. (1944) *The Economics of Control: Principles of Welfare Economics* (New York: Macmillan) pp. 314–15.

Sun, Yefang (1979) 'Some Theoretical Problems in Socialist Economy' (in Chinese), as reviewed by Lin, C. in *China Quarterly*, 98 (June 1984) pp. 357–61.

Tardos, M. (1986) 'The Conditions of Developing a Regulated Market', *Acta Oeconomica* 12.

3 The Affinity Between Ownership and Coordination Mechanisms: The Common Experience of Reform in Socialist Countries

János Kornai*
HUNGARIAN ACADEMY OF SCIENCES, BUDAPEST,
HUNGARY AND HARVARD UNIVERSITY, USA

1 INTRODUCTION

The title of the session in which this paper was given, 'The Theory of Markets in a Planned Economy', suggests two alternative approaches. One is that of a *normative* theory – that is, the elaboration of a theoretical blueprint for an economy, relying upon both the plan and the market. Whatever might be the significance of such an approach, this paper takes as its basic themes the other approach, namely *positive* analysis. A reform process is under way in several socialist countries. The course of thought applied in the paper is based on the hypothesis that in all reform countries it is possible to identify certain common tendencies. Of course, each reforming country constitutes a unique case, and one must look hard to find suitable ways of discerning common patterns of reform in countries as diverse as Yugoslavia, Hungary, China, Poland and the USSR. One must accomplish another equally difficult task as well, that is the task of properly evaluating the cases of failed reform such as the one which was attempted in 1968 in Czechoslovakia. Nevertheless, there exist many common lessons, and in this paper we will attempt to delineate some of them.

The reader is urged, however, not to take these lessons at face value, and to be very cautious before he accepts and applies them. Clearly, the small number of reforming countries which we have mentioned do not add up to a statistically significant sample, and the period of observation is, in most cases, much too brief to provide a basis for a well-founded positive *theory* of reform. What can be attempted is much more modest and is nothing more than an outline of a few preliminary conjectures which will have to be tested against future historical development.

Since the objective of the analysis is to offer a few *general* observations, we will not attempt here to support the conjectures with empirical evidence.[1] In other words the emphasis is less on a purely factual description and more on the outlining of a specific approach to the analysis of these well-known facts.

One more reservation must be stated in advance. The issues to be discussed in the paper have many political ramifications. Decisions concerning ownership and coordination mechanisms are, of course, strongly linked to the questions concerning power, political institutions and ideology. Apart from a few short hints, this paper does not elaborate on the political aspects of the topics.[2]

2   TRANSFORMATION WITHOUT A STRATEGY

If we look at the history of the countries mentioned, we find that without exception, reform blueprints or programmes were in circulation before the actual period of the reform. In many cases, these blueprints were prepared by scholars. As a matter of fact, for the first example of such an academic proposal for transformation within socialism one can go back as far as Oscar Lange's famous proposal for market socialism and to the debate to which his idea gave rise in the 1930s. Some blueprints were also prepared by the leadership in charge, that is to say by party and government officials in Yugoslavia, in Hungary, in China, in the USSR and in other countries. Finally, there have also been instances of programmes published illegally or semi-legally by dissident politicians, such as those by the authors close to the unofficial trade union Solidarity in Poland, as well as by opposition intellectuals in Hungary and in the Soviet Union.

While all these reform proposals are interesting historical documents, and while some of them have exercised a certain influence on the course of events, the reality of the reforming countries never did, and does not today, correspond to any of the blueprints. In fact, even the officially publicised intentions of the party and of the government were usually not consistently realised, and the deviations from the original programme were sometimes so large that they bore no resemblance to the initial guidelines. Of course, history stands witness to other cases of discrepancies between intent and outcome: the fate of the French Revolution reflected little of the ideas which the *Encyclopédists* along with Rousseau had been discussing in their works, and the Soviet Union in the 1930s turned out to be a country quite different from the one which Marx or the participants of the revolutions of 1917 had imagined.

It is ironic to note, nevertheless, that major transformations in centrally planned economies go on without being based on a central plan. There is a Chinese adage which talks of 'crossing the river by touching the stone'. The reform process in socialist economies conforms exactly to this image: whole societies have proceeded to cross the deep water without accurate knowledge about the final direction by a process of moving from one stone to another. Because of this lack of strategy, the reality of reform in socialist countries is characterised by historical compromises, by movements backwards as well as by movements forwards, by periods of euphoria and of optimism alternating with periods of lost illusions and of frustrations. It also often turns out that, in spite of the best efforts, some changes cannot be preserved. At times, people learn the limits of reformability by, figuratively speaking, running against a stone wall. In any case, the limits of transformability of a society can be accurately gauged only once one begins to transform it.

Under such circumstances it becomes extremely important to observe what evolves *spontaneously* in the transformation process. Marx used the German term 'naturwüchsig' (as grown in nature) to characterise spontaneous historical processes. These are phenomena which appear not as a consequence of governmental orders or of administrative pressure but follow the free will of certain social groups.

The study of 'naturally grown' changes is all the more important since individual freedom of choice typically increases as a consequence of reform. True, certain restrictions imposed by unchangeable taboos remain. Nevertheless, spontaneous changes reflect to some extent the voluntary decisions and revealed preferences of various social groups.

Exactly this approach distinguishes the present paper from many other studies. Most of the work on reform in socialist systems deals with the normative issues, and even in the realm of positive analysis, the intentions and actions of the leadership and the apparatus are discussed. This paper would like to draw the attention to another, not less important, point of view: what is going on spontaneously, not at the orders of the leading groups or even in spite of their orders.

3 THE EVOLUTION OF A PRIVATE SECTOR

In this endeavour, our first focus should be on the evolution of a private sector. Let us remind ourselves briefly of the period in which the first reform proposals were elaborated. When, for example, the áuthor began to participate in the Eastern European thinking on reform in the years 1954, 1955, and 1956, all of the scholars who took part in the debate were almost exclusively concerned with the questions of reform as it applied to the state-owned sector.[3] Discussions turned around the issues of how to give more autonomy and stranger profit-based incentives to the state-owned firms, of how to decentralise economic administration while, at the same time, maintaining state ownership in all but the most marginal sectors of the economy. These were the views of the radical reformers of those days.

Taking a thirty-year leap in history, it turns out that, quite in accordance with the previous section of this paper, history has taken quite a different course from the one outlined in the original blueprints written by academic economists. In the author's opinion, in all the socialist economies in which reforms have had time to develop, and especially in Hungary, in China and in Poland, the emergence of a significant private sector is the most important result of the reform in the economy.

The most important inroad of private activity in socialist economies occurs through private farming. There exists a variety of forms. Either the land has been reprivatised *de facto* (as, for example, under the Chinese 'family responsibility system'), or private farming has never been abolished and survives all kinds of political changes, as for example in Yugoslavia or in Poland. In Hungary, the role of the household plot and of private farming has also increased in the wake of the reform. In addition, typically there also exists some kind of family subcontracting within the agricultural cooperative.

In addition to these private and semi-private agricultural businesses, we find legal, tax-paying private businesses in various other sectors. A significant private sector has emerged in various branches of the service, transport and construction industry; to a lesser extent private business operates in manufacturing as well.[4] There appear different forms of income derived from private property, for example, from the renting out of private homes in cities or from privately-owned second homes in recreational areas.

In addition to the formal private sector, various types of informal 'moonlighting' often appear; unlicensed, and perhaps illegal, but none the less tolerated activities proliferate in the service, commerce, transport and construction sectors. Reform economies also experience a significant increase in elaborate do-it-yourself activities, such as the building of one's own house with the help of one or two professionals and that of some friends.

In some countries, and in some sectors, such as housing and agriculture, it even happens that property owned by the state or by some other social organisation is sold or leased to individuals. The idea of genuine reprivatisation in the British way – that is to say, the idea of the sale of the stock of state-owned companies to the public – came up, for instance in the Hungarian and Chinese discussions of reform. In practice, however, the larger part of the growth of the private sector takes place as a result of entrepreneurial initiative sometimes based on private savings but sometimes almost exclusively on the labour input of the individual.[5]

It must be stressed that the government typically does not have to convince its citizens to enter the private sector by a propaganda campaign. Usually, after certain prohibitions on private activity are lifted, the private sector begins to grow quite spontaneously with individual enterprises sprouting up like mushrooms in a forest after rainfall. The explosion of private activity is all the more notable as it often follows a period of brutal repression of any form of private venture. As soon as the repression against private activity is terminated in the reform countries, the private sector immediately begins to expand in a genuinely spontaneous manner. People do not have to be cajoled or coerced in order to choose this way of life.[6] In fact, they are immediately attracted by the higher earnings, by the more direct linkage between effort and reward, and by the greater autonomy which the private sector offers. The third reason – namely the prospect of greater autonomy in private activity – in particular should not be underestimated.[7]

Private activities generate relatively high income because they are able to meet demand left unsatisfied by the state-owned sector. A craftsman, or the owner of a corner grocery store or indeed of a small restaurant is typically in the middle income group in a private enterprise economy. But here, in the environment of a chronic shortage economy the same activities catapult these people into the highest income group, not because they are particularly smart or greedy, but because of the rarity of the service that they provide. The price which they get for their output is just the *market clearing price* in the small segment of the economy where a genuine market operates. They can be grateful to the state-owned sector and to the fiscal and monetary systems which create supply and demand conditions leading to free market prices significantly higher than the official prices in the state-owned sector.

The dimensions of this growth of private economic activity are even more remarkable if one takes into account the fact that the private sector must adjust to the hostile environment of the half-heartedly reforming socialist economy. Despite some improvements, the daily life of private businesses is still characterised by a multitude of bureaucratic interventions and restrictions. The private sector has limited access to material supply, and almost no access to credits and to foreign exchange. Material, credit and foreign exchange is often acquired in illegal or semi-legal ways.

A further sign of hostility is the jealousy of people who are suspicious of growing income differentials. This eny of individuals who suddenly come to earn more than others, while it occurs in all systems, is likely to be all the more divisive in a society in which people have been brought up to consider equality to be a major social desideratum. Finally, further difficulties are caused by the absence of legal institutions for the consistent protection of private property and for the enforcement of private contracts, as well as the lack of political movements and associations devoted to the articulation of the private sector's interests. Even dissident groups are, so to say, reluctant to step forward and advocate the interests of private business and private property. And that leads to the ideological aspects of the issue.

Can one justifiably assume that this small-scale private activity inevitably leads to capitalism? It is very tempting simply to answer 'no'. Thus, if we were now in a meeting called upon decide on the pragmatic question of how many licenses to give to private taxi cab owners, this author would not at all object to the argument that private taxi cabs are not genuine capitalist ventures, and that Hungarian, Soviet and Chinese socialism will not be endangered if a few more such cabs are allowed on the road. Nevertheless, if we want to be objective, it is not possible to dismiss the above question so easily.

Using now the terminology of Marxian political economy, we may classify the overwhelming part of private sector activities in socialist economies as small commodity production. Roughly speaking, the decisive distinction between small commodity production and genuine capitalism in the Marxian sense is that the former uses only the labour input of one individual, together perhaps with that of his family members, whereas the latter uses hired labour regularly and thus becomes exploitative as it seeks to extract the surplus from the employee. In this context, the ideology and practice of socialist countries has been very much influenced by Lenin's frequently quoted dictum that 'small production engenders capitalism and the bourgeoisie continuously, daily, hourly, spontaneously, and on a mass scale' (Lenin, [1920], 1966, p. 8). In the author's opinion, Lenin was absolutely right. If a society allows for the existence of a large number of small commodity producers, and if it permits them to accumulate capital and to grow over time, a genuine group of capitalists will sooner or later emerge. To appreciate this fact, the reader is asked to imagine for a moment what would happen if private producers had the same access to credit and to all kinds of inputs as the state-owned enterprise in a socialist economy and, moreover, were to be treated equally by the tax and subsidy system. Without any doubt, the more successful private businesses would begin to accumulate and grow. Thus, the negative answer to the question as to whether small commodity production breeds capitalism in pragmatic discussions of particular cases is already predicated on the assumption that the government will not allow private business to grow beyond a certain critical threshold. In other words, the growth of the private sector in a socialist economy is not only hampered by the excessive red tape of an ubiquitous and omnipotent bureaucracy; the sustained growth of private businesses also runs counter to the ideological premises of the system, and will therefore be held in check by the ruling party and by the government who are not willing to tolerate a significant capitalist sector.

There are different ways of imposing constraints on the private sector's ability to grow. Sometimes these constraints simply take the form of legal restrictions (such as, for example, the form of an upper bound on the number of people which may be employed in a legal private enterprise, or of a limit on the amount of capital which may be invested in private businesses). Obstacles to growth may also be incorporated in the tax system. The extent of taxation of a particular activity at a given point in time can vary quite substantially, thus providing the authorities with an additional tool for keeping the private sector under control. The author has talked to Hungarian private craftsmen who pointed out to him the exact level of taxation up to which they would be able to uphold the private venture, and beyond which they would have to abandon it and return to work in the state-owned sector. Of course, these critical reservation thresholds may vary from sector to sector, from period to period, and from business to business. But it is important to note that they exist and that they impose institutional limits on the survival of a private firm. The most powerful upper limit on accumulation is uncertainty and the fear of future nationalisation and confiscation. Memories of past repression are alive, and the individual might be scared that he and his children might one day be stigmatised as 'bourgeois' or 'kulak'.

As a consequence of this situation, economies of scale cannot be enjoyed due to the limits on capital accumulation. It might be socially more reasonable in the given political and ideological climate to waste one's profits rather than to put them to productive use. In historical accounts of capitalist economies, we are used to reading about the parsimony of the founders of family businesses who endeavour to bequeath their wealth to future generations. In accordance with the picture painted in Thomas Mann's novel *Buddenbrooks*, we begin to associate wastefulness only with the second and subsequent generations of a family line of capitalists. By contrast, waste in family businesses in socialist countries often begins on the very first day of their existence, given that it is quite uncertain whether the venture will have a prolonged existence even within the individual founder's own lifetime.

The social environment of the private sector also results in myopic behaviour. The private firm is typically not interested in building up a solid goodwill with its customers for its products or services, because its owners feel that they might not even be in business the following year. Thus, in the extreme, given the overall environment of the sellers' market, private firms may be quite dishonest with their customers so as to reap the largest possible amount of one-time profit. To the extent that consumers are used to the queues and to the shortages in the state-owned sector, it is generally easy for the private firm to keep its customers, even though its employees might hardly be more forthcoming and polite than the employees of its counterpart in the state-owned sector, if there is one. Instead of raising the overall standards of service of the sellers under state ownership in the direction of those of a buyers' market, the standards of a new small private venture drop downward to those of sellers in a chronic shortage economy.

Private ventures have to adapt to the use of bribery, too, in the acquisition of the necessary inputs. Cheating is needed not only to acquire inputs, but also to defend the business against the state. Many individuals joining the private sector are not entrepreneurs, but adventurers. Such is the natural process of selection under the given conditions.

These circumstances set the trap for the social position of the private sector. Daily experience supplies arguments for 'anti-capitalist' demagoguery and for popular slogans against profiteering, greediness and cheating.[8] Such propaganda fuels further restrictions and interventions which lead to further deterioration: to capitalism at its worst. We therefore face a vicious cycle. It is reminiscent of a marriage between an anti-Semite and a Jewess, or between a racist and a black woman. Husband and wife irritate each other, may even hate each other but they know they must live together because of strong common economic interests. The contemporary socialist system needs the active contribution of a private sector, otherwise it is not able to deliver the goods to the people. Socialism has apparently arrived at a stage in history when it is unable to survive in its pure, strictly non-capitalist fashion and must coexist with its self-acknowledged arch-enemy not only worldwide but within its own borders as well. In other words, the system is heading towards a *mixed economy* where various forms of public and private ownership will operate side by side. The formulation of the problem makes it clear that this is an issue of extreme political importance, but in keeping with the brief compass of this paper, we will not discuss it any further.

4 THE PERSISTENCE OF BUREAUCRACY

The state-owned sector remains the dominant sector of the economy in Eastern Europe and in the Soviet Union, and in China as well, though not to the same extent. As China proceeds on the road to industrialisation, however, the role of state-owned enterprises is likely to increase.

The central idea of the original reform blueprints had been the abolition of the command economy – that is, the elimination of mandatory output targets and mandatory input quotas. At this time, Yugoslavia and Hungary are the only countries which have more or less consistently implemented these proposals. In China, USSR and Poland they have been realised only partially.

The initial expectation of the reformers had been that, once the administrative system had been abolished, there would be a momentary vacuum which would then be filled by the market mechanism. In other words, bureaucratic commands would be instantaneously replaced by market signals. The underlying assumption of this position was that of a simple complementarity between the two mechanisms of coordination, namely bureaucratic and market coordination.[9] However, this expectation, which was shared by the author in the 1950s, has turned out to be naive. What actually happened was that the vacuum left by the elimination of administrative commands, and thus by the elimination of *direct* bureaucratic coordination, was filled not by the market, but by other, *indirect* tools of bureaucratic coordination.

The role of the market, which had not been completely eliminated even under the classical socialist planning system, has of course increased in the wake of the reform. However, the role of the bureaucracy continues to remain pervasive, and is asserted in many different ways.[10] To summarise in a nutshell, the role of the bureaucracy remains paramount in the selection and in the promotion of managers, and in the decision making power with regard to the entry and the exit of firms. And while the bureaucracy has reduced or completely relinquished direct administrative control over the quantities of output and input of state-owned firms, it can still control them by informal interventions, through formal state orders and informal requests, and also through administrative price setting and through the extremely strong financial dependence of the firm on its superior organs. Thus the state-owned firm has remained strongly dependent on the various branches of the bureaucracy, on the ministries in charge of production, on foreign trade authorities, on the price control office, on financial bodies, on the police, and so on. The party organisations also intervene frequently in the affairs of firms. A change has taken place in the form, but not in the intensity, of dependence.

In our description of the private sector, we have used the terms 'spontaneous' or 'naturally grown'. Here, we shall emphasise that the persistence of the bureaucracy is a spontaneous and natural outgrowth of the system as well.[11] The Central Committee or the Politburo does not have to decide to maintain as much of the bureaucracy as possible during the process of reform. On the contrary, the bureaucracy may grow *despite* sincere attempts to reduce it, and in the face of dramatic campaigns to get rid of it, such as the one which took place during the cultural revolution in China. The current Soviet *perestroika* (restructuring) again sets out as its goal the reduction of the size of the bureaucracy; yet, the experience up to now does not allow us to place a lot of confidence in the possibility of checking the natural growth of the bureaucracy, even if drastic methods are employed. A self-reproduction of bureaucracy can be observed in the sense that, if it is eliminated at some place, in one particular form, it will reappear at another place in some other form. This permanent restoration of bureaucratic control is explained by many factors. One is, of course, all the material advantage associated with bureaucratic positions, namely financial benefits, privileges and access to goods and services in short supply. Even more important is the attraction of power. And here we arrive at a highly political issue again. The relative shares of the role played by bureaucratic and market coordination are not simply a matter of finding the most efficient division of labour between two neutral forms of control. The bureaucracy rules the socialist economy. Allowing the genuine functioning of the market means the voluntary surrender of an important part of its power.

The most important consequences of this situation are the limits imposed on the reformability of the state-owned sector by the systemic tendency of self-reproduction of the bureaucracy. We might be able to appreciate this point more clearly by considering the question of the constituency for reform. In the case of greater state tolerance for private economic activity, this constituency is large and well-defined. It consists of all citizens of a socialist country who choose to, or at least would like to able to, have the option to work in the private sector, as enterpreneurs or as employees.

On the other hand, nobody is an unqualified winner in the decentralisation of the state-owned sector. Every person involved with the state-owned sector gains as well as loses as a result of genuine decentralisation. Each member of the bureaucratic apparatus may gain autonomy *vis-à-vis* his superiors, but at the same time may lose power over this subordinates. A reduction in paternalism and a concomitant hardening of the budget constraint[12] entails advantages as well as disadvantages for the managers as well as for the workers of a state-owned firm. They gain in autonomy, but at the same time lose in protection. While it is typically true that people are not in favour of, or are at best indifferent with regard to, the protection of others, they usually like to be protected themselves. In a capitalist economy, this ambivalent feeling towards protection is best reflected in the complex attitude towards free trade being evaluated favourably when it allows a company to market its own products in foreign markets with only minimal tariffs, but being less eagerly welcomed when it results in foreign competitors entering the company's domestic markets. In a socialist economy, every individual working in the state-owned sector has these schizophrenic feelings with respect to the soft budget constraint, to paternalism, and to protection. While high taxes are disliked, subsidies, even if the firm is not now receiving them, may come in handy in the future, and can therefore not be opposed quite firmly. Shortages, while they inconvenience the firm as a buyer, suit it as a seller. Thus it turns out that neither the bureaucrats, nor the managers, nor indeed the workers, are enthusiastic adherents of competition or of the marketisation of the state-owned sector. Some enlightened government officials and intellectuals may come to the conclusion that a hardening of the budget constraint and a decrease in paternalism is needed so as to improve the performance of the economy. However, there are no strikes or street demonstrations in favour of increasing economic efficiency at the expense of state protection. As a result, there does not exist a grassroots movement for the decentralisation of the state-owned sector.

Since on the one hand there is strong inducement to maintain the bureaucratic positions, and on the other hand there is no unambiguous constituency against their maintenance, the final result is the permanent reproduction of bureaucratic coordination.

5 ALTERNATIVE FORMS OF SOCIAL ORGANISATION

After this discussion of the private sector and of the state-owned sector and of the role of the bureaucracy and of the market in a prototype reforming socialist economy, let us now approach the theme of this paper from a somewhat more general point of view. Consider Figure 3.1.

When referring to state ownership *1*, we have in mind the classical case of bureaucratic centralised state ownership, *2* is private ownership, while *A* and *B* refer respectively to bureaucratic and to market coordination.

Two *strong* linkages exist between the ownership form and the coordination mechanism. Thus, it is common to encounter classical, pre-reform socialist economies which combine state ownership with bureaucratic control and classical capitalist economies which combine private ownership with market control. These two simple cases might be looked upon as historical benchmark models. It seems quite natural, that when economic units based on private ownership operate in the market both as sellers and as buyers, that they would be motivated by the incentives of financial gain and would be highly responsive to costs and to prices. Similarly economic units under state control are operated by the bureaucracy, using bureaucratic instruments.

By contrast, we can observe that in the reforming socialist economies, the private sector, while mainly controlled by the market, is also subject to bureaucratic control, as symbolised by the dotted line from *2* to *A*. Yet this attempt to impose bureaucratic control on private activities does not and cannot work smoothly due to the basic incongruity of this pair.

In addition, there exist other, generally also inconsistent, attempts to coordinate the state-owned sector via market coordination (the dotted line from *1* to *B*). This idea was of course at the centre of the blueprint of market socialism. However, it turned out not to be possible to decrease the dominant influence of the bureaucracy. The influence of the market on the coordination of state-owned firms is full of frictions, as we have already seen in the earlier sections of this paper. In spite of the efforts of reformers to strengthen the linkage of *1* to *B*, there is an inclination to restore the linkage of *1* to *A*: bureaucratic coordination penetrates and pushes out the influence of the market.

To sum up: the relationship between the latter two pairs – namely

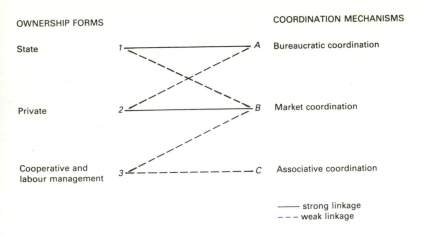

Figure 3.1   Strong and weak linkages

the relationship between *1* and *B*, and between *2* and *A* – can be characterised as *weak* linkages.

The notions 'strong' and 'weak' linkages do not imply a value judgement and do not indicate any preference on the part of the author. These are descriptive categories. In accordance with the general philosophy of the paper, a linkage between an ownership form and a type of coordination is strong if it emerges spontaneously and prevails is spite of resistance and countermeasures. It is based on a natural affinity and a cohesion between certain types of ownership and a certain types of coordination mechanisms respectively. The adjective 'weak' refers to linkages, which are to some extent artificial and not sufficiently strong to resist the impact of the stronger linkage. Weak linkages are pushed aside by the strong ones time and again, whether the intellectual and political leaders of the reform like it or not.[13]

6   THE WEAKNESS OF 'THIRD FORMS'

Is there a 'third way'? First, let us turn to the issue of ownership. In row *3*, where the Figure 3.1 refers to cooperatives and labour management, we must emphasise the non-private, but also the non-bureaucratic character of social ownership, such as that found in genuine communes or in instances of genuine workers' management.[14] The idea of cooperative socialism has long been part of socialist thinking. As for coordination of type *C*, the term 'associative mechanisms' is the collective name of a set of potential mechanisms. It is probably easiest to define the set in a negative way, as any mechanism of coordination which operates neither through the bureaucracy nor through the market, but which is based on self-governance, on free associations, on reciprocity, on altruism or on mutual voluntary adjustment.

The literature on socialism is rich in proposals which suggest that socialist society be based on cooperative ownership, and on non-market, non-bureaucratic associative coordination. In referring to this tradition of thought Marx coined the somewhat derogatory term 'Utopian Socialism'. Early representatives of this line of thinking have been Proudhon, Fourier (to an extent), Owen, and others.

The literature does not always couple *3* and *C*. Some authors place the emphasis on *3*, others on *C*, while in some cases, the two are considered together. Ideas of this kind come up frequently in the context of the reform discussions in socialist countries.[15] The whole Yugoslav experience constitutes an attempt, albeit a highly imperfect one, to move in the direction of this third way to socialism away from the exclusive reliance on state or private ownership and on the bureaucracy or on the market. The Chinese cultural revolution may be looked upon as an attempt to smash the bureaucracy and to proceed to a non-bureaucratic kind of socialism without the introduction of market elements. But neither of these two great historical experiments leads to conclusive results. In both cases the transformation was forced upon society by the political leadership and although at the beginning the initiative from the top had enthusiastic support among at least a part of the population, it was subsequently institutionalised and forced through, without countenancing any deviation from the central party line. Therefore the fact that something resembling ownership form *3* was and still is the dominant form in Yugoslavia or that the rhetoric of Mao's Cultural Revolution reasserted principles similar to coordination mechanism *C* does not allow us to reach any conclusions concerning the true strength of these forms.

Let us apply instead the criterion proposed previously and look at whether cooperative ownership and associative coordination grow *spontaneously and naturally* during the reform process of socialist systems. This question is meaningful, because the establishment of genuine voluntary cooperatives, voluntary adjustments and other forms of associative coordination are not prohibited in these countries. Small cooperatives are far better tolerated by the system than private economic activities. And altruism and non-commercialised reciprocity are of course legal in any system.

However, we can observe that, while *3* and *C* exist and did exist even at the peak of bureaucratic centralisation, these forms have not experienced a spectacular growth after the command system had been abolished. When beside centralised state-ownership other forms were permitted, private ownership gained ground rapidly. While the elimination of direct bureaucratic control left a momentary vacuum, this vacuum has been filled mainly by indirect bureaucratic control, as well as with some form of market coordination. Cooperative ownership and associative coordination play only an auxiliary role at most.[16]

Let us sum up our *theoretical conjectures* concerning the strengths or weaknesses of the forms of social organisation. While ownership forms *1* and *2* are robust, *3* has few followers. Similarly, while coordination forms *A* and *B* are widely applied, *C* operates only in a rather restricted area of affairs. And in contrast to the strong linkages between *1* and *A*, and between *2* and *B*, all other potential linkages from *1*, *2* and *3* on the ownership side to *A*, *B* and *C* on the coordination mechanism side are weak.(Figure 3.1 shows with dotted lines only four of the potential weak linkages. There are, of course, others.)

The validity of conjectures concerning the strength or weakness of certain ownership forms, of coordination mechanisms and of linkages between ownership and coordination mechanism is an *empirical* matter. As indicated in the Introduction, the present paper does not provide empirical evidence. Yet these conjectures can be accepted, modified or rejected by inference from empirical studies reported in the available literature or conducted in the future. In any case, the issue of the validity of empirically testable conjectures must be strictly separated from the normative issue: political and moral preferences over the set of alternative forms of ownership and coordination mechanisms.

It must be admitted that the observations concerning the weakness of third forms are drawn from a small sample observed over a brief period. Perhaps twenty or thirty years from now, researchers might be able to observe that this tendency was stopped and that history took an alternative route. History is always unpredictable. But as long as no contrary evidence is provided by experience, it is worth while to keep in mind the observations concerning the strength or weakness of the alternative ownership forms and coordination mechanisms.

It is fully understandable that various social groups and intellectual currents advocate a wider role for third forms. These efforts may have beneficial effects, provided that those who make such suggestions do not nourish false hopes and do not strive for the dominance of non-state and non-private ownership, and of the non-bureaucratic and non-marketised coordination. It would be intellectually dishonest to hide the weakness of third forms.

7   ABOUT NORMATIVE IMPLICATIONS

No search for a third form of ownership and/or for a third form of coordination mechanism allows one to evade the real tough choices. Hence, we really need to decide what the relative importance of the two robust forms of ownership – state versus private – will be. Closely allied to this will be the choice concerning the relative shares of the two robust coordination mechanisms: that is, bureaucratic versus market coordination.

Here a *caveat* is needed. In the discussion of reform ideas it has not infrequently been observed that critical propositions generated as the positive (descriptive) analysis of an existing socialist system acquired a *normative twist*. The logical structure of this normative twist is as follows: 'If you say that the phenomenon *A* has harmful effects, then it implies a value judgement and a prescriptive suggestion as well: the elimination of phenomenon *A* eliminates the harmful effects. Therefore phenomenon A should be eliminated'. This train of thought is logically false and also dangerous. Even if one can prove that phenomenon *A* has harmful effects, it does *not* follow from this proposition that (1) the elimination of phenomenon *A* is at all feasible under the given conditions, and (2) that the elimination of phenomenon *A* is a sufficient condition for the elimination of the harmful consequences.

And now we can return to the ideas elaborated upon in the present paper. The author would like to avoid normative twists to his own positive analysis. The positive (descriptive) statements to the effect that both state and private ownership are robust forms, and that each of them has a strong linkage either to bureaucratic or to market coordination does *not* imply the proposal that society must give up state ownership and shift to private ownership. Such an extreme normative conclusion ('restore capitalism!') is not implied. Nor does the paper suggest that we are faced with an 'either–or' type of binary choice between mutually exclusive forms: either state ownership cum bureaucratic coordination, or private ownership cum market coordination. The ideas presented in the paper can, however, be construed to entail the following:

1. State and private ownership can coexist within the same society. Yet in the present political, social and ideological environment this is an uneasy symbiosis, loaded with many dysfunctional features.

2. The decision concerning the actual shares of state and private ownership, and the associated decision concerning the combination of bureaucratic and market coordination are both dependent on the ultimate value judgements of those participating in the choice. The paper does not comment on these value judgements, nor on the political and ethical criteria underlying the choice. Consequently, it cannot offer unambiguous suggestions. What it tries to do is much more modest: it offers *conditional predictions* based on the theoretical conjectures about the strengths and weaknesses of various possible linkages between ownership and coordination mechanisms. This paper merely warns: let us not have illusions and false expectations. Once one arrives at a large share for state ownership, one gets a 'package deal', and the package then inevitably contains a large dose of bureaucratic coordination. Another warning is also needed: if one really wants a larger share for market coordination, one must *ipso facto*, accept a larger share for private ownership and for individual activities. But a desired coordination mechanism, (say market) does not come about without a significant backing of the appropriate ownership form (say private ownership). Likewise, one cannot get the desired ownership form (say public) without getting its associated form of coordination (say bureaucratic coordination). Such is the *Realpolitik* of reforms.

The usual slogans demanding state ownership cum market entail a misunderstanding or engender a naive, false expectation which will certainly be disproved by the bitter track record of experimentation with half-reforms. We might even say that some economists and policy makers have used this catch-phrase as a tool of mass manipulation, or, to apply a less pejorative formulation, as an educational instrument. ('After a long period of telling $2 \times 2 = 8$, it is reasonable to say at first $2 \times 2 = 6$. Declaring immediately that $2 \times 2 = 4$ causes too much of a shock.') But then, must every socialist country tread the painful path of gradual disenchantment? Is it really hopeless to expect that the latecomers to the reform process might learn from the disappointments of those who have gone before them?

3. Those who sincerely want a larger role for the market must allow more room for formal and informal private activities, for free entry and for exit, for competition, for individual entrepreneurship and for private property. Only a radical extension of the private sector creates favourable conditions for the marketisation of the whole economy, including more effective market signals and more powerful profit incentives for state-owned firms. Movement in that direction – namely in the direction of the extension of the private sector – is the most important yardstick of economic reform. Without such movement reform slogans pay only a lip-service to decentralisation and market-coordination.

How far can a socialist system go in the uneasy symbiosis with private ownership and individual activities? The answer to this question is more a political or an ideological issue than a question of economics – and the analysis of these aspects goes far beyond the theme of the present paper.

Notes

* Earlier versions of the paper were presented at the New School for Social Research (New York), at Harvard University (Cambridge, Mass.), at the European University Institute (Firenze) and at WIDER, the World Institute for Development Economics Research (Helsinki). I should like to express my thanks to the participants of the seminars at these institutions for valuable comments and to Mária Kovács, to Carla Krüger and to Shailendra Raj Mehta for assistance in the transcription and editing of the lecture. The support of the Hungarian Academy of Sciences, of Harvard University, of WIDER and of the Sloan Foundation is gratefully acknowledged.
1. There is a voluminous literature concerning the description and the analysis of reform processes in the various socialist countries. To men-

tion only a few examples: J. P. Burkett (1989) on Yugoslavia, J. Kornai (1986a) and L. Antal *et al.* (1987) on Hungary, D. H. Perkins (1988) on China, Iu. N. Afanas'ev (ed.) (1988), E. A. Hewett (1988), G. E. Schroeder (1987) and N. Shmelev (1987) on the USSR.

2. The author is working on a book entitled: *The Political Economy of Socialism*, where the relationship between political structure, ideology, ownership forms and coordination mechanisms is explored in detail.

3. See, for example, the following sample of the earliest papers advocating a decentralisation based reform in Eastern Europe: B. Kidric (see his papers from the 1950s in the (1985) volume) for Yugoslavia, Gy. Péter (1954a, 1954b, 1956) and J. Kornai [1957] (1959) for Hungary, and W. Brus [1961] (1972) for Poland, E. Liberman [1962] (1972) for the USSR and Sun Yefang (1982) for China.

4. Private business partnerships, owned and operated by a group of people belong to the private sector, along with business owned and operated by single individuals or by a family. In the Soviet Union such partnerships are called 'cooperative', although everybody knows that they are in fact private business partnerships.

5. About the formal and informal private sector see G. Grossman (1977), I. R. Gábor (1985), C. M. Davis (1988), S. Pomorski (1988) and B. Dallago (1989).

6. Perhaps the USSR, and especially the Soviet agricultural sector is an exception. Here the memory of the terror which accompanied mass collectivisation and the 'liquidation of kulaks' is so deeply imprinted on the collective conscience that it has been passed on from generation to generation and many individuals are still diffident about starting individual farming or any other kind of private business.

7. On Hungarian television, the author once watched a programme about a man who had been a lawyer in a state-owned enterprise, but who had decided to leave his job to open a small private restaurant – just so as no longer to have a boss tell him what to do. The same reason was given by former members of an agricultural cooperative who had chosen to quit and had opened a small regional food-processing plant.

8. It is ironic that some politicians and journalists in the reforming socialist countries, (sometimes even in the 'new left' circles within oppositional groups) argue against high prices and profiteering on *moral* grounds. It is not recognised that it is inconsistent to declare the desirability of a market and at the same time to refuse the legitimacy of a price generated by the very same market mechanism.

9. The term 'bureaucratic coordination', here as in other works of the author is used in a value-free sense, without any negative connotation as in many Eastern European writings and speeches. It refers to certain types of controlling and coordinating activities. The main characteristics of this mechanism include the multi-level hierarchical organisation of control, the dependence of the subordinate on the superior and the mandatory or even coercive character of the instructions of the superior.

10. In the spirit of note 9, a word of explanation is needed concerning the term 'bureaucracy'. This notion is also used in a value-free way, without

implying any negative judgement whatsoever. It denotes the hierarchical apparatus in control of all social and economic affairs and includes not only government officials and managers, but the functionaries of the party and of the mass organisations as well.

In other words 'bureaucracy' refers to a certain *social group* different from other groups in society, and 'bureaucratic coordination' refers to a certain *coordination mechanism*, different from other mechanisms, such as, for example market coordination. Conceptual distinctions not withstanding there is, of course, close linkage between these two phenomena: the bureaucracy applies bureaucratic coordination methods to govern those who are subject to its power.

11. As before, the term 'natural' is not used here in the sense of American advertising, where it is a synonym of words such as good, wholesome and non-artificial. Rather we use it to denote a phenomenon which reproduces without government support, and sometimes even in spite of policies designed to oppose it, simply as a consequence of the social situation.

12. The terms 'soft' and 'hard' budget constraint are discussed in the author's works (1980, 1986b).

13. There are many other combinations of *1, 2, A* and *B* worth considering. For example, if in an economy the private sector is strong and stable, and the linkage of *2* to *B* is the dominant one, a certain segment of the economy can be successfully subjected to the linkage of *1* to *B*. In other words, in a basically private market economy the state-owned sector can adjust to the rules of the market.

14. In accordance with the definitions used in the present paper, private business partnerships in the Soviet Union cannot be regarded as genuine cooperatives. They belong to Form *2* and not to Form *3*.

15. Of course, cooperative ownership can be linked not only to coordination mechanisms of type *C*, but to the market mechanism as well. For example Yugoslavia experimented with a coupling of ownership form *3* (labour management) with both coordination mechanisms *B* and with mechanism *C* (market and 'associative' coordination). Large segments of the economy were coordinated in the usual way by the market mechanism. At the same time, so-called 'social compacts' were arranged to establish direct contacts between the representatives of producers and of consumers; they were expected voluntarily to make mutual adjustments. While the official policy alternated in the emphasis given to mechanisms *B* and C, in fact bureaucratic coordination mechanism *A* was prevailing all the time, and was in a latent fashion the dominant force.

16. Ownership form *3* and coordination mechanism *C* are associated in many writings with certain political ideas such as administrative decentralisation of government activities, the increased role of local governments, participatory democracy and self-governance, corporative ideas of various sorts, and so on. Again the discussion of these aspects is beyond the limits of the present paper.

References

Afanas'ev, Iu. N. (ed.) (1988) *Inogo ne dano* (There is No Other Way) (Moscow: Progress).

Antal, László, Bokros, Lajos, Csillag, István, Lengyel, László and Matolcsy, György (1987) 'Change and Reform', *Acta Oeconomica*, 38(3–4) pp. 187–213.

Brus, Włodzimierz [1961] (1972) *The Market in a Socialist Economy* (London: Routledge & Kegan Paul).

Burkett, John P. (1989) 'The Yugoslav Economy and Market Socialism', in Bornstein, M. (ed.) *Comparative Economic Systems: Models and Cases* (Homewood, IL and Boston, MA: Irwin) pp. 234–58.

Dallago, Bruno (1989) 'The Underground Economy in the West and East: A Comparative Approach', in Bornstein, M. (ed.) *Comparative Economic Systems: Models and Cases* (Homewood, IL and Boston, MA: Irwin) pp. 463–84.

Davis, Christopher M. (1988) 'The Second Economy in Disequilibrium and Shortage Models of Centrally Planned Economies', *Berkeley–Duke Occasional Papers on the Second Economy in the USSR*, 12 (July).

Gábor, István R. (1985) 'The Major Domains of the Second Economy', in Galasi, P. and Sziráczky, Gy. (eds) *Labour Market and Second Economy in Hungary* (Frankfurt and New York: Campus) pp. 133–78.

Grossman, Gregory (1977) 'The "Second Economy" of the USSR', *Problems of Communism*, 26(5) pp. 25–40.

Hewett, Ed A. (1988) *Reforming the Soviet Economy. Equality versus Efficiency* (Washington, DC: The Brookings Institution, 1988).

Kidric, Boris (1985) *Sabrana Dela* (Collected Works) (Beograd: Izdavacki Centar Komunist).

Kornai, János [1957] (1959) *Overcentralization in Economic Administration* (London: Oxford University Press).

Kornai, János (1980) *Economics of Shortage* (Amsterdam: North-Holland).

Kornai, János (1986a) 'The Hungarian Reform Process: Visions, Hopes and Reality', *Journal of Economic Literature*, 24(4) (December) pp. 1687–1737.

Kornai, János (1986b) 'The Soft Budget Constraint', *Kyklos*, 39(1) pp. 3–30.

Liberman, Evsey G. [1962] (1972) 'The Plan, Profits and Bonuses', in Nove, A. and Nuti, D. M. (eds) *Socialist Economics: Selected Readings* (Harmondsworth: Penguin Books) pp. 309–18.

Lenin, Vladimir Il'ich [1920] (1966) *Left-wing Communism, an Infantile Disorder* (Moscow: Progress).

Perkins, Dwight Heald (1988) 'Reforming China's Economic System', *Journal of Economic Literature*, 26(2) (June) pp. 601–45.

Péter, György (1954a) 'Az egyszemélyi felelos vezetésrol' (On Management Based on One-Man Responsibility), *Társadalmi Szemle* 9(8–9) (August/September) pp. 109–24.

Péter, György (1954b) 'A gazdaságosság jelentoségérol és szereperol a népgazdaság tervszeru irányitásában' (On the Importance and Role of

Economic Efficiency in the Planned Control of the National Economy), *Közgazdasági Szemle*, 1(3) (December) pp. 300–24.

Péter, György (1956) 'A gazdaságosság és a jövedelmezoség jelentosége a tervgazdaságban, I–II' (The Importance of Economic Efficiency and Profitability in Planned Economy I–II), *Közgazdasági Szemle*, 3(6) (June) pp. 695–711 and 3(7–8) (July–August) pp. 851–69.

Pomorski, Stanislaw (1988) 'Privatization of the Soviet Economy under Gorbachev I: Notes on the 1986 Law on Individual Enterprise', *Berkeley –Duke Occasional Papers on the Second Economy in the USSR*, 13 (October).

Schroeder, Gertrude E. (1987) 'Anatomy of Gorbachev's Economic Reform', *Soviet Economy*, 3(3) (July–September) pp. 219–41.

Shmelev, N. (1987) 'Avansy i Dolgi' (Credits and Debts), *Novyi Mir*, 6 (June) pp. 142–58.

Sun Ye-fang [1958–1961] (1982) 'Some Theoretical Issues in Theoretical Issues', originally published in the period 1958–61. Edited and translated by K. K. Fung under the title: *Social Needs versus Economic Efficiency in China* (Armonk: M. E. Sharpe).

Comment

Aleksandar M. Vacić*

ECONOMIC COMMISSION FOR EUROPE

The theory of markets in a planned economy is discussed in some detail in three reports presented to the conference – those prepared by János Kornai (Chapter 3 in this volume), Włodzimierz Brus and Kazimierz Laski (Chapter 2 in this volume) and the Institute of Economics of the Academy of Sciences of the USSR, the latter presented to the audience by Leonid Abalkin, Director of the Institute (Chapter 1 in this volume).

These three reports approach the issue in different and to some extent diverging ways, which makes the task of the discussant challenging and professionally interesting. An attempt will be made here to discuss them in a logical sequence, taking into account also comments regarding the role of market forces in planned economies made in other reports. Before turning to the various views presented in the reports, it should be pointed out that almost all look at the issue in close conjunction with past and ongoing economic reforms. This makes them interesting not only theoretically but also from the viewpoint of economic policy.

1 CO-ORDINATION MECHANISMS AND THE OWNERSHIP STRUCTURE

In his paper devoted to the affinity between ownership and co-ordination mechanisms, János Kornai begins with several assumptions significant for the design of his approach. Most earlier discussion of economic reforms tended to follow a normative rather than a positive approach. This often makes it difficult to grasp real developments in individual countries, and at the same time usually leads to an underestimation of differences in their real economic situations. Reform blueprints or programmes were in most cases (Kornai claims, in all cases – a view which I do not share)[1] in circulation before the actual period of the reform, but the reality of

55

reforming countries has never corresponded to any of the blueprints.

Irrespective of their initial ambitions and varied efforts to implement them, all reforms have shown that there are *limits to the reformability* of societies and that these limits can be accurately gauged only in the course of implementation. Of all the components of national economies, the least transformable is the state sector, where traditional economic, juridical and political forces are the strongest. Given its large share in the total economy, the low transformability of the state sector imposes limits on the general scope of real economic reforms and regularly brings about departures from the original reform programmes. Accordingly, it appears much more interesting to monitor real processes of economic reform rather than reform blueprints, the more so as any transformation tends to evolve spontaneously, in keeping with the natural forces ruling economic development.

Along these lines of reasoning, the main message contained in the report presented by Kornai is that any substantial extension of the role played by market forces in a planned economy depends on *diversification of the ownership structure* – and primarily on the extension of the sector based on private property. In this sector alone market forces tend to appear with surprising vigour even in countries where there have been no private activities other than those based on individual plots for years or decades. Private farming, legal, tax-paying private businesses in other sectors, various types of informal, 'grey' economy, or varied activities based on property owned by the state but leased to individuals could be cited as usual forms of such activities.

In assessing the potential effects of increasing *private economic activities*, two points seem to be important. The emergence of a significant private sector was the most important immediate result of the reforms, especially in the most reform-oriented countries such as Hungary, China and Poland. This is also true for the Soviet Union, although – owing to the many years of marginalisation of the private sector – the share of the private sector in that country remains much smaller than in the other three economies mentioned. On the other hand, it appears that prospects for a lasting expansion of the private sector – and of the market forces in parallel with it – are not so good, as private economic activities continue to be discouraged by a number of obstacles and constraints. Almost everywhere private business faces a multitude of restrictions and bureaucratic interventions caused by the absence of clear-cut juridical regulations or the lack of legal institutions to protect private property and enforce private contracts, by hostility which originates in the jealousy of people who are suspicious of growing income differentials, by the lack of effective political support at the level where decisions concerning this sector are usually made, etc.

Furthermore, given the uncertainty about the scope and time horizon for future tolerance of the private sector, economies of scale cannot be enjoyed due to limits on capital accumulation. Thus the private firm is typically not interested in a lasting expansion of its activities or development of solid relations with its customers, but rather in reaping a high income over a short period of time.

Due to the above-described and various other juridical, political or economic constraints, including discrimination in respect of the availability of numerous raw materials in short supply or of credit facilities, the small-scale private sector cannot threaten the overall nature of the existing socialist countries. Nevertheless, Kornai claims that one cannot deny that it sows some seeds of economic practices typical of capitalist economies. In many countries there has been public concern about the potential effects of such developments for the traditional set of values of the socialist system. But in most reform-oriented economies this is no longer strong enough to prevent further development of this sector. To use Kornai's words, 'Socialism has apparently arrived at a stage in history when it is unable to survive in its pure, strictly non-capitalist fashion and must coexist with its self-acknowledged arch-enemy not only world-wide but within its own borders as well'.

In another way, and in a much broader scope, the relevance of the multisectoral economy for the real influence of market forces in a socialist economy is highlighted in the report presented by Dong Fureng (Chapter 12 in this volume). His detailed description of the different attitudes of various regions and individual social strata in China shows that the market economy can be disliked or even rejected in milieux where it previously never existed. This shows that market forces can be effective on a large scale only after the overall development level of a subsistence economy is overcome and the social division of labour makes outdated the primitive common property or other informal constraints usually imposed in traditional pre-capitalist rural life.

However, even if sectors other than the state sector – private, cooperative, mixed, etc. – become significant, this does not in itself guarantee a change in the main *mechanism of communication* in socialist countries. In fact, contrary to expectations that the extension of the private sector will inevitably bring about a contraction of bureaucratic coordination in favour of market forces, Kornai claims that state coordination remains – either directly or indirectly – the main coordinating channel in the state sector while the market is the strongest channel in the private sectors. The relations between state ownership and market coordination and private property and bureaucratic coordination, to use the author's words, remain the weak linkages, putting the overall role of market forces much below expectations.

A third option put forward in some socialist economies – that of *cooperative ownership and associative coordination* – in spite of its unexpected failure in Yugoslavia, continues to attract many economists, János Kornai included. Thus Yugoslav economists still seem to owe international public opinion an explanation of why the Yugoslav path, once considered almost optimal, brought about such unexpectedly bad results. The usual claim – that it was not market forces but rather their compression by re-emerging informal direct planning at the level of conflicting individual federal states, which has brought the Yugoslav economy to a state of stagflation since the mid-1980s – seems to be close to the hearts of reformers and reform-oriented scholars in other socialist countries and elsewhere.[2] But the assessment has to be supported by tangible arguments, and even more by long-awaited new economic reforms which would bring the country back on to the right track. Meanwhile, other forms of cooperative property and associative coordination now offered by new legislation in several countries – even though they are not intended to become the dominant form – have to be monitored carefully and interpreted in a balanced way.

Another very important issue for the general role to be played by market forces in a planned economy is the question of the *degree and the ways of participation in the international division of labour*. The reports submitted by Marie Lavigne, Oleg Bogomolov and Thomas Wolf (Chapter 14, 13 and 10 in this volume) indicate that the overall situation in this respect seems to be far from clear. In fact, even in the mid-1980s, when the third wave of economic reforms in the European centrally-planned economies started, there appeared to be two different approaches. One of them considered opening everyday economic activity at the enterprise level to direct influences of the international markets not only a component of the reform process but even the most important part of the reform. In the other case, the internal economic reforms are still interpreted as the main concern, assuming that external economic relations remain a derived issue, to the extent that even far-reaching economic reforms at home would be compatible with maintenance of the state monopoly in the foreign trade area. Judging by recent developments, the second approach seems to be losing ground. But – as shown in the report of Marie Lavigne – the relationship between the two aspects of the reform and even the real meaning of some changes in the regulations concerning foreign economic ties in many cases remain uncertain.

2 THE GREATER ROLE OF MARKET FORCES – BUT IN WHAT MARKETS?

If most economists now agree that a greater role should be played by market forces in reformed socialist economies, the next question is in what markets, whether just in the goods market or also in the capital market and the labour market. Although touched upon in several reports, this issue is discussed in detail only in the report submitted by Włodzimierz Brus and Kazimierz Laski (Chapter 2) and in a very interesting retrospective – in the light of the experience of the Hungarian New Economic Mechanism, usually referred to as NEM. Although formally limited to the Hungarian experience, this report is highly instructive as regards the challenges and dilemmas of the market arrangements faced in Hungary which, *mutatis mutandis*, are largely similar to those of other reform-oriented countries, including Yugoslavia. Several problems seem to be of particular interest.

First of all, given the very strong inheritance of non-market or even anti-market interpretation of the nature of the traditional socialist economic system, nobody thought in the early stages of economic reforms in all reforming countries that the presence of capital and labour markets was a crucial issue. Put another way, because of the rigidity of the traditional central planning, with all its unfavourable effects on the everyday life of the population, the main problem was to provide a legitimation for acceptance in principle of the market, leaving details of its scope for future stages. Although from a purely theoretical point of view this may appear simplified or even super-ficial, historically this attitude can be understood. Finally, the very fact that even today, in the fourth year of *perestroika* and the third wave of economic reforms, apart from Yugoslavia, the economic system aimed for by economic reforms can be called *a market economy* – rather than a *commodity production* – in only two countries, demonstrates that the past continues to influence the present and in some instances to shape its framework.

On the other hand, the brief review of the earlier theoretical debates – including Lange, Lerner, Dobb and Baran – presented in the Brus and Laski paper shows that even the revised Marxist thinking about an optimal organisation of the socialist economy, which had to some extent included the influence of the market, did not envisage any place for a genuine capital market. Thus, the discussion about the necessity of extending market influences from the products market to the capital market and also to the labour market appears to be a more recent phenomenon resulting from the experience of the most reform-oriented countries, Hungary included. The basic claim of Brus and Laski, very near to their general conclusion, is that 'the Hungarian NEM provides us with the decisive proof of the virtual impossibility of expecting product markets to operate properly without simultaneously opening up the markets for factors of production, especially the capital market'.

Leaving aside details and purely theoretical considerations, the main argument in favour of the *capital market* is based on the historical experience of the Hungarian NEM and other countries with reformed socialist economies. Partial reforms, limited to goods market, without a capital market, necessarily restore the decisive role of the centre in determining the rate of accumulation, in the allocation of investment resources and thus in the shaping of structural change in the economy through sectoral and spatial allocation policies. Moreover, this continued strong, albeit indirect, role of the centre does not emerge by chance, but rather as a reflection of the vacuum left in the functioning of the reformed economy when direct allocation from state investment funds is abolished but no other mechanisms for the direction of the accumulation funds of enterprises have been created. Thus either general investment funds (such as the OIF – General Investment Fund – and RIFS – Republican Investment Funds – in Yugoslavia), or specialised banks with similar functions and under direct control of the centre (such as the Investment Bank, Agricultural Bank and Foreign Trade Bank in Yugoslavia, and similar establishments which exist in other reforming countries, Hungary included) appear as logical, seemingly reform-oriented solutions. Similar to critical observations of Kornai and Brus concerning their viewpoints of that time, this author must admit that at that time he also wondered whether it was possible for a socialist economy to introduce either capital or labour markets on a large scale without compromising some of the generally-shared foundations of the system.[3]

Brus and Laski give a great deal of evidence that all the reforms remain incomplete and subsequently reversible as long as they are limited only to the products market. Put simply, without an effective capital market the centre maintains its decisive role in one of the crucial areas – that of investment and/or expansion of production or its restructuring, reducing the role of enterprises to the maintenance of existing capacities or their gradual extension without major technical or structural change. In turn, such a role of the centre limits competition to that between enterprises within individual sectors or branches, as they are unable to expand into other areas of activity. Furthermore, combined with the unquestioned role of the centre in decision making on the nationwide rate of accumulation, which also implies a relatively rigid control of wage differentiation, leaving the capital allocation function with the centre, ultimately disables the elementary disciplinary function of the market to distinguish between the most successful enterprises, the average, the mediocre or simply loss-making ones.

The protective role of the centre in respect of enterprises that on purely economic grounds should sooner or later have been closed down thus turns into a tutelage function in respect of the most successful enterprises, which can always be reproached for abusing their advantage in the market. A single mention of an enterprise in a such context in a speech by a prominent leader, or a similar comment in the editorial article in a daily or a weekly, is sufficient to wipe out the efforts of years and to prevent other directors from embarking on genuine enterpreneurial paths. The logic of 'Medium is beautiful', by preventing the striving for the above-average, necessarily pulls down the average, bringing it sooner or later to the level of mediocrity. It is not surprising, therefore, that all comparative analyses of the performance of individual groups of countries – such as developed market economies, newly industrialised countries and centrally-planned economies – have brought evidence of the poor performance of the latter group. In the United Nations Economic Commission for Europe, for instance, such studies have been undertaken at least three times in the 1980s. All of them reached similar conclusions – a declining competitiveness of the east European countries and the Soviet Union in the western markets;[4] below-average if not marginal effects of the investment goods imports on their export performance

in the global economy;[5] and also poor performance of the east
European countries in the west European markets during the process
of its integration.[6]

The lack of a capital market inevitably also reduces the scope for
the *labour market*, and not fortuitously. In other words, even if it is
assumed that a labour market is just the reverse side of the fact that
people have a right to choose their jobs and to change them many
times in their lifetime, in the traditional socialist surroundings employees feel very uneasy if they are to be either hired or fired by their
former colleagues. This applies even in a situation where there is still
a shortage of labour on a nationwide scale. People seem to prefer
dealing with state employment establishments rather than to rely on
market chances. Security of employment, even if it does not provide
an income sufficient to guarantee minimum welfare, appears to have
a much higher significance for the average worker than might be
assumed on purely economic grounds – a case where sociologists can
help economists to understand human nature better than they usually
do when designing their theories.

3   'SOCIALIST MARKET ECONOMY' – AN EXCUSE, A TACTICAL SLOGAN OR A NEW TYPE OF MARKET ECONOMY?

The final sentences of the last paragraph brings us to the last question, and at the same time the question one might have started with:
if historical experience has proved that socialism cannot survive
without the market economy and if market forces are to be extended
not only to products but also to factors of production – how then can
requirements stemming from the market logic be combined with
achievements of the socialist economic system, such as full employment, free health services and education, secure jobs, etc.? A simple
answer to this question might be that these achievements have in any
case been overestimated or unevenly distributed, and as such are
non-existent. But the experience of the reforming countries, including the Soviet Union, clearly shows that they are much more deeply
rooted than one may have assumed. Another answer might be that
the socialist economies, if genuinely reformed, will simply turn into
'normal' – that is, market and consequently capitalist – economies,
thus repeating, this time from the other side, that any developed
market economy is in fact a capitalist economy.

In this respect the reforming socialist economies, as evident in both national debates and international reviews, do not have the same stance. Some of them clearly say that, notwithstanding the advantages of market economies in respect of economic efficiency, they still give priority to the broader social values built into their system. Others seemingly no longer feel it necessary to explain in theoretical terms where they are moving; they just continue to move and wait for the natural process of development to determine both the path and its name. A third claim is that what they have in mind is not just a market economy, but rather a *socialist market economy* – an explanation that used to be very popular in Yugoslavia and seems to be increasingly referred to in the Soviet Union, see for example Chapter 1 in this volume.

The first position is clearly unsustainable in the longer term. Indeed, there is evidence that a preference for the existing economic arrangements, with everybody else reforming, is no longer comfortable for anybody. Accordingly, even the countries in which there have recently been no actual or announced economic reforms claim that this reflects the fact that they had sufficient reforms in previous years. The second position may postpone necessary answers for a few years or so, but an answer will in the longer run be required by both domestic and international public opinion. Thus the crucial question to be answered is whether the most reform-oriented countries are evolving into capitalist (market) economies or whether they are creating a new type of market economy, a socialist market economy.

Although no definite answer could be given to this question, for the moment the option for a new, socialist type of market economy seems to be closer to the hearts of national leaders and scholars of most reforming countries – at least in that none of them has claimed that the objective is to restore the capitalist market economy. Moreover, in the papers presented to the conference this choice is explicitly pointed out and explained in detail by L. Abalkin (Chapter 1 in this volume) and by Ante Čičin-Šain (Chapter 8 in this volume). It is also indicated in the report by Béla Csikós-Nagy (Chapter 7) and indirectly present in the comparisons between the old and the new Polish systems described in detail by Zdzisław Sadowski (Chapter 4). This choice has been also shared for years by the author of these comments and presented in his writings.[7] But things are far from being solved by the option for a socialist market economy, even if this choice is supported by everybody, everywhere.

The point is that the interpretation of the socialist market economy as the objective of the reformed economies proves to be very vulnerable in at least two ways. For one, the socialist market economy has been frequently interpreted in various ways which would practically deny it the character of a market economy. Some arguments of that nature seem to be present also in the report submitted by the Institute of Economics of the Academy of Sciences of the USSR. For another, many rational pragmatic steps towards the establishment of markets, notably in respect of capital and labour markets, have usually been rejected as incompatible with the socialist market economy. Finally, some of the basic assumptions of the real economic systems based on the theory of the socialist market economy proved to be Utopian or simply idealistic. An illustration of this is the Yugoslav scheme of the mid-1970s, which assumed that the worker can be simultaneously 'a competent producer, an entrepreneur and qualified decision maker in the major fields of social and political life' – to use the words of Čičin-Šain. For such qualities to be present in every worker, and exercised at the same time – while in all developed market economies they are subject to special training and exercised separately – the Yugoslavs must all be very talented, if not geniuses. Both potential distortions in the interpretation of the very concept of the socialist market economy thus in fact point to their common denominator – a lack of coherence in basic assumptions and inconsistencies in various aspects of the juridically defined economic system based on them. Thus the theory of a socialist market economy remains an area open to new contributions.

Although this conclusion might sound pessimistic, and further progress along the path of market economy is not easy, I think that the worst may already be behind us. In fact, there has recently been considerable agreement on at least five major points shared by a vast majority of reform-oriented economists.

First, a market economy is not in itself a capitalist economy and the extension of market forces in socialist countries consequently does not necessarily bring about the capitalist economic system.

Second, the socialist economic system is in no respect just the opposite of the capitalist one. Since the latter has reflected developments in all the preceding social and economic systems, the rejection of all elements of the capitalist economic system necessarily impedes the functioning of many institutions which are component parts of modern civilisation.

Third, the market forces in socialist countries, actual or potential but in any case badly needed, have nothing or very little to do with the market inherited from pre-revolutionary times and/or capitalism. Instead, they originate in both the production and the consumption arrangements of the contemporary socialist economies themselves. Viewed from this angle, the market economy is not extraneous but immanent to socialist economic systems worldwide.[8]

Fourth, the evolution of the socialist economies towards the market economy may make them closer to the capitalist economies and even bring about elements of the capitalist economic system within them while not threatening the socialist economic system as such.

Fifth, both the capitalist and socialist economic systems are subject to historical change. Consequently, new, more profound and historically better supported understanding of socialism may emerge, providing a basis according to which the real nature of each society will no longer be judged just by the words used in its constitution or by the prevailing type of property rights, as these have proved to be far from reliable for any theoretical thinking.

To sum up, given the experience of the seven-decade-long history of socialism, at the turn of the century any further opposition of the socialist to the capitalist market economy hardly makes sense as it is exactly the prejudice that the former should be the opposite of the latter that prevented the socialist countries from attaining many things that would otherwise have been easily achieved. Instead, at least for genuinely reform oriented socialist economies, it seems much more important to understand the logic and identify the mechanisms of contemporary developed market economies – including their comprehensive macroeconomic policies – and to apply them gradually and in a balanced way, with due considerations for the overall level of economic development of each country and the broad social values shared by its population.

Notes

* The views presented in this text are those of the author alone and do not necessarily coincide with those of the United Nations Economic Commission for Europe, where he is Director of the Division for Economic Analysis and Projections.
1. In contrast to early departures from the traditional socialist economic system, which usually require a long preparation and are frequently

reversed, at later stages new reform packages may be introduced at once and prepared with not much participation of the general public. The 1965 Yugoslav economic reform, for instance, was implemented in the latter way, although national authorities later on claimed that some 2000 economists participated in its preparation. One should, of course, distinguish between the discussion on alternative ways of reform *before* they are implemented and the usual wages of justification *after* they start.

2. An attempt to explain the origins of the Yugoslav economic and social crisis was made in my article 'Why the development in Yugoslavia deviated from the socialist self-management market economy' (Vacić, 1985–6). The subject seems to have been of interest to economists of many other socialist countries as, in addition to its primary publication in Serbo-Croatian and its English edition referred to above, it was also published in Hungarian (see Vacić, 1985–6). A more detailed explanation of the origins of the Yugoslav malaise is offered in my book (1989) *Jugoslavija i Evropa: Uporedna analiza privrednog razvoja Jugoslvije, 1971–87 (Yugoslavia and Europe: a Comparative Analysis of the Economic Development of Yugoslavia 1971–87).*

3. The Yugoslav substantive debate in this respect already took place at the beginning of the 1970s and resulted in two considerably different concepts, represented by the books *Privredni sistem Jugoslavije (Vacić, 1972)* and *Privredni sistem Jugoslavije* (Vacić, 1973). At that time I shared the view that both capital and labour markets existed *de facto* in Yugoslavia and should be further developed, albeit as a part of the historically-formed Yugoslav economic structure rather than as a reflection of the socialist economic system in a theoretical sense.

4. See ECE (1983).

5. See ECE (1987).

6. See ECE (1989).

7. See Vacić (1978).

8. I came to this conclusion in the process of reconsideration of the theory I was taught during the preparation of my Ph.D. thesis and explicitly formulated it in the resulting book (Vacić, 1966). 'Irrespective of the fact that market relations existed in the capitalist economic system also and that all socialist countries inherited a system of market relations, so that one may to some extent speak about a continued existence (preservation) of market relations in socialism, transformation of the output of labour into a commodity is a normal, regular and typical feature of socialist economic relations. In this sense, assuming that up-to-date developments of socialist countries have manifested general laws of socialism as a system, one can say that market economy is immanent to socialism'.

References

ECE (Economic Commission for Europe) (1983) 'Exports of manufactures from Eastern Europe and the Soviet Union to the developed market economies, 1965–81', in *Economic Bulletin for Europe*, 35(4) (Pergamon Press for the United Nations) (December) pp. 441–534.

ECE (1987) 'Eastern imports of engineering goods, 1960–85', in *Economic Bulletin for Europe*, 39(4) (December) (United Nations) pp. 49–97.

ECE (1989) 'The effects of West European integration on imports of manufactures from Eastern and Southern Europe', in *Economic Survey of Europe in 1988–89* (New York) pp. 64–86.

Vacić, A. M. (1966) *Uzroci robne proizvodnje u socijalismu* (Origins of Market Economy in Socialism) (Belgrade: Naučna Knjiga).

Vacić, A. M. (1972) *Privredni sistem Yugoslavije* (Belgrade: Institut za ekonomiku investicija).

Vacić, A. M. (1973) *Privredni sistem Yugoslavije* (Belgrade: Institut društvenih nauka).

Vacić, A. M. (1978) *Robna proizvodnja i socialistički privredni sistem* (Market Economy and Socialist Economic System) (Belgrade: Savremena administracija) 2nd edn (1984).

Vacić, A. M. (1985–6) 'Why the Development in Yugoslavia Deviated from the Socialist Self-management Market Economy', *Eastern European Economies*, 25(2) (Winter) originally published in Serbo-Croatian in *Socijalizam*, 26(11) (1983). Also published in Hungarian, *Közgazdasági szemle* 31(5) (1984); Polish, *Życie gospodarcze*, 20 (1699) (13 May 1984) and Slovak *Ekonomický časopis*, Bratislava, 35(4) (1988).

Vacić, A. M. (1989) *Jugoslavija i Evropa: Uporedna analiza privrednog razvoja Jugoslavije, 1971–87* (Yugoslavia and Europe: a Comparative Analysis of the Economic Development of Yugoslavia, 1971–87) (Belgrade: Ekonomika).

Comment

Pekka Sutela*
UNIVERSITY OF HELSINKI, FINLAND

I will discuss the papers starting with Abalkin (Chapter 1 in this volume), then looking at Brus–Laski (Chapter 2) and ending with Kornai (Chapter 3), not because this is the alphabetical or numerical order, but because there seems to be what the Marxists would call a 'logical–historical' connection between the papers. To put it crudely and somewhat unjustly, Academician Abalkin's paper reflects what I take to be the dominant mode of discussion in contemporary Soviet reform debates. At the same time its posing of questions – and many of the answers, too – is very like the theoretical framework of 'early Brus', criticised in the paper by Professors Brus and Laski. Their paper, on the other hand, depicts a theoretical transition from questions of the economic mechanism to the deeper problems of ownership and motivation. Professor Kornai's paper, finally, gives a leading Hungarian economist's view of these problems.

There is much to be welcomed in Academician Abalkin's paper. It shows how crucial old dogmas are being abandoned and proposals for a far-reaching market creation strategy are outlined in current Soviet reformism. At the same time, unfortunately, the discussion is also teasingly vague and even contradictory. This is also characteristic of much of current Soviet economics.

As an example, take the issue of settling with old dogmas. Markets, Abalkin emphasises, are immanent to socialism. To argue otherwise would be to follow conceptions alien to the true spirit of Marxism, he continues, without mentioning that actually the perspective of marketless communism is one of the characteristic features of Marxian socialism. Certainly it should be possible to criticise Marx where that is his due.

One reason why markets are necessary, Abalkin argues, is their fundamental democracy: the right to choose is a prime precondition of developing one's personality. This, presumably, is the motivation behind Abalkin's definition of markets. They are said to have two fundamental characteristics: direct relations between producers and consumers and the existence of choice among potential transaction partners, 'competition between producers'.

This is not a satisfactory definition of markets. It does not discriminate between market exchange, gifts and reciprocity – certainly an important consideration for the centrally-managed economies. In denying the existence of monopoly markets Abalkin actually applauds monopsony when citing Galbraith. Furthermore, Abalkin's definition does not begin to tackle the issues of the various intermediary forms between markets and hierarchies like subcontracting – or leasing, to take another example close to the Soviet experience.

There is another crucial weakness in Abalkin's discussion. He seems to think that specifically socialist markets could exist. They would exclude hired labour, include social guarantees and also combine markets with planning. This is hardly satisfactory. First of all, a denial of hired labour excludes the pluralism of ownership forms so eloquently defended by Kornai. It is not even congruent with the new Soviet cooperatives, which do hire labour. Furthermore, applying the definition by negation for exploitation given by Abalkin somewhat later, in many cases the spread of hired labour in the USSR would make exploitation less, not more. Abalkin's denial of hired labour under socialism can thus only be a relic of a dogma.

Neither do Abalkin's two further constituent elements for socialist markets clarify the discussion, especially as he earlier failed to give a satisfactory definition of markets. Therefore he is in fact offering no reasons for believing in the existence of 'socialist' or 'capitalist' markets. There can only be markets, functioning with differing efficiency within different institutional frameworks.

Given the vagueness of Abalkin's fundamentals, the unclarity of his discussion on 'the objective laws of markets' is no surprise. Neither do all of his more practical recommendations convince the reader.

It would be somewhat unfair to end the discussion of Abalkin's paper in such sceptical tones. The deepness of dogmatism from which Soviet economics has to rise is huge, and remembering this Abalkin's paper is a progress report. But it cannot be the last word on Soviet economics, and any reform programme outlined on such theoretical foundations must fail to convince.

The paper by Professors Brus and Laski is especially interesting, remembering the influence 'young Brus' has had on reform thinking in the centrally-planned economies. Their paper argues that the creation of goods markets is not enough; they must be complemented with capital and labour markets to function efficiently. Here Brus and Laski also see the main teaching of the two decades of Hungary's NEM.

I accept the main argument of the paper. While noting that the discussion on labour markets in the paper is much less conclusive than that on the capital markets, one can add at least two more reasons for the necessity of functioning capital markets. They can be thought about as a risk-spreading device and also as a way of offering alternative assets for economic agents easily taking the road of conspicuous consumption in the course of reforms. Accumulation, after all, is as much Moses and the prophets for socialism as it is for capitalism, and one of the main problems in the transitional period is in safeguarding the environment for long-term non-state investment. This is a crucial topic addressed by Kornai.

The paper by Brus and Laski – quite properly – leaves the questions of creating capital markets aside. Even if that is not their topic, two comments may be pertinent. First of all, capitalist experience shows that widely different kinds of financial markets may function with a sufficient efficiency, given different economic histories and developmental phases. The same might well be true of the reformed economies, too. Therefore, attempts to enforce a textbook model of efficient capital markets may well prove utterly disappointing, especially in small countries, where capital markets are necessarily thin and opening of these markets a high-risk project. Developing an oligopolistic bank-centred financial system – but with a strong and independent central bank – is probably the wiser course. But – and this is the second point – reform makers in these countries perceive an urgency before the deluge. They will probably not be content with letting markets develop; they are going to commit themselves to creating markets, and mistakes are always to be expected.

Neither do I have much to quarrel with in Professor Kornai's well-written and beautifully argued paper. The discussion on the weakness of cooperative forms of ownership is especially welcome, as misunderstandings concerning the so-called cooperative sectors of some capitalist countries, especially those in Northern Europe, seem to be widely spread and propagated among socialist reformers. Cooperatives may well be a good way of breaking the monopoly of state ownership, given the still existing doctrinal constraints portrayed in Academician Abalkin's paper, but their long-term potentials should not be seen in too bright a light. This is especially because of the differences in the way in which cooperatives, on the one hand,

and joint-stock companies, on the other, can raise their equity capital.

Kornai's paper, naturally, is theoretical or, if you like, speculative in character. Its main message, the natural ability of private forms of entrepreneurship to advance once the various barriers set by the centrally-managed system have been abolished, should be open to empirical verification. I don't know if the existing evidence, incomplete as it may be, really is as conclusive as Kornai makes it to be. Even he, importantly, notes that his thesis may not hold in the Russian case, where any social basis for private entrepreneurship has been uprooted by the most ruthless means for decades.

It is, I think, appropriate to end by making a note of doctrinal historical importance. Professor Kornai has, seemingly, come to adopt many of the basic arguments of the Austrian side of the great socialist planning debate of the 1930s. This probably better than anything else shows how far the economic discussion in some of the centrally-managed states had advanced from the somewhat innocent days of the 1950s and 1960s, when the discussion was largely set in terms of rationalising the economic mechanism of the state sector. Still, there are grounds to expect that these countries will have to live with a dominant state sector in the foreseeable future, too. The questions of its internal functioning, as well as of its relations with other forms of ownership, therefore also have to continue to pre-occupy the reformists.

Note

* Financial support by the Yrjo Jahnsson Foundation is gratefully acknowledged.

Comment

Don Patinkin
HEBREW UNIVERSITY OF JERUSALEM, ISRAEL

Let me start by saying that I see the main justification of my serving as a discussant of the papers by Brus and Laski (Chapter 2 in this volume) and by Kornai (Chapter 3) to lie in the fact that I am the oldest student of Oskar Lange at this conference. Lange was one of my teachers when I was a graduate student at the University of Chicago in 1943–4, and indeed one of my courses with him dealt with the subject that is a main theme of these papers as well as of many others at this conference – namely, the use of the market mechanism in a socialist economy.

I am afraid, though, that I have only one comment on that aspect of these papers; namely, I fail to find in them an adequate discussion of bankruptcy, of the automatic penalty costs of economic failure that are a necessary concomitant of the successful introduction of the market mechanism into a socialist economy.

Let me now correct two doctrinal matters in the paper by Brus and Laski. The first relates to their statement that '[s]cepticism with regard to the use of the rate of interest in a socialist economy was strengthened by the implications of Keynesian economics'. This is just not so, for in Keynes *General Theory* (1936) and afterwards, and *a fortiori* in his earlier *Treatise* (1930), Keynes continued to stress the importance of the rate of interest in influencing investment decisions. My second relates to their reference to Kalecki's statement that 'the rate of interest cannot be determined by the demand for and supply of new capital because investment "finances itself" regardless of the rate of interest'. Kalecki (1965) made this statement with reference to a capitalist economy, and so it in itself cannot be cited as an indication of his view of the role of the rate of interest in a socialist one.

Kornai has emphasised how bureaucracy has persisted despite reforms. Perhaps we should in this context enunciate 'The Law of the Conservation of Bureaucracy' – which may also reflect even the conservation of the same bureaucrats, albeit in different contexts. Observation shows that such a law holds also for non-socialist countries. As a case in point I can cite my own country, Israel, where the advent of the Likud to power over ten years ago, with one of its promises being to reduce the number of government employees, has been followed only by an increase in their number. In brief, once any political party reaches power, it is loth to give up one of the important attributes of that power, which is the power to appoint and employ people.

I am struck by the fact that the countries in the lead in carrying out reforms involving reliance on the market mechanism are the relatively new socialist countries – China, Hungary and the like. I see this as another instance of the advantages of a latecomer to a process, which has long since been noted with reference to economic development. In this case the advantages of the relatively new socialist economies may stem from the fact that they still have memories of the functioning of a market economy, and even more so from the fact that there has been less time for a bureaucracy to entrench itself.

References

Kalecki, M. (1965) *Theory of Economic Dynamics* (London: Allen & Unwin) 2nd edn. published in the USA by Monthly Review Press (1968).
Keynes, J. M. (1930) *A Treatise on Money* (London: Macmillan).
Keynes, J. M. (1936) *The General Theory of Employment, Interest and Money* (London: Macmillan).

Part II

The New Concept of Planning: Interaction with Markets

4 The New Concept of Planning: Interaction with Markets

Zdzisław L. Sadowski
UNIVERSITY OF WARSAW, POLAND

1 INTRODUCTION

The purpose of this paper is to shed some light on what seems to be one of the crucial aspects of the economic reforms now going on in several countries of the socialist group. The essence of these reforms is a transformation of the economic system from one governed by central planning to one largely governed by the market. The transformation presents formidable and historically unprecedented problems, both intellectually and technically. One of these problems is, very naturally, that of what role, if any, should be assigned to planning in the desired future system.

There is no ready answer. The present reforms are processes of change which were set in motion without any fully developed and accepted theory or even vision of the new desired system. This is understandable in processes strongly influenced by spontaneous developments, intuitive *ad hoc* decisions and socio-political pressures. In the course of changes, new areas of doubt are continuously opened, leading to a search for new answers. One knows in one's heart what was wrong with the old system. One does not know how exactly the desired system should and can look like, given its heritage.

In what follows I offer an interpretation based on my own experience in dealing at both the theoretical and the practical level with problems involved.

A reform of the economic system implies a shift from a given set-up 'A' to a new one 'B' with different characteristics. The set-up 'A' is the point of departure. The set-up 'B' is the desired system. The road from the one to the other is the process of transition.

The idea of a new concept of planning clearly belongs to the description of the desired set-up '*B*'. But it can hardly be dealt with properly without ascertaining what the process of reform is all about. I therefore propose to deal with it in three parts which follow.

2   THE POINT OF DEPARTURE

The countries now engaged in reforms worked for several decades in a system of central planning which will be referred to in this paper as 'old' or 'traditional'. The main features of this old system were centralised resource allocation and direct management of the economy by central decision making. The theoretical claim was that central planning was capable of achieving optimum allocation of resources by maximising a goal function, given the constraints. This claim was eventually disproved by showing that it suited only a model of 'perfect planning', where the central decision making body would be omniscient, omnipotent and consistently benevolent. It was shown that none of these three conditions could be met in actual practice

With regard to performance, what may be considered debatable is only how far the logic of the old system may be suitable for early stages of industrialisation. What is now beyond doubt is that, with the growing complexity of an expanding industrial economy, central management visibly failed to create enough adaptability of producers to changing market conditions and to provide sufficient incentives to innovation and technological progress. As a result, it tended to petrify the established economic structures and proved unable to secure structural adjustment between supply and demand both with regard to consumer and producer goods. A shortage economy resulted which eventually undermined the meaning of planning itself. Rather than by the plan, the economy became governed by current arbitrary decisions made under the impact of competing shortages.

The visible deficiencies of the old system led to a search for new solutions. This was started a few decades ago, in the 1950s. The accumulated experience of this search, including its failures, constitutes an important feature of the situation at the start of the present wave of reforms.

All the endeavours to reform the system made since the late 1950s were aimed at providing some autonomy of decision making to individual state-owned firms and at making broader use of market instruments. Some success along these lines was achieved in Hungary where the reform started in 1968 led to considerable improvement in the working of the consumer goods market but the system of management remained largely centralised for many years. Similar endeavours undertaken in Poland in 1956 and 1973 failed. The reason for these failures was later found in the basic inconsistency of the reform programmes. It was assumed that autonomy of state-owned firms and broader use of economic incentives in running the economy were compatible with the basic formula of resource allocation by the central plan, that is, by administrative decision. The autonomy of the firm was understood as the right of the firm to make its own decisions solely with regard to the implementation of plan-imposed objectives. This proved insufficient.

The idea was therefore gradually adopted that a much deeper change was needed, leading to a market system of resource allocation and implying freedom of enterprise instead of limited autonomy for firms, with all the corresponding changes in the socio-political sphere. This, of course, must have led to doubts whether or not the need for any form of central planning remained.

3   THE DESIRED FUTURE SYSTEM

Thus, defining the role of central planning in the new system requires answering first the question: what should make one think that there would be a need for it in a predominantly market economy? It is obvious that in a system of free market allocation of resources there remains no place for central planning in the old sense of setting detailed production plans in physical terms as obligatory to all producers. The bureaucratic hierarchy involved in setting such planned tasks and disaggregating them to reach individual firms and then watching after their implementation loses it *raison d'être*.

But this does not seem to make a case for the tendency which is observable in various quarters to treat the plan and the market as fully alternative methods of running the economy which exclude each other. In the dominant understanding of the reform it is considered necessary to combine both methods. Why?

Before answering, it would be useful to consider the relationship between the concept of central planning and that of a socialist economy. In many minds the old system of central planning is treated as synonymous with a socialist economy. Scrapping the old system would therefore imply scrapping the socialist economy in order to restore a still older system – that of capitalism. In this paper it will be assumed that the essence of the present reforms is to seek a new qualitative shape of the system which should remain socialist in its basic orientation towards objectives of social justice, though the definition of the latter presents certain difficulties. Thus the new concept of planning is to be a constituent part of a new type of socialist economy.

So now comes the answer to the earlier question. For reasons primarily connected with motivation towards efficiency and innovation, it is considered necessary to reintroduce a predominantly market economy performing through the market the functions of allocation and distribution. On the other hand, for reasons primarily connected with social welfare and non-economic social objectives, it is considered necessary to preserve the responsibilities of the state in influencing by means of deliberate policies the performance of the market in the shaping of socio-economic development. For this central planning would be an organising tool.

In this new role, however, central planning would no longer be supposed to deal with exhaustive coordination in physical terms. Its main focus would be on determining types of policies and policy instruments to be used in pursuing the adopted objectives.

The responsibilities of central planning in the desired system would thus be the following:

1. The setting of objectives for long-term development, such as: the desired growth patterns of private and public consumption, the desired structural changes in the economy, the development of export potential, the promotion of energy-saving technologies, the expansion of particular growth-promoting industries, the development of social infrastructure, education, health services, etc.

2. The determination of the broad strategy for pursuing these objectives in terms of policies with regard to the expected and desirable: patterns of output in selected areas; volumes and composition of the main monetary flows, that is the revenues and expenditure of the state budget and regional budgets, the balance of payments, the expected revenues and expenditure of firms and those of the general public.

3. The determination of specific policy measures and instruments (financial, monetary and direct controls) such as: prices and incomes policies; tax policies; investment policies; quality regulations; purchase policies in some areas, etc.

There is some formal resemblance between the formulation of these responsibilities and those of central planning in the old system. But the difference is that in the new concept planning does not serve to determine any obligatory patterns of resource allocation. It does not lead to the setting of any obligatory tasks for individual firms nor any other bodies. Instead, it is supposed only to provide a consistent picture of the disposable resources of the economy and to plot them against a limited set of objectives. The objectives can be treated as obligatory only to the government which is duty bound to try their best to attain them. But the firms, whether public or private, are entirely free to act on grounds of their own wisdom.

This type of planning is, however, not purely indicative, as it is supposed to serve the implementation of the adopted strategy by means of the designed policies. The term 'strategic planning' is sometimes used to denote its nature. The unavoidable need for flexibility calls for making use of various time horizons in planning the policies. But the basic concentration of attention is on long-term development patterns.

In the desired system resource allocation is done fully by the market. Prices are determined freely by the market mechanism, with the possible use of subsidising consumption or production of some items of particular social significance, such as milk or passenger transport services. The banking system is composed of independent banking companies while the central bank makes use of its monetary policy to control the total money supply. The producing firms are fully free within the law to make their own decisions in all areas and act on an unrestricted contractual basis.

Thus, in the desired situation, the influence of central planning on the working of the economy is of an indirect nature. In its interaction with the market, the plan will serve to influence only selected market variables, the selection being done as a part of the planning exercise. The main idea is that government policies should be orientated to affect the course of basic economic flows but not to interfere with the behaviour of individual decision makers.

Planning will therefore serve to influence such areas of functioning of the market as:

1. The volume and composition of consumers' demand mostly by:
   – taxes and subsidies
   – incomes policies
   – social welfare policies
   – housing policies.

2. The directions, volume and composition of capital formation, mostly by:

- direct decisions on some projects, particularly in social and technical infrastructure
- tax incentives or barriers
- environmental policies
- influencing credit policies of the banking system
- creating special credit facilities or other forms of supplementary financing.

3. The level and composition of market supply of goods and services, mostly by:

- taxes and subsidies
- foreign trade policies
- influencing credit policies of the banking system
- exhortations to the firms
- some direct controls, mostly concerning quality.

4. The price determination, mostly by:

- taxes and subsidies
- anti-monopoly policies.

A basic precondition for the appropriate working of this new system of planning is that development objectives adopted in the planned strategy must be determined with broad public approval. It is therefore necessary to combine this system with a fully democratic political set-up which would be capable of arriving at such approval.

The system of interaction between the market and the plan described leaves much scope for varied determination of the actual scope of policy interference with the working of the market. The general position would be that three parts of the economy should be distinguished:

(a) a large part left entirely to spontaneous interplay of market forces
(b) the part indirectly influenced by policies designed within the plan
(c) the relatively small part directly managed by central decision making, particularly related to some investment projects run either by central government bodies or some authorised agencies.

4 PROBLEMS OF TRANSITION

The processes of change in the countries where they are most advanced have shown that a distinction is needed between the discussion of the desired system and that of the road leading to it. A realistic programme for the reform cannot just be formulated solely in terms of a vision of the desired state of affairs. This would be pathetically insufficient. This applies to almost every aspect of the reform, including the new concept of central planning.

Problems of transition are different from those of the desired system, and without trying to understand them the discussion of the latter would remain purely academic. The main problem is that the traditional system left a heritage in the shape of a well-rooted structure for the management of the economy. This heritage has to be entirely disposed of or substantially changed. There is just no way to leap over from a system of centralised resource allocation to a market one.

The basic economic reasons are the following:

1. The old system did not make use of prices as scarcity coefficients; the inherited set of price relationships is therefore totally unsuited to the needs of a market system. One cannot rely on market signals for optimum resource allocation as long as these signals are false. But the adjustment of the price structure has to be a relatively lengthy process.
2. The old system established a high degree of monopoly throughout the economy. This was done because for management by the bureaucratic hierarchy it was more convenient to have a higher rather than lower level of concentration of output. The shift from this situation to a competitive market is cumbersome and takes time. Meanwhile, the inherited situation hampers adjustment of the price structure and the opening of the market to free price formation. The problem is less acute in countries with a favourable balance-of-payments position.
3. The old system was connected with a high level of income redistribution through the state budget; this can hardly be reduced abruptly for social reasons.
4. The old system maintained large pockets of inefficiency in the form of high-cost producers; such firms can hardly be closed or easily restyled, both for reasons of their share in total supply and of the needed massive redeployment of labour.

Apart from these economic factors, an important hampering role is played by non-economic components of the heritage, notably the organisational structure and the political system. These also have to evolve in order to facilitate economic change.

For all these reasons the transformation of a centrally-planned economy of the old type into a system based on an interaction of the market and the plan has to be a time-consuming process of gradual change in a multitude of areas. What has to be gradual first of all is the adjustment of the price structure and the system of price formation. The effect on the price levels and the cost of living of gradual liberation of price formation from the rigidity of central administration needs cushioning by maintaining areas of price control. At the same time the process of demonopolisation has to be gradual as well, with many areas of the economy not quite prone to penetration by new entrants in view of the obsolete price structure and hence inadequate profitability. This only shows important feedbacks emerging in the process of adjustment.

But from this it follows that typical of the period of transition is the unavoidable coexistence of areas where market allocation mechanisms are already at work with those where administrative control over allocation has still to be maintained with a view to its gradual dwindling away. A good example of a very difficult area is provided by access to foreign exchange in a country with a serious payments deficit like Poland. The process of change was started by the introduction of a uniform official rate of exchange into an economy where it just did not exist, the old system having been based on multiple rates. This was combined with starting price adjustment towards aligning commodity prices with those of the world market. But a swift move to establish market exchange rate which would equilibrate supply with demand for foreign exchange would result in rapid adjustment of the domestic price levels of an intolerable scale. Therefore the attainment of an equilibrium rate has to be gradual. Until it can materialise, free access to foreign exchange cannot be granted and a system of rationing has to be maintained.

One cannot, of course, be blind to the traps involved in the gradual process, particularly to the danger of enhancing price inflation without attaining the basic objective of equilibration. But this is a further complication of the problem.

The problem is that, as long as administrative forms of resource allocation have to be maintained in some areas, the new concept of strategic planning interacting with market allocation can hardly materialise in practice. The current economic policies and the system of planning itself continue to be overburdened by the need to deal with the prevailing supply shortages. It is the difficult and narrow path leading out of the shortage economy that is more decisive for the successful materialisation of the new concept of planning than a detailed vision of the desired system.

5 The New Concept of Planning: Duality with Market Forces

Michael Kaser
INSTITUTE OF RUSSIAN, SOVIET AND EAST
EUROPEAN STUDIES, UNIVERSITY OF OXFORD, UK

CONCEPTS OF DUALITY

Nearly thirty years ago Jan Drewnowski, in a seminal, but neglected, paper 'The Economic Theory of Socialism: A Suggestion for Reconsideration' (1961) proposed the division of any monetised economy into 'the zone in which state preferences are supreme (the zone of state influence), the zone in which individual preferences are supreme (the zone of individual influence) and the zone in which state and individual preferences meet (the zone of dual influence). To determine which part of the national economy belongs to which zone means to define the nature of the economic system in question' (p. 350). He pointed out that historical cases have existed where one of the two preference functions has been virtually exclusive of the other – Soviet 'War Communism' of the 1920s or the capitalism of a century ago – and that shifting the boundaries between them and with the intervening preference zone is constrained by property rights.

In formulating a state preference function he had recourse to another concept of duality, shadow prices – 'a price system connected to and consistent with the plan targets expressed in physical quanties' (p. 349) – and perceived the dual preference zone in a socialist economy as that in which certain economic activities were subject both to the state's quantity planning and to market-formed prices. He saw 'degrees' of the marketisation of a centrally-planned economy as different blocks of quantity plans were decontrolled. In a footnote he envisaged a practice whereby 'prices are fixed by the state and quantities determined by consumers' preferences' (p. 352), but did not elaborate; such relations are theoretically familiar from the

Lange–Lerner and Kornai–Liptak 'two-level' models.

Other features of duality have long been characteristic of socialist economies. The most important, and the longest-examined by Western analysts, is the two-tier price system. A set of wholesale prices can be established which compensate enterprises for their cumulated labour costs (direct labour costs and material inputs which resolve into Marxian 'live' labour costs plus the consumption of 'embodied' labour through capital depreciation charges). Another set, that of retail prices, can be established which clears the market of planned quantities of goods and services, given household purchasing power and planners' knowledge of consumer preferences. That such price relativities or such macroeconomic equilibrium have not been achieved is not the topic of this paper, but the literature on this aspect of disequilibrium economics is considerable.[1] Another substantial zone of dual pricing is among the 'coloured markets' generated by the differential access by groups of buyers and sellers within a 'shortage economy'.[2] A third relation of duality is of procurement from collective farms under compulsory deliveries (in the USSR with a premium from 1965 for supplementary deliveries and from 1989 in convertible currency for those exceeding the 1981–5 average) and sales to the collective-farm market which are at unrestricted prices. This relationship is another manifestation of two-tier pricing – until the 1960s procurement prices constituting a tax but subsequently a subsidy.

A fourth zone of dual prices arises from the *Preisausgleich* system of foreign trade:[3] a monopolist foreign trade corporation buys goods for export from a domestic enterprise at the wholesale price but receives the export proceeds in foreign currency which are converted at a disequilibrium exchange rate. As applied in the USSR until 1986, the practice involved as many exchange rates as there were traded goods and services, just as the domestic two-tier price system required as many rates of turnover tax as there were goods sold at retail. The process of economic reform in Eastern Europe started to rectify such disorderly practice before change took place in the USSR. Thus Hungary in 1968 simultaneously applied an 'internal exchange rate' for the external market and a set of *ad valorem* turnover taxes for the internal market; taken in conjunction with a wholesale price reform, effective at the same time, the three transaction areas – external, households and enterprises – became rationally interrelated. The application of internal exchange rates began in 1967 in Czechoslovakia consistently with a wholesale price reform and spread throughout Eastern Europe during the 1970s.[4] The internal exchange rate as such was merely a concealed currency depreciation (as Hungary recognised in embodying the implicit premium/discount in the official rate in 1976 and Czechoslovakia in embodying its *cvrček* in the devaluation of January 1989), but when it was at two (or for a time in Poland three) levels of premium/discount, a further exhibition of duality came into use. These so-called 'directional multipliers' (coefficient by partner–country group) were intended to dissuade exporters by a discount on the official rate from selling exports to the 'easy markets' of other socialist countries and to encourage by a premium exports for convertible currency. The same effect could patently have been obtained by differentiating the respective exchange rates, but it was judged politically important to maintain the notional cross-rate of the valuta rouble (then at par with CMEA's 'transferable rouble') to the dollar.

While 'directional duality' was only a veiled form of depreciating the rate to the rouble against the rate to the dollar, the coefficients introduced in the USSR in 1986 were multiple exchange rates and were rendered useful by the disparity of wholesale price relativities from those ruling in the world market. The extent of the divergence of the two price sets and the revelation of still wider divergence as the system was implemented is evident from the known range: initially there were 1500 coefficients ranging from 0.3 to 6.0, that is a range of 18 times, but by late 1988 the number had doubled to 3000 and the range had widened to 0.2 to 6.5. A decree of December 1988 forecast the abolition of the coefficient system after a revised set of wholesale prices had been in operation for at least one year (when the effects of the new prices would have worked through to enough foreign trade transactions for a single, but of course devalued, exchange rate to be applied). For private and tourist transactions from 1 November 1989 a surcharge of 1000 per cent raised the rate from 62.6 US cents to the valuta rouble to 6.26 roubles. The re-introduction of a tourist or 'non-commercial' rate came nearly thirty years after the tourist rate was abolished (when on 1 January 1961 all domestic rouble values were divided by ten but the valuta rouble divided by only 2.5) in a devaluation which merged it with the commercial rate.

2   THE 'DUAL TRACK' ENTERPRISE

All four examples of duality in the recent operation of socialist countries apply to clearly-defined sets of transactions, often by separate enterprises, with respect to a homogeneous good. Thus the foreign trade corporation transacted in the external sector in valuta roubles and in the domestic sector in domestic roubles, the margin at the official exchange rate being absorbed (as a subsidised loss or a tax) in a purely accounting report. What is novel about the 'dual track' practice for state enterprises is that the bounds are infinitely variable within a single enterprise for a homogeneous good.

The term 'dual track' enterprise was introduced by the present writer in a journal article (Kaser, 1987); but the operational relationship had appeared as part of the Chinese economic reform in 1984, was applied in the USSR and Bulgaria in 1988 and in Czechoslovakia in 1989. It is everywhere seen by those governments as a transitional form for transactions as 'plan indicators' yield to 'commodity market relations', but during that period its use raises interesting issues of enterprise optimisation. The present writer put the novelty as follows, namely that the Soviet non-farm reform was 'taking a form which is Chinese in origin rather than one previously tried in Eastern Europe – the limiting of state orders (*goszakazy*) to a given enterprise to less than its productive capacity. Enterprise management can thereby choose whether at current prices and demand it is profitable to use all or only part of its capacity. Gradually the sellers' market (or 'shortage economy'), which has prevailed in the Soviet Union since 1930 and in China since 1958, should cover a relatively small area of transactions, because a buyers' market will be encroaching within the state sector itself – let alone as the private and cooperative sector is allowed to enlarge. The central authorities retain the right to locate the frontier between the two markets, but each state enterprise would know its place for a given period under a 'long-term normative'. Such 'normatives' are already embodied in the financial legislation for Chinese and, in draft, for Soviet state enterprises. The reform would set an output quota which is less than its productive capacity and permit any production in excess of that quota to be sold freely by the enterprise.' 'Dual-track' production allows the central planning authority to keep a predetermined volume and mix of products to guarantee current inputs for other enterprises' quotas and to substantiate plans for civilian investment, for export and for defence spending. At the same time, by producing above-quota goods only when there is a demand for them, enterprises respond to market forces' (Kaser, 1987, pp. 405–6). In the three European countries Bulgaria, Czechoslovakia and the USSR, the 'dual track' is in due course to be replaced by market relations, but because quantities demanded and supplied at the fixed price will vary between the *goszakazy* and the residual *khozzakazy*, profit maximisation cannot be the sole criterion for enterprises on (to continue to use the Soviet terminology) 'full cost accounting'.

3 COMBINATIONS OF FIXED AND FLEXIBLE PRICES

The dual track enterprise is confronted by choice among quantities while prices – on both tracks – remain fixed. Some state enterprises in China may sell their market-oriented output at flexible prices (and correspondingly buy inputs from similarly-authorised enterprises at flexible prices) while the controlled quantities (state orders) are sold, and inputs bought, at fixed prices. Soviet collective farms under *perestroika* rules of 1985 can sell up to 30 per cent of their crop at whatever price they can obtain before obligatory deliveries are completed; previously flexible prices could be obtained only after procurements at the fixed price had been fully honoured. In other countries, Albania alone excepted, cooperative farms enjoyed the option of flexible-price sales in parallel with obligatory quotas at fixed prices.

It is generally agreed by governments of hitherto centrally-planned economies that the transition to flexible prices will take a considerable time. The Chinese authorities which had been progressing rapidly in that direction since 1978 in agriculture, since 1981 in foreign trade and since 1984 in the non-farm sector, were impelled by rising inflation in 1988 to suspend further price decontrol for two years. The Soviet objective would seem to comprise fixed and flexible prices for a considerable period. Mr Gorbachev at the Plenum of the Party Central Committee in June 1987 called for 'all types of prices and tariffs to be reconsidered in their aggregate; the organic connection between wholesale procurement and retail prices and tariffs should be ensured during a radical reform of the price system. It is necessary consistently to reflect in them the socially-necessary expenditure on the production and marketing of output, its consumer-oriented properties, the quality of output and effective demand'. He went on to speak of a combination of 'stability and flexibility' and the Law on the Enterprise, enacted just afterwards, allows centrally-fixed, negotiated and free prices. Immediately subsequent interviews with the price authorities demonstrated the extent of price reform envisaged. The Director of the Goskomtsen Research Institute suggested that wholesale prices would have approximately to double, although engineering goods would not need much change, and that in retail pricing foodstuffs would increase significantly, although turn-over tax cuts might bring down the prices of manufactured consumer goods. The Chairman of Goskomtsen spoke of existing 'prices play-ing little role in creating balance between supply and demand, leading to continual shortages both for retail and wholesale goods' (Kaser, 1988). The theoretical presentation of fixed pricing when quantity relationships operate within a market and other prices are flexible has been considerably developed:[5] it has always applied (subject to the constraint noted in the following paragraph) to the combination of fixed wages and free choice of occupation in most socialist countries, but partial price decontrol will evoke new combi-nations of quantity constraints and supply effects.

Another area of much contemporary concern in theory is of principal–agent relations. The application of this analytical tool to Soviet practice has been particularly developed about the incentives or instructions evolved to compensate for the inadequacy of the information available to the principal (planning office or ministry) but influencing resource allocation by the agent (the director of a state enterprise). There are notably numerous Western studies of the ratchet effect.[6] While wholesale prices are fixed by the principals, in implementation of quantity planning – Grossman (1968) felicitously called fixed prices 'crypto-physical magnitudes' (p. 5) – the principals can have rational expectations about outcomes in values and quan-tities. An early contributor to this set of analyses, Hirsch, even considered competitive pricing to be 'hardly conceivable in a planned economy (Hirsch, 1961, p. 121). With partial decontrol, information on flexible price options open to the agent will not be available to the principal when setting the 'state orders'.

A further set of issues arise among the supply-side approaches usually termed 'post-Keynesian economics'.[7] The rigidities which must be relaxed as flexible quantities and prices are authorised may be classified by form of market – of labour, of capital and of goods.

Except for historically brief, abnormal periods – for example, from immediately before to some time after the Second World War in the USSR, during the Cultural Revolution in China – or for certain categories, notably collective farmers and graduates of tertiary edu-cation, the socialist countries have not compulsorily directed labour; politically-motivated use of forced labour has had its economic spin-off and has been sporadically discussed as such by economists.[8]

Labour has been as mobile as housing and information allowed among offers of employment at non-negotiable wages. To modify the strictly fixed wage scales China has introduced a 'floating wage' to permit greater wage flexibility upwards and the compulsory conversion of state enterprises into worker-cooperatives to permit flexibility downwards. The Soviet Law on the Enterprise, effective from January 1988, extends wage flexibility *pari passu* with aggregate financial autonomy. The emergence of trade unions rivalling the official organisations in Hungary and Poland relaxes their monopoly of wage negotiation. These and other relaxations, including modification of job security and even unemployment, are introducing new search costs into the systems. The Soviet authorities reinstituted, after an absence of four decades, employment offices and short-term unemployment benefit.

Capital markets have begun to be considered in socialist countries, but the issues so far made in China, Hungary, Romania and the USSR are fixed interest bonds. What in the market economies is termed equity rationing is complete in the socialist states save in the cooperative sector, but credit rationing is being relaxed by the disarticulation of the 'monobank system'. Allied to capital markets is a market for land, never forbidden in Eastern Europe, but precluded in the USSR and China under state and cooperative exclusivity in the one and by the people's communes in the other. Both these latter countries now permit leasing (in each for some 50 years, with inheritable tenure), limited in the USSR to leases from collective and state farms (which are thereby perpetuated) but by an initial per household distribution in China, following complete abolition of the communes.

Finally markets for goods and services are the most free but the non-diversification rule for state enterprises, particularly in the USSR, limits adjustment. Everywhere the persistence of the industrial ministry system and the protection from foreign competition still exercised allows monopoly power which in turn wards the government away from price decontrol.

This paper has sought only to raise issues: their solution is crucial to the success of market-oriented reform in the socialist countries.

Notes

1. Notably in formal terms by Barro and Grossman (1971, 1974) and in empirical application to the socialist economies by Portes and various co-authors, particularly Portes and Winter (1978, 1987) and Portes, Quant and Yeo (1988).
2. The convenient term 'coloured markets' is due to Katsenelenboigen (1977) and the 'shortage economy' to Kornai (1981).
3. The *Preisausgleich* term is not strictly appropriate but was borrowed from GDR usage; the practice was originally explained by Pryor (1963).
4. The first full account and the use of the term 'internal exchange rate' is in Kaser (1979).
5. In addition to the work cited in note 1, other early studies were Backhouse (1980) and Nissanke (1979).
6. There is extensive reference to the literature and a further development of the ratchet effect in Darvish and Kahana (1989).
7. A useful survey is by Greenwald and Stiglitz (1988).
8. The first full study was by Swianiewicz (1965), and a decade later there was a notable controversy in the pages of *Soviet Studies* and the *Slavic Review*.

References

Backhouse, R. E. (1980) 'Fix-price versus Flex-price Models of Macroeconomic Equilibrium with Rationing', *Oxford Economic Papers*, 2, pp. 210–23.
Barro, R. and Grossman, H. (1971) 'A General Disequilibrium Model of Income and Employment', *American Economic Review* (March) pp. 89–93.
Barro, R. and Grossman, H. (1974) 'Suppressed Inflation and the Supply Multiplier', *Review of Economic Studies*, pp. 87–104.
Darvish, T. and Kahana, N. (1989) 'The Ratchet Principle: A Multi-period Flexible Incentive Scheme', *European Economic Review* (January) pp. 51–8.
Drewnowski, J. (1961) 'The Economic Theory of Socialism: A Suggestion for Reconsideration', *Journal of Political Economy* (August) pp. 341–54.
Greenwald, B. C. and Stiglitz, J. E. (1988) 'Examining Alternative Macroeconomic Theories', *Brookings Papers on Economic Activity*, 1, pp. 207–60.
Grossman, H. (1968) *Money and Plan* (Berkeley Calif.: University of California Press).
Hirsch, Hans (1961) *Quantity Planning and Price Planning in the Soviet Union* (Philadelphia: University of Pennsylvania Press).
Kaser, M. C. (1979) 'La politique du taux de change dans le pays membres de la Banque Internationale de coopération économique', *Revue d'études comparatives Est–Ouest* (December) pp. 159–76. The English original (presented to a conference in Aix-en-Provence in 1979) was circulated as *Papers in East European Economics*, 58.

Kaser, M. C. (1987) '"One Economy, Two Systems": Parallels between Soviet and Chinese Reform', *International Affairs* (Summer) pp. 395–412.

Kaser, M. C. (1988) 'Reform in the USSR and China', *Pacific Review* 1.

Katsenelenboigen, A. (1977) 'Coloured Markets in the USSR', *Soviet Studies*, 1, pp. 62–85.

Kornai, J. (1981) *The Economics of Shortage*, 2 vols (Amsterdam and New York: North-Holland).

Nissanke, M. (1979) 'The Disequilibrium Model in a Controlled Economy', *American Economic Review* (September) pp. 726–32.

Portes, R. and Winter, D. (1978) 'The Demand for Money and for Consumption Goods in Centrally-planned Economies', *Review of Economics and Statistics* (February) pp. 8–18.

Portes, R. and Winter, D. (1987) 'Macroeconomic Planning and Disequilibrium, Estimates for Poland 1955–80', *Econometrica* (January) pp. 19–41.

Portes, R., Quant, R. and Yeo, S. (1988) 'Tests of the Chronic Shortage Hypothesis: The Case of Poland', *Review of Economics and Statistics* (May) pp. 288–95.

Pryor, F. L. (1963) *The Communist Foreign Trade System* (London: Allen & Unwin).

Swianiewicz, S. (1965) *Forced Labour and Economic Development* (Oxford: Oxford University Press).

Note on Yugoslavia

Dragomir Vojnić
INSTITUTE OF ECONOMICS, ZAGREB,
YUGOSLAVIA

1 INTRODUCTION

Yugoslavia is now in the process of its third socio-economic reform. The first reform started in the early 1950s with the inauguration of workers' self-management. The second reform began in the mid-1960s, in 1965 to be precise, and the third in the early 1980s with the adoption of the Long-Term Programme of Economic Stabilisation in 1983.

The main task and goal in all the reforms was to increase economic efficiency and political democracy – that is, to improve the quality of life. The basic theoretical and methodological orientation in all the reforms was towards increasing the motivation of all economic subjects and individuals for productive and constructive work.

This increase of motivation for productive and constructive work was always based on changing the relationship between the market and the plan in favour of a more market-oriented economy. All the reforms stressed the need for an open economic model, giving firms greater freedom in decision making regarding their business and development policies.

Increasing the scope and freedom of decision making is one of the key preconditions for the development of the socio-economic and political model based on socialist self-management.

However, according to the Yugoslav experience, the greatest uncertainties and blockages concerned the role and position which commodity production and the market (as well as the plan) can and should have in the organisation of a socialist economy and society.

One can easily understand that these questions are not only economic but also political in nature.

Enlarging the role of commodity production and the market (hence reducing the function of command planning) and, on this basis, strengthening the independence, autonomy and freedom of economic subjects (that is, enterprises) in business and developmental decision making, has direct implications for the nature and structure of power and for the distribution and redistribution of socio-economic power. The Yugoslav experience shows that the reform of socialism is not possible unless it goes beyond the economy to include the entire political sphere. This was well confirmed by the 1965 reform. At that time, the Yugoslav economy and society were more than ready for a complete and radical socio-economic and political reform.

The lack of will on the part of the political factor and ideological forces to pursue a general democratisation of the country's economy and society caused the failure of the reform in the late 1960s.

The failure of the reform was followed by a variety of deformations (such as underestimation of the role of commodity production and the market) which eventually pushed the Yugoslav economy and society in the late 1970s and early 1980s into a severe crisis, in which they still find themselves.

The ideas that inspire the third reform, and that from part of the Long-Term Programme of Economic Stabilisation, are similar to those that gave birth to the 1965 reform. Those ideas are: a model of an open economy, greater emphasis on export expansion, development of domestic technology and creative technology transfer, greater motivation through the greater freedom of economic subjects in their business and development decision making, and a system of planning based on the logic of economic compulsion and market laws. This represents an orientation to indicative planning with firmer measures and instruments of economic policy.

2   THE PERIOD PRIOR TO THE 1983 PROGRAMME

During this period, all the weaknesses of the economic system were especially prominent, particularly those of the planning system and development policy with its typical characteristics of autarkic development. Yugoslavia did not react adequately to the energy crisis and the recession in its international environment, or to any other changes in international economic, especially financial, trends and relations. The social cost of development in the period preceding the crisis (that is, until the late 1970s and early 1980s) was extremely high. This can best be illustrated by the marginal capital coefficient trends.

In the 1956–60 five-year period it was necessary to invest 2.4 dinars in the economy to increase the social product by 1 dinar. In the following five-year period, 1961–65, the capital coefficient rose to 2.9, and it continued to rise in the ten-year period 1966–75 to reach 3.6 at the end of that period. In 1976–80, on the eve of the crisis, the capital coefficient deteriorated further and reached 4.3.

Based on the high gross investment rate in the capital assets of its economy (24 per cent), financed to a large extent by international borrowing and domestic deficit, Yugoslavia recorded a relatively high rate of growth of the social product (5.4 per cent).

In the five-year period preceding the current crisis Yugoslavia made such mistakes in its economic and development policy that soon pushed it into the group of worst-indebted countries in the world. Yugoslavia's overall foreign debt is in the region of 20 billion US dollars. The current account deficits amounted to 3.7 billion US dollars in 1979 and 2.3 billion in 1980.

The contribution of technological progress to the rate of growth of the social product dropped from 34.4 per cent in 1965–74 to 7.4 per cent in 1974–84. At the same time, the contribution of technological progress to the rate of growth of the industrial social product decreased from 53.8 per cent to only 19.1 per cent.

It goes without saying that both the capital coefficient values and the contributions of technological progress continued to follow extremely unfavourable patterns in the crisis period of the 1980s.

The high social cost of development becomes quite apparent when viewed in a comparative light. If Yugoslavia had had the same or similar social costs of development (expressed in the form of capital coefficients) in the twenty years preceding the crisis as some other countries with similar structural characteristics, such as Spain, Portugal, Greece and Turkey, its 1980 social product would have been approximately twice as big as that actually realised in that year.

Instead, owing to the mistakes made in the 1980s, Yugoslavia found itself in the position of overinvestment and overindebtness. Overinvestment and overindebtedness are often considered as the causes of the crisis. This is not correct, however, and it shows a failure to distinguish between causes and effects. The causes of the crisis are in fact much deeper; they are multidimensional and can be explained only in a multidisciplinary way.

3   THE 1983 LONG-TERM PROGRAMME
OF ECONOMIC STABILISATION

In preparing the Long-Term Programme of Economic Stabilisation
Yugoslav socio-economic science pointed out the essential causes of
the crisis and indicated the ways and means of overcoming it. The
synthetic external symptom of the crisis of socialism is the low degree
of economic efficiency and political democracy. The overcoming of
the crisis requires such radical changes which in fact mean a reform of
socialism, which in turn means a general democratisation of socialist
economy and society.

The five-year period since 1983 (that is, since the Long-Term
Programme was adopted) has been marked by considerable vacillation. The nature of the vacillation has been twofold, reflecting the
inertia of dogmatic views and indoctrinated social consciousness.

The fact that reform cannot be confined to the economic sphere,
leaving out the reform and democratisation of the economy and
society as a whole, is already fully recognised. However, the suggestion that this implies the need for the reform of socialism itself
provoked a massive resistance in the parts of society which perceived
the reform as an attack on socialism itself and its basic foundations.
The problem is all the greater as resistance comes not only from the
state and party bureaucracy (as usually suggested in simplified and
vulgarised statements) but also from part of the working class as well.

The second cause of vacillation and resistance to reform has been
the existing structure of the Yugoslav economy as a result of the
many years of autarkic development. The synthetic expression of the
accumulated structural problems of the Yugoslav economy is found
in low economic efficiency, low competitiveness, high production
costs, high social costs of research and development, inadequate
participation in international economic relations and exchange, continuous problems of external liquidity and high indebtedness, great
technological and economic lag (especially in comparison with developed European countries), huge financial instability, losses and
deficits, and escalating inflation. Such structural characteristics cannot be a sound basis for export expansion, and they act as a cause of
resistance to reform.

Quantitative criteria and sectoral priorities in areas such as energy,
food and raw materials have been dominant in the concept of development and long-term development policy, owing to the weaknesses

and defects in the functioning of the overall economic system, and particularly of the system of planning.

What has just been said is equally true of the overall concept and strategy of development, long-term development policy, and many individual investment projects and decisions.

4 REFORM SINCE 1988

Based on the platform formulated in the Long-term Programme of Economic Stabilisation in 1983, the reform of the socio-economic and political system started in 1988. The bases of the reform are the conclusions of the First Conference of the Yugoslav League of Communists and the amendments to the 1974 Yugoslav constitution (which in fact represent a constitutional reform).

The reform of the economic system has already started on this basis. A reform of the League of Communists has also been announced. It can generally be said that this third major Yugoslav reform is based on three pluralisms: (1) pluralism of the market; (2) pluralism of ownership; and (3) political pluralism.

The pluralism of the market refers to the function of an integral market and market evaluation and formation of prices for goods, capital and labour. In this connection, special attention is to paid to the reform of the banking system, as well as to other preparations for the introduction of a functional financial and securities market (including bonds, shares, etc.). The price of domestic capital (interest rates) should be formed by market laws, as well as the price of foreign capital. Thus, a relatively successful foreign exchange market was put into operation in 1988. A significant improvement was achieved in the overall balance of payments situation.

As for the labour market, special attention is to be paid to remuneration according to the market evaluation of work results. The basic approach to this question should be to end egalitarianism (that is, equalising wages across the board) because it expresses such relations in which those who do not work exploit those who do, and any prospect of progress is blocked.

The new approach will create a competitive situation among those employed, and between them and the unemployed Yugoslav citizens. The institution of socialisation of losses is to be abandoned.

This reform offers free access to the process of production for all interested economic subjects regardless of the sector of ownership. Equally, it will force out of business those economic subjects that consistently run losses.

The pluralism of ownership means equal treatment of all types of ownership, social as well as private, cooperative, combined, and joint ownership. Special attention is to be paid to creating conditions that will stimulate joint ventures with foreign partners and other forms of direct investment of foreign capital.

Political pluralism is not to be automatically equated with the pluralism of political parties. Such pluralism will be achieved in particular through reforms within the League of Communists, whose reform was envisaged thirty years ago when the Yugoslav Communist Party changed its name to the League of Communists. The reform of the League of Communists will involve especially the demonopolisation of the League's functions in government, politics and appointment policy. Also, other socio-political organisations, such as the Socialist Alliance, the labour unions, youth organisation, veterans' association, etc. will be freed of their present role of transmitting Party policy and decisions. In any case, the reform of the League of Communists is crucial for the country's overall reform in the direction of a general democratisation of the economy and society. This reform is an indispensable precondition for an increased economic efficiency and political democracy, and for the overcoming of the crisis. It will affect the entire planning system and overall concept of development and development policy. The planning system and development policy should be based on the functions of an integral market.

The development policy should be based on qualitative criteria, such as capital formation capability, profitability, net foreign exchange inflow, etc. Such criteria should be applied to every investment project or investment decision.

In the light of these criteria, all elements of the system of natural economy must be abandoned, and the elements needed for a sound economic system and development policy based on commodity production and an integral market must be introduced. This means a system in which everything is subordinated to the main goal, that of producing values as the characteristic of all market-oriented economies, instead of the production of things (commodities), which is the characteristic of the natural economy.

Having all this in mind, the reform of the planning system will strengthen the concept of indicative planning and stress the role of the economic and development policy.

The essence of the structural policy should be structural changes and adjustments as the most important vital task and objective. Yugoslavia cannot hope to solve any of its existing crucial problems without undergoing significant structural changes and adjustments. This is particularly true of the problems of insufficient dynamism of production and escalating inflation.

Besides the problems already mentioned relating to the pluralism of the market, pluralism of ownership and political pluralism, the reform has a special task to establish adequate macroeconomic control mechanisms in the financial, especially fiscal and monetary, sphere.

The fundamental problems in this sphere (as János Kornai has said) appear in the transition from the soft budget constraint to the hard budget constraint. In the market economy, as is well known, the monetary and fiscal sphere must function as a state within a state, so to speak. The Yugoslav experience shows that problems related to the overall financial system, and especially the monetary and fiscal system, are central to reform. There are good reasons to believe that these problems will be the toughest to overcome in the reform of the economic system and socialism.

In conclusion, it should be stressed that an adequate reform of the financial complex, especially of the monetary and fiscal sphere, is crucial for overall reform, including the reform of the planning system in the sense of indicative planning, the strengthening of the role of economic and development policy, the introduction of the necessary structural changes, the development of the model of an open economy, and the domination of economic criteria, mechanisms and economic compulsion.

Our Yugoslav financial system is in a deep crisis, which is reflected in unbearable financial instability. An accurate assessment of the financial position and of the causes of financial instability is a precondition for the definition of an appropriate method and deadline for financial rehabilitation, itself an indispensable requirement for the implementation of clear development criteria. The mechanisms of the financial system must be such as to have a stimulating effect on capital formation in the country, the flow of foreign capital into the country, and a more rational use of corporate and private funds. For this reason the financial sector should receive priority treatment in the reform.

The basic social commitment to a market economy model and the system of socialist self-management requires further elaboration of an economic system which will secure greater motivation and initiate greater autonomy of firms in day-to-day business operation and developmental decision making, flexibility and variety of ownership and organisational patterns in accordance with technological needs, and prompt adjustment to domestic and foreign demand. Such objectives will be supported by a system of social planning adapted to the needs of an open market economy, autonomy of economic subjects, and pluralism of forms of ownership.

·All these efforts are accompanied by a lively legislative activity. Several pieces of legislation, including the laws on enterprises, foreign and joint investment, banking and planning, were adopted at the end of 1988 and in the first few months of 1989.

It should be said, finally, that the third Yugoslav reform seems to be better prepared in the professional and scientific sense than earlier reforms, given that it now encompasses both the economic and the political sphere.

Comment

László Csaba*
KOPINT-DATORG INSTITUTE FOR ECONOMIC
INFORMATICS AND MARKET RESEARCH BUDAPEST,
HUNGARY

THE DUAL-TRACK TRICK AND RADICAL REFORMS IN SOCIALIST COUNTRIES

First and foremost I should like to pinpoint the remarkable intellectual and *conceptual similarity* of the two papers in chapters 4 and 5 of this volume. While Kaser focuses on historical and international aspects, Sadowski dwells on contemporary and domestic Polish aspects of what is paraphrased as the 'dual-track enterprise'. This sounds very much like economic common sense: since the 1950s and 1960s there is something close to a consensus view in East and West that in reality only mixed economic systems prove to be viable.

Experiences of the 1970s and 1980s, especially the lack of any radical breakthrough that was expected from reforms, may cast some doubt over the 'dual-track enterprise', where elements of various economic systems coexist side by side for a substantial period of time. When we have addressed the question why reforms in socialist countries – from Yugoslavia to China – have resulted in limited success only; when we ask why, after a decade or so, each reform shows some *fatigue*, the basic issue pertains to the validity of the underlying assumption. Is it true that elements of various economic systems may be mixed more or less according to our own taste and preferences?

In view of the empirical evidence from the 1970s and 1980s it does not seem entirely senseless to rehash the age-old dispute between the majority gradualists and the minority liberals over how to change a system. The latter have always maintained that economic systems possess basic features determining their congruence and thus the basic mode of functioning of the given economic order. Allowing for a variety of concurring interpretations, observance over time of the 'one step forward – two steps backward' type of reform, one is tempted to raise a very traditionalist question. Is not the basic issue whether the market is merely a supplementary instrument, or, on the contrary, the fundamental form for coordinating interests and decisions both at the macroeconomic and microeconomic levels? Is the market an *instrument of, or an alternative to, bureaucratic coordination* (Kornai, 1984)? This is a question which in economic policy cannot be addressed so diplomatically as it usually is at international gatherings. When we are confronted with the issue of indicative versus compulsory planning, or with the role of central agencies in deciding over investment projects in physical forms (to cite two major points from Sadowski), we are clearly in an either – or situation: *tertium non datur*. While the central agencies continue to set investment priorities *in concretu*, they are continuing mandatory planning practices despite their declarations of intent stating the contrary. Kaser's argument on state orders turns, in fact, in my favour. It is no accident that there remains no room for *khozzakazy* (commercial orders) (cf. the figures given in Bogomolov's paper, Chapter 13 in this volume). If the basic system continues to be that of a shortage economy, the intention to cut back the share of central resource allocation gradually is bound to remain wishful thinking. If prices are partially decontrolled they will indeed provide information to decision makers about imbalances in the economy. However, if this is not coupled with the *motivation* to act accordingly, the central agencies will be tempted to suppress various forms and carriers of these unpleasant pieces of news, and will continue to act in their previous manner. The recent Soviet price controls and various decrees limiting the cooperatives may serve as novel examples for this.

My conclusion is that various *systems do not seem to mix in reality so easily* as was commonly postulated in the 1950s and 1960s – among others by Drewnowski and Brus. Certainly, a fully-fledged liberalisation of the economy often entails such high social expense that it may be feasible only under extreme historical circumstances (as in 1948 in the FRG or in 1980 in Turkey). However, the need for a political compromise in implementing reforms should not be canonised and generalised as a theoretical maxim, as a justification for eclecticism.

We must at this point consider the *role of vision* in economic reforms. Interestingly, Sadowski cautions against 'pathetic theorising'. In the meantime he concedes with equal justification that in the Polish reforms of 1982 not even available evidence from economic theory was utilised; instead improvisations prevailed in policy making. This paradox underlines the importance of vision. Without at least a general concept about the major elements of the then new economic system to be introduced, without having a clear idea about what fundamental items of the old system are to be changed in a congruous manner, as a package, central agencies lack their compass in trying to struggle their way through the troubled waters of a crisis-ridden economy.

Certainly, the approach of '*Sozialkonstruktivismus*' would be anything but helpful. There is no evidence that a bunch of clever people could indeed devise an 'ideal' socio-economic system that would work, while there is ample evidence of how much harm such self-appointed prophets could cause. However, without knowing where to get to, without having a fairly definite idea about sequencing policy and systemic measures, no radical reform vocabulary might result in meaningful rearrangements of economic behaviour at micro- and macro-levels. The role of vision is to help systematise and sequence the reform measures.

What is resistant to change? Given the extreme slowness of systemic change, given the recurring discrepancy between radical blueprints and lukewarm implementation in several countries over longer periods of time, this is an issue that deserves a thorough scrutiny. Sadowski points to resistance posed by the management structure. This is certainly true, but is only a part of the story. Even in a comment like this I think three further dimensions should be added to the picture.

(a) Resistance of '*real economic structures*' – fixed assets, qualifications, infrastructure etc. is important. Let us recall that in Poland several of the Gierek investments are still under completion in line with the current five-year-plan. Let us remember that in Hungary a growing share of investments has been going to the primary sectors. In the case of a real adjustment policy, 30–50 per cent of existing fixed assets would have to be simply written off in some sectors. Thus it is clear that the material composition of national product is not really favourable to systemic change.

(b) The role of *socio-political lobbies* should also be mentioned. Especially under the current condition of a low level of economic transparency it is very easy to manipulate decision makers and the public. It should be noted, though it cannot be proved in this comment, that redistribution by the state takes place in the interests of the socially strong – for example, the large mining companies – rather than favouring the socially weak. Last but not least, regional differences as well as the decay of infrastructure pose hurdles in the way of economic readjustment along market signals.

(c) Socialism in all countries developed as an *autarkic economic system*. Without going into the causes of this situation it should be taken as a starting point. In an institutionally closed economy there is hardly sufficient pressure to adjust economic behaviour to international competitive norms. Given the prevailing mono-polised structure of production and trade, the easier way is always open to most economic agents. Therefore it is always more appealing to bargain with authorities than to reorganise the activities of companies. Economic seclusion is a result of historic development, posessing strong legitimation as an ideo-logical value, in terms both of nationalism as well as of conven-tional leftist propositions aiming at invulnerability from the capitalist world markets. Therefore overcoming isolation and opening up the socialist economies is a long-term socio-political process, implying much wider-ranging changes than the intro-duction of a uniform marginal rate of exchange.

It seems to me that an economic policy and reform relying on an embedded 'double-track conviction' *will never succeed in opening up the respective country, thus it will never result in a real market economy*. The arguments of Sadowski against a realistic rate of exchange – neglecting contrary experiences of other countries like Portugal, Turkey and South Korea – may very well illustrate this point. Therefore one has to raise the issue of reformability of the entire system. If a dozen of the developing countries have actually managed to change from bureaucratic to market regimes, then countries with a historically higher level of development should not find it by definition impossible to master the same task. The real issue is what makes the norms of behaviour of economic agents change? The answer here can of course be shorthand only. Let me restrict myself to the four decisive factors:

(a) First and foremost the *property rights issue* should be settled in a satisfactory manner. Recent Hungarian experience (Csaba, 1989) seems to run counter to the conventional expectation – voiced by Kaser – that pluralism in labour relations would alleviate wage demands. In fact, since the property rights issue is mostly debated rather than solved, wage pressures have become stronger than ever. Traditional labour unions become more militant due to competition. Moreover, they join forces with management and with the sectoral and regional organs to counter attempts by the Bank and the Ministry of Finance to keep wages down.

(b)   Not only a vision, but a *strategy of transformation* is needed. This implies planning in a strictly indicative manner, at the same time as producing concrete timetables of sequencing economic policy and systemic measures. It does require restraint not to try and define what is 'socially necessary' in concrete terms/ projects.

(c)   Not only a strong, but a legitimate government is needed. Moreover, one that is willing to implement a policy of change that will first bite and only later produce results.

(d)   Opening up the economy as a policy turn is a *conditio sine qua non* for the viability of a reform process. Of course, opening can work only if a set of further conditions are met in parallel. Among these the most relevant ones are: monetary policy is not accommodative (Wolf, 1988), fiscal spending is under tight control, inflation is being fought through import and antitrust policy rather than through price controls, an 'equilibrium' rate of exchange is being introduced, and investment allocation follows scarcity signals as transmitted by prices.

Such a mixture of systems – according to developing country experience – does work. True, it also produces a large number of socio-economic problems. However, these will emerge in a situation where *the cake to be distributed actually grows*. Thus the proposed reforms do contribute to curing the fundamental economic ills of Eastern Europe, which lie precisely in the fact that the cake does not grow. Moreover, under current arrangements, without radical re-forms there is no chance for it to grow in the long run either (Winiecki, 1988; Csaba, 1988).

Note

At the time of the conference I was Alexander von Humboldt Fellow at the University of Munich.

References

Csaba, L. (1988)   'CMEA in 2000', *The Nordic Journal of Soviet and East European Studies*, 1.

Csaba, L. (1989)   'The Recent Past and Future of the Hungarian Reform; An Overview and Assessment', in Wallace, W. and Clarke, R. (eds) *The Hungarian Reform: The Second Decade* (London: Longman).

Kornai, J. (1984)   'Bureaucratic and Market Coordination', *Osteuropa-Wirtschaft*.

Winiecki, J. (1988)   *Economic Prospects in East and West* (London: CRCE).

Wolf, T. (1988)   'The Simultaneity of Effects of a Devaluation: Implications for Modified Planned Economies', *Acta Oeconomica*, 31 (3–4).

Part III

Cost Determination and Price Formation

6 Reform of the Soviet Price System

Morris Bornstein*
UNIVERSITY OF MICHIGAN

Rather than presenting an abstract discussion of price reforms in a hypothetical socialist centrally-planned economy, this paper considers the concrete case of the Soviet Union. It examines in turn the three main components of the price system: state industrial producer prices, agricultural producer prices, and retail prices. For each, it briefly analyses some important features of current pricing practice; discusses recent and prospective changes; and, by way of illustration, identifies some unresolved issues.[1]

1 INDUSTRIAL PRODUCER PRICES

In the USSR industrial producer prices – usually called 'industrial wholesale prices' (*optovye tseny promyshlennosti*) – are based on the branch average cost of production (*sebestoimost*) and a profit markup. The former includes direct and indirect labour, materials, fuel and power, amortisation allowances, and various overhead expenses. The profit markup is supposed to provide a 'normal' rate of profit (in relation to capital) for the branch as a whole. But the profitability rate may be above or below 'normal' for an individual enterprise, depending upon its product-mix and the relationship of the actual cost of its output to the planned branch average cost.

Quality differentials, and the superiority of new products over earlier models, are supposed to be reflected by a set of surcharges (*nadbavki*) and discounts (*skidki*). The surcharges increase (or the discounts decrease) the prices and profitabilities of products of higher (lower) quality. Thus they affect a product's relative contribution to an enterprise's gross and net value of output, as well as to its profits and bonus funds related to profits.

Soviet industrial producer prices are set primarily from the cost or

111

supply side and usually do not also reflect demand or scarcity. Surcharges and discounts inadequately reflect differences in quality and technological level. Hence, enterprise plan assignments often are expressed in physical units in an effort to secure the desired output of products that price–cost relationships make 'disadvantageous' for the enterprise. Also, administrative allocation, rather than price rationing, is commonly used to distribute raw, intermediate, and finished goods. Finally, cost and price increases in industry may not be fully passed along in corresponding changes in agricultural producer prices or state retail prices.[2]

According to official statements, new industrial wholesale prices (and freight rates) are to be introduced on 1 January 1990. The calculation of costs for the new prices will include a 140 per cent increase in the charges (on the wage bill) for social insurance. Other changes include higher charges for geological survey costs, reforestation, the use of water, and environmental protection measures. Rental payments will be raised in the oil, gas, and other extractive industries. A labour tax and a larger capital tax will be paid out of profits (Pavlov, 1987, p. 22, and Komin, 1988a, p. 93).

Scattered, often preliminary statements indicate that coal prices will be raised 100 per cent and oil and gas prices 100–150 per cent (Komin, 1988b, p. 113). Electricity rates will rise 45–65 per cent (Maiorets, 1988). Similar increases are likely in the prices of metals and petrochemicals. The average increase in prices of construction materials will be about 30 per cent (Shcherbakov, 1988). The overall price level for the output of machine building and metal working is to remain basically unchanged. However, prices of raw-material-intensive output will rise, while prices of R & D-intensive products will fall. For example, prices on electronic and computer products are to be cut by an average of 15–20 per cent (Komin, 1988a, pp. 94–5). Percentage increases in freight rates, by mode of transport, are to be as follows: rail, 30–35; road, 20–25; river, 30–35; and coastal shipping, 35–45 (Stepanenko, 1988).

On the whole, the envisioned changes in industrial producer prices correspond more to a 'revision' than to a 'reform'. In Soviet pricing terminology, a reform (*reforma*) refers to a basic change in the way prices are constructed, whereas a revision (*peresmotr*) adjusts many prices without altering the fundamental scheme for price formation. By these standards, Soviet industrial producer prices are deemed to have been 'reformed' in 1966–7 (Schroeder, 1969) but only 'revised' in 1982 (Bornstein, 1985).

For instance, no fundamental changes are indicated in the latest methodological instructions for pricing new machinery, equipment, and instruments ('Vremennaia metodika', 1987) and new products of the raw material branches ('Metodika', 1988).

There is to be greater use of 'contract' prices (*dogovornye tseny*) for producer goods, to be negotiated between producer and user enterprises within the framework of detailed regulations established by the USSR State Committee for Prices ('Polozhenie', 1988). But such contract prices are not likely to provide much of an improvement in the pricing of producer goods, for several reasons (V. Kim, 1988b, p. 34). First, they apply only to the relatively small share of output on which prices are not set by state pricing agencies. Second, contract prices are to be related to reference ('base') prices established by pricing agencies. Third, these agencies prescribe detailed rules for the determination, agreement, registration, and modification of contract prices. Fourth, after two years the contract price is to be replaced by a centrally-set price. Thus, in the assessment of a Soviet pricing expert, the regulations concerning contract prices 'tie enterprises hand and foot, and do not even let them "sneeze" in the pricing sphere' (V. Kim, 1988a).

Another problem area is the establishment of domestic industrial producer prices for exports and imports. At present, the Soviet relative price structure differs markedly from that on the world market, and Soviet official exchange rates are considerably overvalued (at least in relation to convertible currencies). If the domestic producer prices for exports (imports) were equal to the prices paid by (to) foreign trading partners converted into roubles at the official exchange rates for the respective foreign currencies, many Soviet enterprises would have substantial losses or unusually high profits on planned foreign trade transactions.

To avoid these consequences for enterprises, the Soviet authorities use a complex set of adjustment coefficients to achieve the exchange rates applied in settlements for some export and import transactions of Soviet enterprises. There are about 3000 'differentiated currency coefficients' (*differentsirovannye valiutnye koeffitsienty*) – hereafter called DCCs. The DCCs apply primarily to various kinds of machinery and equipment.[3] The DCCs vary by currency area, by product group, often by individual product, and sometimes by particular Soviet enterprise. The size of the DCC is intended to assure a 'normal' profit for the enterprise in the fulfilment of its assigned export or import transactions (Doronin, 1988). The DCCs are reported to range from 0.2 to 6.6 (Bunich, 1988, p. 7). For example, if the official rate is 0.6 roubles per dollar, a DCC of 2.0 for an export transaction makes the actual settlement rate 1.2 (2.0 × 0.6) roubles per dollar, raising the enterprise's sales revenue and profits in roubles.

The use of DCCs is supposed to be curtailed gradually, after the introduction of new industrial wholesale prices in 1990, and devaluations of the rouble, in 1990 and 1991, in settlements with Soviet enterprises for their transactions in convertible currencies. However, the authorities are likely to continue very detailed adjustment of the prices of many tradables, through DCCs or explicit subsidies and taxes (Kuznetsov, 1988; Golovatyi, 1989).

2   AGRICULTURAL PRODUCER PRICES

Soviet collective and state farms sell their output to state procurement organisations at 'purchase prices' (*zakupochnye tseny*). The procurement organisations resell this output at industrial wholesale prices – either to the light and food industries for processing, as in the case of grain and wool, or directly to the trade network when further processing is not needed, as in the case of eggs. The basic principle is that agricultural purchase prices should cover the costs of farms operating in 'normal' conditions and provide them a profit that can be reinvested to expand their capital stock of buildings, equipment, reproductive livestock, and inventories.

Sales assignments for agricultural products are given to large numbers of farms whose production costs vary widely because of differences in natural conditions, such as soil, topography, rainfall, temperature, and length of growing season. The Soviet practice is to differentiate the prices of many commodities geographically by price zones, in an effort to capture for the state differential rents arising from more favourable natural conditions.[4] These zonal prices are set with reference to the average costs of production in each zone. The aim is to provide, for each product, lower prices but higher profitability in low-cost areas, and higher prices but lower profitability in high-cost areas. In addition, weak farms, with low profitability or losses, get surcharges on the base zonal prices.

Nevertheless, many farms deliver livestock, potatoes, eggs, and other products at a loss. One-third of the farms had a profitability rate (relative to cost) below 10 per cent and 13 per cent of the farms operated at a loss, according to a 1988 source (V. Kim, 1988b, p. 30).

Moreover, the financial results of farms have been bolstered by subsidies on industrial inputs to agriculture. These subsidies have covered the difference between the industrial wholesale prices received by the producer and the lower 'release' prices at which goods and services have been sold to farms. This 'dual-price' scheme has applied, for example, to motor vehicles, agricultural equipment, mineral fertiliser, concentrated feed, and electricity.

According to an April 1989 decree, new agricultural purchase prices are to be introduced on 1 January 1990 ('O korennoi perestroike', 1989). These prices are to allow for the effects on farms' costs from new industrial producer prices and freight rates (discussed above); the elimination of subsidies on industrial inputs into agriculture; and the introduction of charges for the use of water by farms. For most products, the new agricultural producer prices are to be based on zonal average costs, although the number of zones will be reduced (and their size thus enlarged).[5] With the introduction of the new prices, price surcharges for weak farms are to be eliminated, while explicit rental payments will be collected from some farms in more favourable natural conditions. However, detailed information on the new agricultural producer prices has not yet been disclosed.

The abolition of subsidies on industrial inputs to agriculture is a positive step because it causes farms' costs and profits to be stated more accurately.

In contrast, the Soviet authorities have rejected proposals for new agricultural producer prices based on marginal costs for the country as a whole, or at least for very large climatically-similar zones. Such uniform prices (for a particular quality grade of a specific product) across the country or a zone would be accompanied by a comprehensive system of explicit rental payments by individual farms (see, for instance, A. Kim, 1988).

The official view is that passing higher marginal-cost-based agricultural producer prices along in higher retail prices would involve retail price increases 'running into tens of billions of roubles' (Pavlov, 1989) – or larger budget subsidies to avoid such increases.

3   STATE RETAIL PRICES

There are three principal components in the state retail price. The first is the producer price, namely the industry wholesale price (or, for an unprocessed food product like eggs, the agricultural purchase price plus the markup of the agricultural procurement agency). The second component, covering distribution, includes the wholesale and retail trade margins for planned costs and profits at their respective levels, and transportation charges. The last element is a differentiated excise tax (called the 'turnover' tax) or subsidy, if one is applied to the particular commodity. Turnover taxes are levied on alcoholic beverages and many non-food consumer goods like clothing and appliances. Subsidies are provided primarily for food products and services.

For many years, many consumer goods and services have been sold at prices below the market-clearing level, as shown by widespread and persistent shortages. Hence, various forms of non-price rationing distribute the available supply. They include administrative allocation (for instance of housing), coupons, queuing in actual lines or on waiting lists, influence with sales personnel, access to special stores, and black market transactions.

This excess demand is not reflected in official state retail price indexes, which report only a modest rate of inflation of about 1 per cent per year from 1980 to 1987 (USSR, *Nar. khoz.*, 1988, p. 434).

One explanation of the low rate of inflation depicted by the official state retail price indexes is the long-standing official commitment to retail price 'stability', understood to mean not only stability of the overall retail price level, but also rigidity of many individual prices.

Another explanation is that the published state retail price indexes refer only to changes in the 'permanent' state retail prices of goods, in terms of the index sample's coverage and weights. The indexes do not purport to capture changes in retail prices of five other kinds. (1) The indexes do not cover state sales of services. (2) The indexes do not encompass legal non-state sales of goods or services, such as collective farm market sales and sales by cooperatives. (3) Without a modification in the nominal permanent state retail prices of goods, their effective prices can change when quality is reduced. (4) Without changes in either the permanent state retail prices of goods or their quality, the effective average prices facing households can increase. This occurs when the product-mix is altered to increase the share of higher-priced items and decrease the share of lower-priced items. (5) Some (at least nominally) 'new' goods are sold at 'temporary' or 'contract' prices intended to exceed their permanent prices.

Thus, it is widely recognised, by both professional economists and the general public, that inflationary pressure in the USSR is much more severe than conveyed by official state retail price indexes (see, for instance, Golovachev, 1988).

As noted above, retail prices of most food products, some nonfood consumer goods, and most services have been held down by subsidies.

In regard to food products, according to a recent official estimate, in 1986 the retail price as a percentage of the total cost to the state for assistance for production and infrastructure, and for purchase, transportation, processing, and sale, was as follows: rye bread, 72; beef, 27; pork, 45; poultry; 73; whole milk, 46; and butter, 33 (Semenov, 1988, pp. 21–2).

In the Soviet budget for 1989, subsidies to cover the difference between agricultural purchase prices and retail prices are planned at 87.9 billion roubles, or 17.8 per cent of total budget expenditures (*Pravda*, 28 October 1988, p. 5).

Soviet economists, pricing officials, and political leaders now criticise the heavy subsidisation of the prices of meat, dairy products, and other foods as economically unsound. They point to the burden of subsidies on the budget, on the one hand, and shortages at artificially low prices, on the other.[6]

In this connection, some economists and officials have proposed that the population be 'compensated' for price increases – (1) by offsetting reductions in other retail prices, and/or (2) by increases in money incomes (Parkhomovskii, 1987; Chekhlov, 1988; Lopatnikov, 1988).

The problem with the first approach is to identify the appropriate goods. They should be goods for which the price cuts could come out of turnover tax revenues, in order to satisfy the principle that prices should cover costs (and provide 'normal' profits) for production and distribution. Also, they should be goods for which supplies are ample to meet greater demand at lower prices, in order to satisfy the principle that prices should clear the market. How easily could the government provide such offsetting price cuts to compensate for large increases in the prices of food products?

In the second approach, if the increment to household money incomes is as large as the increase in the value of retail sales resulting from the price increases, there may be no reduction in the excess aggregate demand of households.[7] Whatever the amount of such compensation payments, their distribution across households must be decided. Presumably the compensation payments should be made to households as consuming units, rather than to individuals as workers.

A differentiated scale could provide larger payments per person to households with lower per capita incomes, in an effort to reduce income inequality *per capita* across households. But such payments would alter the income differentials – from differences in wages by occupation, skill level, and productivity – envisioned by the wage reform (Gladkii, 1986).

No similar compensation for retail price increases appears to be envisioned for savings in cash or savings bank accounts. On the one hand, lack of (full) compensation would diminish the purchasing power of savings and the potential effective demand of households for goods and services. On the other hand, greater awareness that inflation can reduce the value of savings could lead households to reduce their voluntary saving.

These problems are recognised by some Soviet economists, who question the advisability of compensation through (1) reductions in prices of non-food consumer goods or (2) payments to households (Deriabin, 1988; Iasin, 1988). Other Soviet economists deem compensation payments economically undesirable but perhaps politically necessary if retail prices are to be raised (Borozdin, 1988, pp. 55–6).

Finally, many economists consider that retail price increases are so politically sensitive that they threaten *perestroika* as a whole. According to Academician Shatalin: 'The new economic mechanism has not yet been formed. And under the present conditions it is a naive and dangerous undertaking to pull it by such a thin and sensitive thread as retail prices' (Shatalin, 1988).

Thus, in March 1989 Gorbachev promised that, despite changes in agricultural producer prices scheduled for 1990, the present levels of state retail prices would be preserved 'for the next 2–3 years' on basic food products like bread, flour, meat, fish, eggs, milk, sugar, butter, and vegetable oil ('Ob agrarnoi politike', 1989, p. 3).

4   CONCLUSION

Proposals for a 'marketising' economic reform in a socialist planned economy commonly call for an increase in enterprise authority for decision making (and a corresponding diminution in central planning and administrative orders) concerning inputs, outputs, and investment. In turn, enterprises are to operate on principles of 'financial viability', with sales revenue covering (at least) operating costs, and even 'self-financing', with much (if not all) investment financed by (retained) profits from an excess of sales revenue over costs. To steer the decentralised decisions of enterprises properly, prices should reflect both costs and scarcities.

At present in the USSR state industrial producer prices, agricultural producer prices, and retail prices often fail to meet one or both of these criteria.

The changes announced so far for industrial producer prices, freight rates, and agricultural producer prices do not indicate much improvement in regard to these criteria. Moreover, the political problems in adjustment of retail prices are severe.

Therefore, the prospective Soviet price system in the early 1990s seems likely to be far from the ambitious goal expressed by the First Deputy Chairman of the USSR State Committee for Prices: 'full reflection in prices of real costs of the production of output, liquidation of the accumulated contradictions and distortions in prices, assurance of necessary flexibility of prices, their establishment in accordance not only with costs but also with demand' (Komin, 1988b, p. 111).

Notes

* This study draws on research supported by several organisations whose assistance is gratefully acknowledged. They are the International Research and Exchanges Board, in connection with a trip to the USSR in 1988, and three units at the University of Michigan: the Office of the Vice-President for Research, the Center for Russian and East European Studies, and the Faculty Research Assistance Fund of the College of Literature, Science, and the Arts. Also, I wish to thank the Soros Foundation for funds for transportation to the International Economic Association Conference in Moscow in March 1989. Permission was kindly granted to use in this study material in Morris Bornstein, 'Problems of Price Reform in the U.S.S.R.', in NATO's forthcoming book, *Soviet Economic Reforms: Implementation under Way*.
1. Space limitations preclude treatment of other aspects of these three components of the Soviet price system, as well as analysis of other categories of prices, such as transport rates and 'estimate' prices for construction.
2. For a more detailed analysis of industrial producer prices, see Bornstein (1987, pp. 96–109).
3. DCCs are not used for fuel, energy, and primary mineral products; consumer goods; or some types of machinery and equipment (Kuznetsov, 1988, p. 43).

4. For instance, there are 132 zones for wheat (Mozhin, 1989).
5. For potatoes, vegetables, and fruits, prices will be negotiated between producers and agricultural procurement or trade organisations.
6. These shortages have various consequences. (1) The effective purchasing power of money incomes (and savings) varies when households have different possibilities to buy goods and services at state retail prices. (2) Too much of households' time is devoted to searching and queueing for goods. (3) Incentives to the labour force to earn more money are blunted by shortages of goods and services on which they wish to spend additional income. For further discussion of these issues, see Bornstein (1987, pp. 126–7).
7. Some of the increase in household incomes from compensation payments might be voluntarily saved.

References

Bornstein, Morris (1985) 'The Soviet Industrial Price Revision', in Fink, G. (ed.), *Socialist Economy and Economic Policy* (Vienna and New York: Springer Verlag) pp. 157–70.

Bornstein, Morris (1987) 'Soviet Price Policies', *Soviet Economy*, 3 (2) (April–June) pp. 96–134.

Borozdin, Iu. V. (1988) 'Problemy radikal'noi reformy sistemy tsen' (Problems of the radical reform of the price system), *Izvestiia AN SSSR, seriia ekonomicheskaia*, 3 (May–June) pp. 45–56.

Bunich, P. (1988) 'Kompas ekonomiki: kuda klonitsia strelka?' (Compass of the economy: where does the needle point?), *Ogonek*, 26 (25 June–2 July) pp. 6–7, 29.

Chekhlov, N. I. (1988) 'Kto vse-taki vyigraet?' (Who will actually gain?) (Sovetskaia Rossiia, (5 February) p. 3.

Deriabin, A. (1988) 'V zerkale defitsita: spros, predlozhenie, tseny' (In the mirror of the shortage: demand, supply, price), *Trud*, (18 May) p. 2.

Doronin, I. (1988) 'Monetary Instruments: Problems of Their Improvement', *Foreign Trade* (Moscow), 4 (April), pp. 33–6.

Gladkii, I.I (1986) 'Perestroika sistemy zarabotnoi platy' (Restructuring of the wage system), *Ekonomicheskaia gazeta*, 43 (October) pp. 6–7.

Golovachev, V. (1988) 'Pochemu rastut tseny' (Why prices are rising), *Trud* (29 September) p. 2.

Golovatyi, A. (1989) 'Valiuta predpriatiia' (Foreign exchange of the enterprise), *Ekonomicheskaia* gazeta, 6 (February) p. 21.

Iasin, E. (1988) 'Tseny i dokhody' (Prices and incomes), *Trud* (14 July), p. 2.

Kim, A. (1988) 'Stoimostnye rychagi intensifikatsiia proizvodstva v APK' (Value levers for intensification of production in the agro-industrial complex), *Finansy S.S.S.R.*, 3 (March) pp. 51–4.

Kim, V. (1988a) 'O sud'be tsenovoi reformy' (On the fate of price reform), *Ekonomicheskaia gazeta*, 52 (December) p. 8.

Kim, V. (1988b) 'Problemy tsenovoi perestroiki' (Problems of price restructuring), *Ekonomicheskie nauki*, 5 (May) pp. 25–35.

Komin, A. (1988a) 'Peresmotr optovykh tsen na promyshlennuiu produktsiu' (Revision of wholesale prices on industrial output), *Planovoe khoziaistvo*, 10 (October) pp. 90–5.

Komin, A. (1988b) 'Perestroika tsenovogo khoziaistva' (Reconstruction of the Pricing Economy), *Voprosy ekonomiki*, 3 (March), pp. 107–14.

Kuznetsov, V. (1988) 'Domestic and Foreign Trade Prices: Their Interconnection in the New Economic Management Conditions', *Foreign Trade* (Moscow), 7 (July) pp. 42–5.

Lopatnikov, L. (1988) 'Chto naidem, chto poteriam?' (What will we gain, what will we lose?), *Literaturnaia gazeta* (20 January) p. 10.

Maiorets, A. I. (1988) 'Otrasl' na puti k polnomu khozraschetu' (Branch on the road to full economic accountability), *Ekonomicheskaia gazeta*, 50 (December) p. 4.

'Metodika opredeleniia optovykh tsen na produktsiu proizvodstvenno-tekhnicheskogo naznacheniia syrevykh otraslei tiazheloi promyshlennosti' (Methodology for determination of wholesale prices on output of producer goods of the raw material branches of heavy industry), *Ekonomicheskaia gazeta*, 3 (January 1988) p. 19.

Mozhin, K. (1989) 'Tseny, zatraty i rynok' (Prices, costs and the market), *Ekonomicheskaia gazeta*, 6 (February) p. 11.

'O korennoi perestroike ekonomicheskikh otnoshenii i upravleniia v agropromyshlennom komplekse strany' (On the radical restructuring of economic relations and management in the country's agro-industrial complex), *Pravda* (12 April 1989) p. 2.

'Ob agrarnoi politike KPSS v sovremennykh usloviakh (Doklad General-'nogo sekretaria TsK KPSS M. S. Gorbacheva na Plenume Ts KPSS 15 marta 1989 goda)' (On the agrarian policy of the CPSU in contemporary conditions (Report of CC CPSU General Secretary M. S. Gorbachev to the CC CPSU Plenum of March 15, 1989)), *Pravda* (16 March 1989) pp. 1–4.

Parkhomovskii, E., (1987) 'Tovary, tseny, my . . .' (Goods, prices, us . . .), *Izvestiia* (19 November) p. 2.

Pavlov, V., (1987) 'Vazhnaia sostavnaia chast' perestroiki' (An important component of restructuring), *Kommunist*, 13 (September) pp. 14–26.

Pavlov, V., (1989) 'Narushen li tsenovoi balans?' (Has the price balance been disrupted?), *Sel'skaia zhizn'*, (12 January) p. 4.

'Polozhenie o poriadke ustanovleniia dogovornykh optovykh tsen na produktsiu proizvodstvenno-tekhnicheskogo naznacheniia i uslugi proizvodstvennogo kharaktera' (Statute on the procedure for establishment by enterprises of contract wholesale prices on output of producer goods and producer services), *Ekonomicheskaia gazeta*, 5 (January 1988) p. 23.

Schroeder, Gertrude E., (1969) 'The 1966–67 Soviet Industrial Price Reform: A Study in Complications', *Soviet Studies*, 20 (4) (April) pp. 462–77.

Semenov, V. N., (1988) 'Tseny i finansy APK' (Prices and finances of the agro-industrial complex), *Finansy S.S.S.R.*, 9 (September) pp. 17–26.

Shatalin, S., (1988) 'Khochu priznat' svoiu oshibku' (I want to acknowledge my own mistake), *Sotsialisticheskaia industriia* (30 October) p. 2.

Shcherbakov, V., (1988) 'Reforma obnazhaet interesy' (The reform reveals interests), *Sotsialisticheskaia industriia* (10 September) p. 2.

Stepanenko, V., (1988) 'Novye tarify na perevozku gruzov' (New freight rates), *Ekonomicheskaia gazeta*, 50 (December) p. 17.

USSR, Gosudarstvennyi komitet po statistike, *Narodnoe khoziaistvo S.S.S.R. v 1987 g.: statisticheskii ezhegodnik* (The Economy of the U.S.S.R. in 1987: statistical yearbook) (Moscow: Finansy i statistika, 1988).

'Vremennaia metodika: Opredelenie optovykh tsen na novuiu mashino-stroitel'nuiu produktsiu proizvodstvenno-teknicheskogo naznacheniia' (Temporary methodology: Determination of wholesale prices on new machinery output for producer use), *Ekonomicheskaia gazeta*, 51 (December 1987) pp. 15–16.

7 Prices Under Socialism in the Light of Economic Reforms

Béla Csikós-Nagy
ECONOMIC ADVISORY BOARD,
GOVERNMENT OF HUNGARY

1 THEORETICAL BACKGROUND TO THE IDEOLOGICAL CONFRONTATION ON PRICES

Identical views on the laws of the market economy and the mechanism of its functioning were held by the British classical economists, Adam Smith and David Ricardo, and the creators of scientific socialism, Karl Marx and Friedrich Engels.

They started from the idea that economics had to cover everything in society which was constrained by some scarcity. It was on this basis that they distinguished free goods and economic goods. Within the world of natural resources they considered renewability as the criterion determining the separation of free goods from economic goods. That is why they considered land as an economic good. There was agreement also that economics had to consider economic goods as the product of human labour, although production was organised through an active combination of land, labour and capital. That is how the classical labour theory of value became the basis of price theory, although non-renewable natural resources (for example, land) also have prices, and the market can function automatically only on the basis of equilibrium, so that price is directly subject in its movements to the laws of demand and supply.

The equilibrium price is here interpreted in the broad sense, since it plays a determinative role in respect of the factors of production, final products and indeed all matters where a value is assigned, for example, exchange rates. In this context, human labour is in a particular situation yet is no exception to the rule. In Marx one can read the following: 'Commodity production imposes itself on the whole society only where work done for hire is its basis, but all the powers lying hidden in it unfold only then' (Marx, 1867).

No set of scientific arguments had been built up historically to require that the political economics of socialism should place price theory on radically different bases. From this angle, the market mechanism could be viewed as a technical framework which was capable of serving different socio-economic systems. In practice, however, things took another turn.

The experts of the political economy of capitalism were of the opinion that by his explanation of the theory of exploitation Marx had 'compromised' the theory of value; the category of value had simply been discarded from economics under the assumption that an investigation restricted to the terms of commodity exchange was sufficient to explain economic phenomena.[1] For all this the basis was created by the Austrian Carl Menger, the British Stanley Jevons and the Swiss Léon Walras through explaining rational producer and consumer behaviour on the basis of the principle of marginality. Thus the theory of marginal utility became an alternative to the labour theory of value.

For their part, the creators of the political economics of socialism discarded price theory. In fact, it was due to a conscious undertaking of the ideological confrontation that in the USSR (a) the law of price was identified with the law of value; (b) the market price mechanism was rated as anarchic and was replaced by the concept of planned price; and (c) the changes in the price level taking place as a function of the plentiful or short supply of money were rated spontaneous, and a policy of reducing the price level was declared.

For revealing the misinterpretations concerning the law of value, it is expedient to recall the discussion organised in 1926 on 'The law of value in the Soviet Union' (*Vestnik Kommunisticheskoy Akademii*, 1926). There it was pointed out by E. Preobrazhensky that the law of value was a mode of regulation related to commodity production and as such it could not be considered as independent of the law of demand and supply. A different standpoint was taken by Bogdanov, who was the first to formulate the thesis on the conscious use of the law of value in socialism, which then became a prevalent concept. He wanted to prove that the law of the free play of demand and supply was just a spontaneous form of the law of value. The essence of the law of value lay, according to his formulation, not in the fluctuation of prices but in those fluctuations tending to a definite norm. In one case the functioning of the law of value was realised spontaneously and in the other more consciously, but it was one and the same law, that of labour inputs. Preobrazhensky pointed out with good reason that Bogdanov mixed up the law of value with that of labour input. In respect of the socialist relations of production, Marx mentioned simultaneously the cessation of commodity production and the need to take account of the labour inputs (Marx, 1905–10).

2 THE CLASSICAL SOCIALIST PRICE SYSTEM AND ITS CRITICISM

The price system of socialism, as it was realised in the USSR, was first described by Maizenberg (1953). The whole issue and its related problems were then treated by studies numerous enough to fill a library. The classical model of price in socialism which emerges from these writings may be summed up in four points.

1. *Prices are regulated by a price authority* in the form of price fixing as far as possible. An important component of such a price system is a central price list, which is used not only for the control of prices but also in national economic planning. No product can be manufactured or put on the market which is not included in the price list. In the case of non-series products, the fixed price is replaced by an obligatory normative calculation.
2. The general objectives of the national economic plan, the relationships between branches of manufacture and economic sectors, and various other factors make socialist price policy appear to form some sort of homogeneous unity. However, *the price system is not homogeneous*. The divisions in the price system of the national economy are manifested in that the domestic price is separated from the foreign trade price; and that the principles of price formation are different for the spheres of production and consumption, and for the state, cooperative and private sectors respectively. The segregation of parts of the price system is based on the hypothesis, among others, that within the category of state property no real commodity relations exist. In this field, price is a technical tool to be used for accounting purposes, for the determination of plan targets in value terms and for checking the plan directives in monetary terms.
3. *The price system is dual-level*. For products within the category of state property the basis of prices is prime cost, and for those

falling outside state property it is value. The dual-level price system is based on the argument that within the range of state property price changes do not affect the financial relation between budget and enterprise, and that from the point of view of compliance with value proportions it is immaterial whether this is realised on the value level or the prime cost level. The former is explained by the so-called 'zero balance solution' and the latter by the 'real prime cost solution' (Csikós-Nagy, 1975).

4. *The classic socialist price system is ultimately the sum of the industrial, agricultural, consumer and foreign trade price policies.* This quadruple division results in a large-scale segregation which is explained by the fact that there are different primary tasks to be met in the four domains, namely: (a) industrial price policy aims to ensure a smooth management of enterprise self-accounting; (b) agricultural price policy aims to influence the suitable evolution of the planned worker/peasant income ratio and of the production pattern of agriculture; (c) consumer price policy aims to promote market equilibrium in consumer articles and to implement the standard of living policy; and (d) foreign trade policy aims to ensure an equilibrium of the international balance of payments.

For the functioning of this price system, the so-called planned price concept provides the ideological basis. According to this concept, inflation and deflation are to be considered as anarchic traits, following from market spontaneity, which are eliminated by the socialist planned economy. According to the planned price concept, in the socialist economy changes can take place in the price relations starting only from the commodity side; however, these are subordinated to the law of decreasing value. Taking a closer look at the price policy goals which have been formulated in the USSR for the perspective development of the price system, the following is emphasised by Jakovets (1975).

(a) The reduction of the level of socially necessary labour inputs and the changes in value relations need to be reflected ever more fully in the price system.

(b) It is necessary to strengthen the stimulating role of prices in the acceleration of techno-scientific progress, in the improvement of product quality, and in a rational utilisation of the resources of production.

(c) The techno-scientific revolution becomes manifest in an enlargement of the product assortment and in an acceleration of product replacement. This process is to be controlled by the price policy by means of limited prices.

Following the Second World War, the countries choosing the socialist economic system built up their planned economies by relying on a utilisation of the USSR's experiences. Hence, their price systems became of an identical type. The criticism of that price system – apart from Yugoslavia – started at around the mid-1950s. Initially it was a mere price-related debate, but later it grew into one affecting the overall economic mechanism.

3   DEBATE ON THE PRICE MECHANISM

The pure price debate unfolded as one on the price centre. In his opening address within the framework of the debate held in 1956 on the issues of the law of value and of price formation in the Institute of Economics of the Academy of Sciences of the Soviet Union, Kronrod criticised the low level of prices of the means of production. Together with others, he advocated creating a homogeneous, single-level, price system (*Voprosy Ekonomiki*, 1957). In the debate, such categories were included as value price, production price, self-financing price, one- and multi-channel price system. In the debate, Strumilin set out from the socialist principle of distribution according to work done. Payment by results and value price are in compliance with this principle of distribution. Malishev, on the other hand, emphasised that the different capital intensity of the various production branches or products must become manifested in the centre of prices.

The debate on value price versus production price was keen, since it was in connection with the theses on the organisation of commodity production in the socialist way. In fact, at the time of the first formulation of the political economics of socialism a definite distinction was made between the capitalist and socialist way of organising production. It was the view that in socialism production is organised by a matching, not of the three factors of production (land, labour and capital), but of the live and dead labour. By the introduction of the production price formula, this thesis had to be abandoned. This was considered by many as an axiom, despite the fact that the factors of production had to be reckoned with in the practical work of organisation.

In practice, the building of socialism bears evidence to the fact that although the categories of capital and surplus value have evolved in capitalism, yet the separation of labour conditions from labour and the functional organisation of production are objective concomitants of the development of the forces of production, and are at the same time a precondition for rational development of the forces of production. The economic mechanism of a developed commodity-producing society simply cannot be described without paying attention to the functioning of capital.

In the USSR it was the price centre, and in Hungary it was the price mechanism, which were the focus of critical analysis. It was necessary to question whether in the system of administrative prices it was feasible to use prices to stimulate either the desirable structure of production or the promotion and direction of technological development. This problem was believed to be avoidable by those who laid emphasis on the fulfilment of obligatory plan figures, plan of production, plan of productivity, plan of prime costs, and so on.

It was made clear by the debates, however, that incentives connected with price always appear when stimulation is related to value targets. To put it another way, a deliberate price-related stimulation can be based only on personal interests in making profits. But price motivates human activity in every case where success is determined in value terms. Thus, for example, a bonus related to productivity distorts the structure of production, as in this case the enterprise management sets the priority as a function of the material intensity of products. In fact, value targets have the peculiarity that they can function only indirectly to achieve objectives.

4   MOVEMENT TO MARKET PRICING IN HUNGARY

All this explains why the debate on the price mechanism has led more and more to a move towards the *market price system*. Considering the process of economic reform in Hungary from this aspect, four periods can be distinguished.

1. In the course of the preparation of the price reform of 1959 the issue of seasonality was the focus of attention. A solution was sought then to the manufacture of products, the demand for which was not foreseen, which emerged fairly often due to the fact that, for example, fashion was not evolving in the way

anticipated, the winter period differed from the average one, and the like. It was hoped to solve this problem by the price reform of 1959 through the introduction of end-of-season sales and by the creation of a reserve fund provided in the trade margin for this purpose.

2. While in the clothing industry, for example, it was seasonality, in the engineering industry it was the evolution, not liable to planning, of technological development that gave rise to concern. What was characteristic of the sub-supplying industries was the need to manufacture products for which demand was unpredictable, causing underutilisation of capacity due to the product replacements carried out in the assembly (end-product) industries. In the period 1959–67 recourse was had to the use of maximum prices in the engineering industry with a view to creating better conditions for the coordination of production interests.

3. An essential transformation of the price system took place in the course of the economic reform of 1968. The price policy had then to make arrangements for gradually extending the allocation role of price to the factors of production. Account was taken of all the negative phenomena of a shortage economy which could be related to the administrative price fixing and which could be considered as manifestations of a repressed inflation. The following indicators were then interpreted as manifestations of inflation: non-controlled increases in the price level, concealed price increases, forced purchases and forced saving.

   The economic reform of 1968 could not fully eliminate these phenomena but pressed them back considerably, notably by first putting an end to the policy of 'manipulated' price stability and initiating a gradual liberalisation of prices, and secondly, applying new solutions for ensuring a relative price stability through introducing on the one hand the category of unfair profit, and on the other hand the institution of the obligation of prior announcement of the intention of price rises for a definite range of products.

4. The price reform of 1980 aimed to create a closer relationship between domestic and foreign trade price relations on the basis that in manufacturing industry international competitiveness (and in convertible exports the realised average profit) should become the measure of the efficiency of the enterprise. This was regarded as a model that, in close connection with the opening up

to the world market, would lead to a real market price system. Value added tax and general personal income tax were introduced in 1988 in this context.

5   MONETISATION AND PRICE LIBERALISATION

A survey of the socialist countries' debates on the system of management may convince the reader of the fact that the communist parties of these countries usually put the matter of price reform on the agenda when the functioning of the socialist economy becomes strained. The view according to which the negative phenomena emerging in the socialist economies can mostly be attributed to deficiencies in the price system and thus that they can be eliminated with the help of a well-formulated price reform, may be regarded as characteristic. On this assumption, many price reforms were carried out without bringing the expected results, mainly due to the fact that no changes took place in the economic policy and the system of management. The concept of price reform conceived as such cannot be interpreted otherwise than as an escape from the real problems, or at least as a postponement of a solution. Price is the most important regulator of economic processes, but its laws of movement, its effects of stimulation, and its role of income distribution are determined by the legal order of the economy, and notably as a function of the extent to which the socialist state can enforce it.

The reason why it is necessary to refer to the efficiency of state regulation is that the laws of commodity production are based on biological, sociological and psychological functions, where man acts with the least display of effort while striving after the maximum profit, and produces a maximum performance only when constrained to do so and on the basis of his own interests. If this is left out of consideration by state regulation, the market will seek those illegal channels where hedonism prevails. But if the second economy is spreading on a growing scale, it implies a simultaneous weakening of social morals and a spreading of the view according to which the course of satisfying needs and personal well-being deviates from the law. This is a highly hazardous perspective, which is sufficient reason for revising the economic management system which has not given due consideration to the realistic manifestations of social life – that is, for putting on the agenda the issue of social and economic renewal.

Two radically different views have evolved regarding the identification of the course for the process of renewal. One seeks perfection of central planning and of the administrative price system as the main road to improving the efficiency of the system, and the other expects improvement by increasing the sphere of action of the market.

The former sets out from the idea that the troubles of functioning of the socialist economy derive, among other things, from the fact that the planners have not yet mastered the science of central management of the economy. According to this view, knowledge of systems theory and improved forecasts, relying on advanced computer science, create the possibility of a better management. Thus, an efficient allocation of the factors of production is believed to be viable by the use of mathematical programming.

The latter starts from the idea that the troubles in the functioning of the socialist economy derive from the setting of targets without giving due consideration to the possibilities of the economy and from an improper mechanism. Those seeking a solution to the problem in this way believe that it is necessary to establish such relations in the market order of the economy as can permit a rational attitude to become preponderant in economic management.

It appears that while in recent decades emphasis was laid on the perfection of planning, now the creation of a socialist market economy is considered as the way leading out of the 'crisis'. This is a realistic alternative. For giving an idea of the underlying reason, it is expedient to call attention to the debate between Böhm-Bawerk and Stolzmann (Böhm-Bawerk, 1914).

Böhm-Bawerk, a representative of the Vienna school, speculated in terms of 'pure economic categories'. Stolzmann, being a socialist, laid emphasis on the 'social categories'. What was considered as determinative by Böhm-Bawerk was that wherever power appeared, it was either crossing or meeting the rules of the law of price. This is how he came to make a distinction between 'economic power' and 'physical pressure' and to relate to all this the possible modes of enforcing the motives acting outside the economy.

The essence of state regulation complying with the market is that the state can do everything whereby it can influence market conditions but it cannot do anything whereby it sets limits to price automatism. In somewhat less sophisticated terms, the state can have a price and income policy and it can have a production and distribution policy, but it cannot use direct price, income, production and distribution regulators. Direct regulation is to take place within the system of the market mechanism.

In this way, a market-conformable economic policy is based on making a distinction between direct and indirect tools. The economic policy complying with the market gives free scope for the evolution of prices and, on that basis, the self-acting regulation of the market – that is, price automatism. The socialist economy cannot have such an economic policy because of overriding normative social values. These can be complied with in certain circumstances by means of the application of direct tools.

But the market mechanism includes elements which are acceptable to the planned version of market regulation. Regulation using direct tools has the major disadvantage that it is insensitive to the changes taking place in the conditions of economic development. Hence, it can turn against the social interest. That is why it is justified to give preference to the indirect tool wherever a goal can be realised by such; and where a direct tool must necessarily be applied, it should possibly be a financial regulator. From this follows, further, the requirement that if some goal cannot be realised by the use of a financial tool, the reality of the goal should be checked before the application of the direct tools in physical terms. It is this philosophy of the system of regulation that is most suitable for excluding from the objective process of systematic development the irrational elements of petty bossing.

All this explains satisfactorily that the socialist system based on a market economy cannot be made feasible without an unfolding of the functions of money. The money function sets definite requirements for the price mechanism, since price is the form of value in money terms. It is true that price deviates from value; nevertheless the price movement keeps output in line with the trend of demand and supply relationships. Therefore, it is a condition of money's function of measuring value that the price be under the direct control of the market. Political preferences can represent exceptions only in well-founded cases. But the price must act as an equilibrium price in such product spheres as well.

The shortage economy cannot be brought to comply with money's function as a means of payment. And this leads on to money's role as a means of accumulation. The motivation for saving money is different for economic units and individual consumers, and it is different again if constrained saving is at issue due to the fact that the use of money comes up against objective obstacles.

All that can be said about the different money functions can be summed up, from another aspect, as follows: the commodity producing economy is a market economy, and the market economy can function along an optimum course only on the basis of the laws applying to the money economy. These laws are based on a rational allocation of resources; rational allocation, in turn, on the market-clearing function of price; and the equilibrium price, ultimately, on the gold standard hypothesis. This applies to every commodity-producing economy, irrespective of the socio-economic system served by the mechanism in question.

That is why it is justified to characterise the reform steps taken toward the socialist market economy as a monetisation of the economy, and not – in accordance with the predominant concept – as a process of decentralisation. To put it another way, the monetisation of the economy is the basic condition of a rational price system and of an efficient price function. In fact, it is the price that transmits information on the situation of the market, stimulates rational behaviour, and regulates income distribution. If the laws of commodity production are approached from the price aspect, these three functions need consideration in an organic unity. That is why price and wage liberalisation on the one hand, and currency convertibility on the other, can be considered as the most important characteristics of a socialist socio-economic development along the market economy course.

6 PRICE THEORETICAL ASPECTS OF UP-TO-DATE ECONOMICS

The socialist market economy has no exactly formulated and paraphrased model going into all details. But it cannot fundamentally be different from that of the up-to-date market economy. Therefore Marxian economists are interested in all scientific research concerning the characteristics of the market economy and serving to improve its efficiency. These researches are more and more related to the problems which arise, on the one hand, due to the increasing share of public goods in GDP and, on the other hand, due to the appearance of environmental products. In fact, these have no market and thus, in contrast to individual products, their distribution can be controlled only by the political mechanism.

Public goods have always existed, although within a much narrower range than currently, and their investigation was initially relegated by economists to the subject of public finance. On the other hand, the appearance of environmental products is of recent origin. It has turned out that the natural resources believed to be available in unlimited amounts can be damaged and even annihilated by man. This results from the fact that large-scale production of certain manufacturing technologies and the pollution of the environment by various products put on the market may exceed the self-purification capacity of water and air.

The greater the share of public goods in the social product the more the significance, from the viewpoint of consumer sovereignty, of what role is played by society in the shaping of political preferences. This is a sufficient reason why, in a modern society, the related issues of the political institutional system and consumer preference cannot be left out of consideration in the examination of the economic processes. In political economy it is necessary to integrate the economics of the market with that of the community. Musgrave (1959) particularly did a lot in this field.

It could be assumed that in this respect the socialist society organised under the direction of the communist party enjoys a definite dominance over the capitalist society. However, it is shown by experience that the tendency of bureaucratisation has distorted the scale of values of socialism. Thus, in a particular way, the alternative ensured by the existence of several parties provides a better chance to the consumers to enforce their system of preferences than in the communist party-led socialist society. It is to be welcomed for this reason alone that the *perestroika* put on the agenda in the USSR combines the reform of the economy with that of the political institutional system. Supposedly, there will be a general tendency both for political democratisation to unfold on the basis of pluralism and for economic decentralisation to unfold on the basis of market economy.

The greater the pollution of the environment the more there is a difference between the social judgement of the evolution of welfare and the growth of the economy measured by traditional methods. The causes of the generation of environmental products, the peculiarities of their appearance, and the possibilities and modes of their elimination is explored by the economics of the environment. The integration of this with the political economy is due to the existence of the economics of welfare and, above all, to the activity of Pigou (1932).

Society, whether organised on a socialist basis or a capitalist one, must reckon with the peculiarities which follow from the triple range of the goods involved in the sphere of the economy. The laws of these are explored by the economics of the market, the economics of public goods and ecology. The general equilibrium theory of the economy is to be founded by an integration of these three spheres of economic management. The quality of life is brought to expression only by the material and intellectual welfare that can be ensured by the preservation of the natural environment.

The collective and the environmental products raise issues of price theory in different ways. In the case of public goods, this is connected with the identification of the sphere of action of the market mechanism. Supplies are to be organised, by the nature of the thing, on a social scale in all cases where conditions are non-existent for the operation of the market. In socialist societies and in a number of capitalist ones, however, the public goods sector also extends to spheres where distribution, from the purely technical aspect, could be seen to by the market itself, since cost and profit are internal, consumption is competitive and the principle of exclusion from consumption can be enforced. In the case of educational and health establishments cost and benefit are internal, yet they appear as public goods. The use of the services of educational, health and social institutions is not unlimited. Practically, it cannot be so as, for example, the demand for acquiring a university level of education exceeds considerably the number of those admitted to university, and furthermore because there always exists the possibility of declaring the right to social benefits at a time when full satisfaction cannot yet be ensured. Since in the system of social consumption the products have no prices, or they are just a fraction of the costs which as such do not provide for a function of selection, it is necessary to establish the criteria of the rightful claim to admission to the university, to the use of social institution services, etc.

If social provision is not determined by the technical criteria of products, then the distinction between commodity and non-commodity can have its roots only in the ideological aspect of the economy. For the organisation of the socialist economy specific social norms have become obligatory. As a general rule – at least from the aspect of principle – the sphere of concept of social provision covers the care of children and the old, education, and the safeguarding of public health. This is realised in socialist society as a dual system of distribution. Distribution according to the work done and one according to need are coexistent. The latter relates to needs of which the satisfaction is a social requirement from the viewpoint of the members of the society and an ethical requirement from the all-social aspect.

In connection with all this, today the question has been put whether not too far-reaching actions were taken in some countries towards narrowing the sphere of action of the market mechanism. It cannot be considered as incidental that, for example, in Hungary, where major progress has been made towards the creation of market socialism, significant changes have taken place in respect of narrowing the range, or reducing the extent, of price subsidisation by the budget.

In the case of environmental products, the issues of price theory are connected with the internalisation of the market externalities. The environmental effects can, in principle, be quantified by a cost–benefit analysis (Mishan, 1931). However, such quantification comes up against difficulties, among others for the reason that not all external benefit and damage can be expressed in terms of money. The passed-on implications of the deleterious side-effects of production and product use cannot always be tracked down. And there are even more difficulties when proofs are needed to achieve recompense for damage by whoever caused it. Nevertheless, many case studies can be mentioned which, despite limitations, produced relatively good results for decision taking. In the case of large-scale projects, this is necessary. The difficulties about internalisation may be overcome by the application of limits of tolerance. In this case, those causing damage are obliged to observe the limit of tolerance or else, in the case of surpassing the normative values, they are liable to pay a progressive penalty.

Those who consider the market mechanism as essential lay emphasis on the selection of those methods which offer most chance for a flexible adjustment to the market, and by means of which, therefore, the costs of eliminating environmental nuisance can be reduced to a minimum.

Note

1. M. Allais, E. Antonelli, C. Bodin, C. Boruilhet, G. H. Bozsquet, G. Cassel, H. Dietzel and P. Stowe and others simply cancelled the categories of value from the vocabulary of economics.

References

Böhm-Bawerk, E. V. (1914) 'Macht oder ökonmisches Gesetz?', *Zeitschrift für Volkswirtschaft. Sozialpolitik und Verwaltung*, XIII.
Csikós-Nagy, B. (1975) *Socialist Price Theory and Price Policy* (Budapest: Akadémiai Kiadó).
Jakovets, J. W. (1975) *Arak a tervgazdaságban* (*Prices in the Planned Economy*) (Budapest: Kossuth Kiadó).
Marx, Karl (1867) *Das Kapital*, vol. 1, *A Marx és Engels munkaja* (The Works of Marx and Engels) vol. 23, p. 558 (Budapest: Kossuth Kiadó).
Marx, Karl (1905–10) *The cries of Surplus Value*, part III, 1963 (Budapest: Kossuth Kiadó).
Maizenberg, L. T. (1953) *Tsenoobrazovanie v narodnom khozyaistve SSSR* (Price Formation in the Economy of the USSR) (Moscow).
Mishan, E. J. (1931) *Cost–Benefit Analysis: An Introduction* (New York: Washington: Praeger).
Musgrave, R. A. (1959) *The Theory of Public Finance* (New York: McGraw-Hill).
Pigou, A. C. (1932) *The Economics of Welfare* (London: Macmillan) 4th edn.
Vestnik Kommunisticheskoy Akademii (1926) 15, pp. 156–254.
Voprosy Ekonomiki (1957) 2 and 3.

Comment

Karel Dyba
INSTITUTE FOR FORECASTING, CZECHOSLOVAK
ACADEMY OF SCIENCES, PRAGUE, CZECHOSLOVAKIA

There seems to be widespread consensus in the profession nowadays that any meaningful market-oriented reform of centrally-planned economies (CPEs) implies *inter alia* a fundamental change in the principles of price formation – that is, a move from basically administrative pricing to basically market-determined or free pricing for most goods and services. This conviction is also reflected in the papers by Csikós-Nagy and Bornstein (Chapters 6 and 7 in this volume), though both authors differ in what they discuss and emphasise. Whereas Csikós-Nagy remains more on a conceptual level and takes the issue of pricing and reform in a broader theoretical as well as historical context, Bornstein in his paper is much less abstract and more technical as he analyses explicitly the current Soviet price reform (or revision), including retail prices, and evaluates it by standards of microeconomic theory.

Csikós-Nagy contends that there are no scientific arguments in the works of Marx and Engels which would suggest that market-determined prices (the market mechanism) are incompatible with a socialist economy. He says that market mechanism is just a technical device which may serve different socio-economic systems. While I agree with the latter statement, I would not go as far as to claim unequivocal support for it in the works of Marx and Engels. Indeed, other readers seem to draw different conclusions from their writings in the sense that market and prices determined by supply and demand (free pricing) are incompatible with a socialist economy. This view, after all, became the 'theoretical' basis of the Soviet price policies in the 1930s (later on also in other socialist countries in Eastern Europe) and opened a way for administrative voluntarist pricing practice with concomitant shortages and inefficiencies.

Csikós-Nagy recalls also the debate on the relationship of value theory and actual prices which took place in the USSR after Stalin's death. This debate about the 'correct' price formula for computing prices of producer goods by a centre (and applicability of the law of value within the state sector) included a broad spectrum of views,[1] up to those of mathematical economists who favoured values and prices based on opportunity costs – that is, prices derived from optimum plans reached by means of input–output method and linear programming. This discussion on pricing in retrospect should be understood in the context of a search for a more efficient socialist economy. Certainly it led to a better understanding of demand, scarcity and marginality aspects in pricing by some economists in socialist countries. Yet it also seemed to generate some illusions on computability of a 'correct' or more 'rational' price vector (of wholesale prices) by a centre for an economy using computers.[2]

In some socialist countries, notably Hungary, the issue of more rational pricing was relatively early understood as a need to move towards some kind of market-determined pricing. From this viewpoint, Csikós-Nagy traces back the major changes in the Hungarian price policy from 1956 to 1988. While this is interesting, it would perhaps be valuable also to hear his ideas on how the Hungarian price system under a long reform period has really been moving closer to a rational market-determined price system for a small open economy. What should be the basic properties of such a system and what steps should one take to get there or which steps taken in Hungary proved to be a blind alley?

Csikós-Nagy identifies the steps towards a socialist market economy with monetisation of the economy and sees the latter as a precondition of a rational prices system and of its efficient functioning. I agree.. However, for small economies like Czechoslovakia or Hungary, I would emphasise more the creation and preservation of a reasonably competitive market structure to avoid monopoly pricing and/or excessive use of resources. After all, it must be considered a kind of monopoly pricing when a producer (who is not a profit maximiser) more or less dissipates potential profits by an excessive use of resources, including labour, or by the use of less efficient methods of production.[3] A competitive structure is obviously impossible to achieve without a real contestability of various domestic markets by foreign economic actors – that is, without a real opening up of the economy.

Finally, let me raise a broader issue which is also addressed in Csikós-Nagy's paper when he argues that without creating a socialist market economy it will be impsossible to reverse the declining economic performance (or crisis) observable currently in most socialist economies. I also subscribe to this view, yet I would like to know in what sense a socialist market economy differs from a capitalist or non-socialist market economy (socialist-market-determined prices from market-determined prices only)? Csikós-Nagy himself struggles with this when he says that (a socialist-market economy) 'cannot be fundamentally different from that of the up-to-date market economy'. So is there to be any difference or not, and in particular as far as pricing is concerned, between a socialist market and a non-socialist market? I would tend to think that the essential attributes of markets in order to function efficiently should be the same in any society – freedom of choice, free entry and exit, well-defined rewards as well as penalties, etc. – and the content of the socialist attribute must be looked for elsewhere.

Turning now to the paper by Bornstein while having in mind a number of papers he wrote on the subject of Soviet price policies and systems, I have to say that my first impression when reading it was that the Soviet price authorities should make use of his extensive knowledge of the history and theory behind Soviet pricing and his critique of it, and hire him to work on administrative reform of the price system. (Maybe with Morris Bornstein's expertise this mammoth and futile task could become manageable after all!).

After that I felt that a proper way of discussing his paper is for me to refer to Czechoslovak experience with price reforms or revisions so as to complement Bornstein's insights and to highlight some points which would further document the futility of the administrative repricing exercise.

It has always been an officially proclaimed target of price revisions or 'reforms' in Czechoslovakia (see Karel Kouba's contribution to this volume, p. 150) to make wholesale prices of industrial and agricultural goods more 'objective' in the sense that they should reflect more properly the real 'social' cost of producing them. So any price reform we had in Czechoslovakia should liquidate price distortions, take into account more demand factors, ensure a 'just' profit margin in prices, etc.

Yet any price reform administered by a centre is by necessity a longer-term process and one needs several years from its start to its completion even in the age of computers. In between, initial information, for example, prices of imported materials, which must be guestimated at the start of the price recalculations, becomes obsolete.

Next, prices finally arrived at are not the prices set on the basis of independent calculations by the price office. Rather they emerge after protracted negotiations between the price office and enterprises after a mutual consensus which satisfies the parties involved is reached. However, this outcome is not beneficial from the point of view of society at large (efficiency, welfare, etc.).

For enterprises, usually any price reform is a welcome exercise because it allows them to pass through various inefficiencies, past cost increases, etc. and to secure what they consider reasonable profits in supplying reasonably doctored information to the price authorities who, after some haggling to derive their benefits, are more or less forced to use it to meet the deadline.

So the point is that an administratively guided process of 'objectification' of prices using cost information supplied by more or less monopolistic producers (who know that this is to be used for setting prices for their products) and outdated extraneous information, because of motivational and technical distortions,[4] does not bring us any closer to what would amount to market-determined prices (under competitive conditions) – that is, to a real price reform compatible with a market-oriented systematic reform.

Bornstein also in a few pages nicely summarises the Soviet retail price problem which is low recorded open inflation, rather high hidden inflation and repressed inflation (monetary overhang) and recalls very candid Soviet discussion of issues of changes in retail pricing. I can only add that while in Czechoslovakia we do not have a forced saving problem (and repressed inflation) – at least there is enough evidence we do not have it (maybe not yet) – we face a similarly distorted retail price structure as the USSR (as measured against standards of open economies in the west) and one naturally wonders how to solve this socially and politically extremely sensitive problem (remember Poland!) in the least costly way. It is a pity that Morris Bornstein does not say what kind of solution he would prefer or how he would proceed to solve the problems involved – although, of course, this by no means disqualifies his clear analysis of them.

Notes

1. For a thorough early evaluation, see Bornstein (1964).
2. These illusions, at least in Czechoslovakia, still survive in pricing poli-

cies. So cost plus prices computed by using input–output models and some extraneous information are being (in 1989) introduced as a part of a current reform attempt, despite theoretical warnings and bad practical experience with this approach towards finding a more rational structure of wholesale prices in the past. So one must have serious doubts as to what extent the newly-computed price vector reflects better even the relative 'social' cost of producing various commodities than the price vector to be replaced.

3. Under the current system of administrative pricing in Czechoslovakia the retail price of the new model of Škoda car is fixed by the Central Price Office. Yet this office more or less accepts the wholesale price as suggested by the company. This procedure of course validates excessive use of resources in the whole process of production of cars.

4. See also comments above related to Csikós-Nagy's paper.

Reference

Bornstein, M. (1964)   'The Soviet Price Reform Discussion', *Quarterly Journal of Economics*, 78 (February).

Comment

Alec Nove
CENTRE FOR DEVELOPMENT STUDIES, UNIVERSITY OF
GLASGOW, UK

The very interesting papers by Béla Csikós-Nagy and Morris Bornstein (Chapter 6 and 7 in this volume), and Karel Dyba's equally
valuable comments, lead me first to make some remarks about price
theory. No one doubts that prices play a key role in the entire reform
process. One cannot see how essential elements of this process,
including full cost-accounting and trade in means of production, can
even begin to function unless and until there is a fundamental change
in pricing and prices.

Here Marxist political economy can be of little help. Marx had
nothing to say about pricing under socialism, since he imagined a
future socialism without markets and so without prices, profits,
'value'. His value theory was used above all as a base for a theory of
exploitation, of the generation of surplus value. The labour theory,
inherited from Adam Smith, served well for this purpose, stressing
the special role of labour as *the* productive factor. Tugan-Baranovsky
used to point out that, if horses could write economics, there would
be a horse theory of value! However, even applied to capitalism
Marx's labour theory could lend itself to misunderstanding, since it
stressed (human) effort and not result. True, for Marx, a good which
was of *no* use had no value, but clearly the same amount of human
labour can be devoted to the production of goods of *different* use-
values, for example, to a better quality or more attractive dress, a
more (or less) productive machine-tool, and so on. Use-value, the
evaluation by the customer, was downgraded both in Marxist theory
and in Soviet practice. Interestingly, the first professor of economics
of Moscow University, A. Shletser, writing in 1810, criticised Adam
Smith's labour theory, arguing that value (*'tsennost'*) arose not
because labour was devoted to the production of a good; labour was
devoted to the production of the good because it had value for the
user, who was therefore prepared to pay for it. Personally I always
liked Alfred Marshall's image of two blades of scissors, value being

143

influenced both by the conditions of supply (cost of production) and by demand, the latter being responsible for short-run fluctuations of price.

The excellent Russian monetary economist, L. Yurovsky, in his book *Denezhnaya politika sovetskoi vlasti* (1928), has a fascinating chapter entitled 'problems of a moneyless economy', in which he set out the discussions of a seminar held in 1919–20 in which intelligent Marxist and non-Marxist economists debated how economic calculation might be possible without money and prices.

Today's reform requires a radical revision of prices. It is, however, also necessary to stress that, as Kornai wrote long ago, no one takes major decisions on the basis *only* of the information contained in price, valuable though this information is. It is only in neo-classical models of perfect competition that every firm can sell anything it produces at the price which emerges from the magic wand of the Walrasian auctioneer. It is only in textbooks that prices conform to the marginal cost principle. In fact most prices in Western capitalist economies are cost-based, resembling average cost-plus prices. But this 'imperfection' matters little because of *competition*, user *choice*, the need to maintain customer goodwill. Any good which does not attract the customer cannot be sold; firms that produce such goods can go bankrupt. To maintain goodwill one must maintain quality, provide after-sales service. It is a weakness of conventional monopoly theory that it usually relates to two dimensions only: quantity and price. Yet, as Soviet and other experience abundantly demonstrates, quality can deteriorate, indeed under monopoly it 'pays' to ignore quality and the precise requirements of the customer. Of course Soviet prices do need radical change; they provide misleading signals as to scarcity and cost. However, perhaps the greatest damage is done by *chronic shortage* (*defitsit*), which greatly strengthens the monopoly position of the supplier. It may be thought that *defitsit* is itself a function of price, that a higher price would lead to a balance between supply and demand. There are, however, two reasons why this may be no solution, at least in the Soviet case and in the short run. One is the fact that some of the shortages are supply bottlenecks, lack of some essential complementary good, as when fertiliser output increases much faster than the supply of bags, storage space and spreading machines. Dr Dong Fureng, our Chinese colleague, cited another such instance, this being shortage of transport facilities to move vegetables and fruit out of Sichuan province (Chapter 12 in this volume). The other problem relates to the survival (despite much criticism) of the gross output or value-of-turnover plan target, the notorious *val*. This can have the perverse effect of actually encouraging the use of dear inputs so as to enlarge the value of gross output, which is also used to measure labour productivity. Evidently, one cannot use prices to restrict demand unless and until this kind of plan-target is finally eliminated from the system.

One must also bear in mind that today's prices are an insufficient guide to investment decisions, which create productive capacity in the future. Future prices and costs cannot be known with certainty. In the real world errors are unavoidable; hence thousands of bankruptcies. To make major investments it is necessary to estimate not only future costs and prices, but also the likely behaviour of competitors and of suppliers of complementary inputs. In an excellent and neglected book, *Information and investment* (1960) G. B. Richardson pointed out that on the assumptions of perfect competition and perfect markets no would know what to do, since in the model the relevant information would be available to all one's competitors and if they too invest, there would be no profit. In the real world, big investment decisions occur because of so-called 'imperfection': because of information not in the possession of potential rivals, anticipated market domination, long-term tie-up with customers, collusion, or government-sponsored coordination, as in South Korea and Japan. These are all ways of reducing uncertainty and risk which would otherwise inhibit investment. The notion that all the necessary information is contained in prices is surely incorrect – though prices do supply vitally important information, especially as to relative costs.

Another possible source of misunderstanding arises from the commonly-encountered assumption that 'markets clear', that in competitive equilibrium there is a macro and micro balance between demand and supply at market-clearing prices. Yet in the real economy such an exact 'match' between demand and supply cannot exist, and this for two reasons. The first is the real process of competition; if all enterprises were fully utilising their productive capacity, they would have nothing to compete with. Real competition means winners *and* losers, and some of the latter at least will have some unused capacity, just as shops have unsold stock. Secondly, in the absence of exact prediction of future demand, there is bound to be excess supply, as a precondition of being able to supply the unexpected. Thus a restaurant with a choice of menu will always need 'excess supply' so as to offer the customers a choice. Exact supply-and-demand balance will be possible only if the supplier imposes the menu on the customers, as was indeed the case in the army when I was a corporal: we ate what was put in front of us! So in the real world, if there is competition and choice, supply must *exceed* demand. As Kornai remarked long ago, it must be difficult to sell. Many if not most Soviet problems today are linked with the consequences of shortage, that is, with the fact that it is difficult to buy. This applies also to the case of the labour market: how can the necessary degree of flexibility be achieved without some unused labour reserves? Yes, unemployment is an evil, and yes, unused productive capacity seems to be evidence of waste. Yet the fact remains that full employment of all resources is either an unattainable *optimum optimorum*, dependent on the unrealistic assumption of perfect foresight, or it must be associated with shortage, this because exact *macro* balance is bound to be associated with micro imbalances (owing to the exercise of choice, which by its nature is not precisely forecastable). The psychological effect of fear of shortage leads to behaviour (hoarding) which exacerbates it. So those who believe that prices should be such as precisely to equate supply with demand may be suffering from textbook-induced illusions. Prices should be (and in the capitalist West are) associated with excess supply, or at least *potential* excess supply.

Once, when I was in Poland, an economist remarked that if the state fixes the prices even of talcum powder for babies' bottoms, there can be no rational price system. My Polish colleague had, I believe, two reasons for saying this. One is the sheer number of prices which have to be determined: if talcum powder is on the list, the list must run to millions, and it is clearly not possible to administer millions of prices flexibly from some central office. The other is that if even talcum powder prices are seen to be the responsibility of government, they become subject to a political process. In a capitalist economy, as in a socialist one, price rises are unpopular, but the public is unclear about whom to blame. In a country where prices are 'official', they are seen to be the responsibility of the government and party, and so there are political obstacles which prevent necessary adjustments – as we have seen in Poland and as we now also see in the Soviet Union (see Morris Bornstein's paper).

Agricultural prices can be the subject of a discussion running to many pages. I will make only one point concerning them, and that is to stress that no one who comes from an EEC country should lecture anyone about rational prices for agricultural products! But seriously, it seems important to note that totally free agricultural prices exist nowhere, and there must be some reasons for this. I suggest two such reasons. One is the so-called 'cobweb': if supply exceeds demand prices fall, the next year's sowing (or number of pigs) is reduced, prices rise sharply, in the following year there is oversupply, prices fall sharply, and so on, with no tendency towards equilibrium. The second is linked with the first: farm or peasant incomes depend directly on these prices, and violent fluctuations are very painful. This accounts for state intervention, (as also does the need to attract rural voters at election time), but there have been instances of unwise price intervention, which can cause either a glut (for example, the West European butter mountain), or shortage when prices seem unattractive to the producers, as has happened in a number of third-world countries and may now be happening in China and causing shortages of rice and wheat. Soviet farm prices have been subjected to criticism, and their irrationality has been used to justify administrative intervention to compel farms to grow particular crops and to keep specified numbers of livestock. Evidently, farms should be free to respond to prices, to adapt their output to their particular circumstances.

Finally, a remark about earlier debates concerning the law of value and the function of prices in a socialist or transitional economy. There were some wide-ranging discussions on the 1920s, in which not only Bukharin but also Trotsky spoke quite eloquently about the need for markets, prices that reflect supply and demand, a stable monetary unit. Trotsky spoke of this in 1922 and 1923, and also (in exile) in 1932 and 1936 (in criticising Stalinist centralised planning). This does not mean that either Trotsky or Bukharin believed in 'market socialism'. They did not regard NEP as already socialist, and both believed (as did virtually all Marxists of their generation) in a future socialism in which plan would replace the market. But in 'the transitional epoch' markets were seen as necessary, and market-based prices, too. There is now much interest in the USSR in the economics and the economists of the NEP period.

Apart from political men such as Trotsky, Preobrazhensky, Bukharin, there were brilliant professional economists: for example Kondratiev, Yurovsky, Bazarov, Falkner, Chayanov, whose lives ended tragically, and whose return to Soviet history and intellectual life is a positive and welcome event.

References

Richardson, G. B. (1960) *Information and Investment* (Oxford University Press).

Yurovsky, L. (1928) *Denezhnaya politika sovetskoi vlasti* (*The Monetary Policy of the Soviet Regime*) (Moscow: State Publishing House).

Comment

Karel Kouba
INSTITUTE FOR FORECASTING, CZECHOSLOVAK
ACADEMY OF SCIENCES, PRAGUE, CZECHOSLOVAKIA

First of all allow me to make a brief personal statement: I am led to do this from a feeling of moral and professional responsibility. For me personally, this is one of the first conferences I am attending after almost twenty years. Two decades have elapsed in which I have been able to follow the development of opinions concerning the subject-matter of our conference only from afar and outside academic life. I would therefore like to make use of the occasion and to thank a number of colleagues and friends who are present at this conference. They have helped not only me, but a number of Czechoslovak economists, to overcome the consequences of long-term isolation from the international economic community. My sincere thanks also belong to other economists who are not among the participants.

I have been able to follow the course of economic reforms and theoretical work only partially and in a haphazard manner. Nevertheless, it seems to me that a certain consensus now seems to predominate. Existing economic reforms in the eastern European countries have not been successful. The present reforms also are not fulfilling the hopes and aspirations invested in them. They have not stopped the development of crisis in eastern European economies. Not only that. Attempts at a transition to a reformed economy have not precluded deteriorating economic performance and a worsening of the economic situation.

1 ECONOMIC REFORM: SUPPLY AND DEMAND PRICING

So far economic reforms have not been successful in changing patterns of behaviour of economic agents and improving macroeconomic performance. This can be achieved only by a substantial change in economic policies and the economic system. From this point of view I have read with great interest the comments written by Béla Czikós-Nagy, especially in his paper on monerisation and price liberalisation (Chapter 7 in this volume). I agree with a number of the author's comments in this part of his paper.

In my opinion the implementation of reforms in a number of countries has not yet overcome an *instrumental approach to prices*, that is, concept according to which prices should serve the intentions of economic policy or even serve as instruments for fulfilling the traditional plan (cf. Brus, 1988). Perhaps we might, in a simplified manner, say that the core of efficient economic reforms is a replacement of traditional planning with a system of free prices of both goods and the factors of production. Hence this would be a replacement of traditional planning with a price system with adequate functions. A full-fledged price system carries out not only an *information* function, but at the same time a *motivation* function and a *distribution* function. Our type economies do not have rational price systems. But not only that. In my opinion in some countries there still predominates a confused approach to solving the problem of rationalising prices. The question is how to replace the coordination function of the traditional play by supply and demand pricing.

It seems evident that this cannot be achieved by traditional price reforms: here I have in mind an administrative revision of wholesale prices at one stroke. Especially attempts at reform in Czechoslovakia have repeatedly demonstrated this unsuccessful stereotype. During the last 30 years there have been seven wholesale price reforms carried out. Three were considered to be necessary initial steps towards economic reform. This was the case in 1958, 1967 and again in 1989. But the outcome of these reforms of wholesale prices have been and are highly unsatisfactory. They do not represent a feasible road to rational prices. They maintain and strengthen the principle of cost-plus pricing and the administrative method of creating prices. The principle of initial equitable profitability brings advantages to obsolete production and does not promote innovations.

Negative experience with this type of price reform has been fully confirmed by the results of Professor Bornstein's detailed analyses of Soviet reforms of wholesale prices (especially Bornstein, 1962, 1985 and 1987).

The conclusions of these careful and detailed analyses of individual reforms (1961–2, 1982) are always the same: 'The new industrial producer prices are still primarily from the cost or supply side. They will not usually also reflect demand and scarcity' (Bornstein, 1985). 'But industrial producer prices are still set primarily from the cost or supply side and do not usually also reflect demand and scarcity . . . State retail prices for goods and services are often below market clearing levels, and frequently also below cost' (Bornstein, 1987). We can find similar conclusions in Bornstein's Chapter 6 in this volume.

Czechoslovak reforms of wholesale prices were and continue to be of the same type, and the same conclusions are valid for them. Moreover, they do not open the road to connecting domestic prices and prices which exist on world markets through the exchange rate.

The existence of this obsolete stereotype of price reform at the same time makes it much more difficult to implement strict financial discipline. It provides opportunities to pay enterprises economically unfounded costs, which are not under the control of a competitive market. The non-existence of a competitive market at the same time makes it possible for prices to change, depending on the money supply, and not under the influence of effective market forces.

The solution is in a transition to free pricing. I am aware of the fact that to speak of free or contract supply and demand prices does not sound very realistic in the existing situation. This might even be interpreted as a loss of feeling for a pragmatic and realistic approach, given the existing states of disequilibrium. But in my opinion to tolerate ineffective and inflationary macroeconomic policies and the deficit financing of increasing redistribution processes in order to maintain inefficient production at the cost of positively functioning enterprises does not represent a healthy realism. Quite the contrary, tolerating such extensive counter-productive government policies and economic activities seems to be the crucial problem of the further development of the reform.

A transition to free prices is very difficult. It assumes among other things a reassessment and revision of giving priority to growth policy in favour of equilibrium. An expansive investment policy is a special barrier to a transition to equilibrium prices. Among other barriers is the non-existence of an effective anti-monopoly policy.

From the point of view of economic policies various options for the transition to free pricing are possible. Feasible options are predetermined especially by the frequency and degree of disequilibrium situations. In the transition to free prices it is possible to use a system of mixed prices, this is, for instance fixed, contractual and free prices.

The transition to equilibrium prices will unavoidably lead to price increases with unpleasant social consequences especially for lower income groups. Here certain compensations are called for. In my opinion the crucial problem of a transition to equilibrium prices is the ability to maintain the permanency of such price changes. The basic prerequisite here is the extension of supply on the basis of the improved motivation of producers. Without this precondition the economy will face the threat of a gradual loss of positive results of increased prices and the subsequent increase in inflation.

The problem of prices is the most crucial problem of the existence and future of economic reforms. A postponement in solving price problems is very costly and means that we tolerate an increase in deficit financing, even greater deterioration in equilibrium on the investment market, for intermediate products and the consumer goods market. A postponement in solving the price mechanism also poses another threat: a loss of general orientation towards a market-orientated reform. An orientation towards an ineffective type of reform will then prevail, which has so far been the predominant case in previous reform cycles.

A reform orientation to mere decentralisation cannot replace the effects of a competitive market and effective macroeconomic policies.

We can conclude that in the economic reforms which have so far taken place we have seen two types of system attempts. So far the instrumental approach to the market has predominated. This approach is typical for an indirectly centrally-planned economic system, or to put more generally in János Kornai's term for an 'indirectly bureaucratically controlled' economy. On the other hand the development of truly market orientated types of reform processes are still only in the initial stages of seeking effective and efficient system changes.

2   THE CASE OF REFORM CYCLES IN THE CZECHOSLOVAK ECONOMY

Our experience indicates that the reform process and its various types of systemic attempts did not take place in the form of direct smooth progressive development. This fact can be clearly demonstrated in the example of the reform waves in Czechoslovakia.

In the reform cycles of the Czechoslovak economy we have seen – to put it as simply as possible – two types of reform process in various modifications.

The first type predominates. This is an indirect centrally-planned

economic system based on the partial decentralisation of organisation, information and decision making.

In various modifications and to various extents it has accompanied
all attempts at reform undertaken so far. It was most marked in the
project of systemic changes in 1959, in the form of Libermann's well
known long-term (that is, five years) 'normatives' of material stimulation. In its pure form, this is a principle which cannot be implemented. It is thus surprising that this idea has survived its time for so
long. It has reappeared in official projects in Czechoslovakia at the
beginning of the 1980s and again in the present project of reform.

The practical implementation of indirect forms of central planning
is based especially on subjecting the price mechanism to the system of
traditional planning. This is an instrumental approach to prices. The
central agency controls prices in an administrative manner and ma-
nipulates them as an instrument of the plan.

From a theoretical point of view this type is based on the simulation of a market for the factors of production, and its functioning is
adequately described by the theory of bargaining in hierarchical
organisations.

The implementation of this type of economic reform does not run
into major political constraints. But it is an ineffective and non-stable
economic system, which usually returns – by recentralisation – to its
initial point of departure, a traditional system.

This fact became evident in Czechoslovakia already at the beginning of the 1960s. It became the point of departure of our work on an
alternative type of systemic change. Thus in Czechoslovakia there
gradually developed at the beginning of the 1960s, in the form of
consecutive steps, the project of a market-orientated reform. The
autonomy and responsibility of enterprises were based on an application of the system of mixed prices. In 1966 three types of prices
were implemented: fixed, limit and free prices; it was assumed that
the share of free prices would increase. A part of the reform project
was an orientation towards the linking of traditionally isolated price
spheres, that is, the linking of wholesale and retail prices. The project
also assumed a number of steps to link domestic prices with prices on
world markets through the US dollar.

Strong correlation and/or interaction between economic and socio-
political factors were typical characteristics of the project. This
project and the initial changes which were actually implemented were
directed towards the renewal of economic and political pluralism in
the spirit of our country's traditions. I am to this day convinced that

after a series of various corrections had been introduced, it could have served as the point of departure for a more rational economic system. In my opinion it could have been the promising embryo for the renewal of a civic society and development of democracy in our country.

But I am not concerned with sentimentality or non-critical reminiscences. I would like to call attention especially to less known facts, which are important from the present point of view.

First of all in economic literature on this subject throughout the world the opinion has predominated that the Czechoslovak economic reform ended in August 1968. This is not true. The preparation of documents for the government continued, in spite of changed conditions, in 1969. The projects of the time saw a certain reduction in the political programme for change. But the programme of economic reform continued to be developed in a substantial manner. On the basis of little-known documents and literary sources we can claim that as a matter of fact the Rubicon of previous reform attempts was for the first time crossed. This was written into the relevant documents and on a preliminary basis the project for the gradual creation of a market of the factors of production, that is, a labour market, a capital market and money market was approved. Anti-monopoly measures were included, and the creation of a competitive environment in the economy was assumed, together with the identification of the sources of inflationary pressures and the outlines of an anti-inflationary policy (cf. Kouba, 1968).

The decision of the authorities entirely to abandon the project for economic reform and to assess it in an entirely negative manner was made only in the period 1969–70. I have always considered this decision to be one of the greatest errors, not only in the economic sphere. It deprived us of the opportunity to gain new experiences from the parallel development of market-orientated reforms in Hungary and Czechoslovakia.

Secondly, I would to call attention to the generally relatively positive macroeconomic performance of the Czechoslovak economy at the end of the 1960s. Here we ought to be very careful, I share the circumspect approach to the assessment of a similar phenomenon, the so-called Golden Age in the development of the Hungarian economy in the period 1968–72. Nevertheless, this fact forces us to ask why contemporary economic reforms are not accompanied by improvements in macroeconomic performance (cf. Dyba and Kouba, 1988).

Under given conditions I do not consider the contemporary reform programme in Czechoslovakia in the 1980s to be an effective type of systemic change. It does not avoid a repetition of the errors of the preceding reforms and it continues in the preceding strong points of domestic reforms in an inconsistent manner; it is also to a great extent oblivious of contemporary economic theory concerning the prerequisites of effective systemic change. It is a hybrid between an indirectly centrally-planned economy and partial market processes. Hence the credibility of the reform programme and economic policies is very low.

The effectively pro-market orientation of the approved blueprint for reform is weak. Its implementation so far is fully in the hands of branch ministries and the central planning agency. Even the stronger aspects of the existing programme of monetisation of the economy tend to degenerate in their hands. Thus we are again faced with the transition to a dominantly ineffective and unstable system of indirect central planning. It is an instrumental concept of market as a tool of the traditional plan. Strong political constraints – stronger than in Hungary, Poland and the Soviet Union – represent a barrier for developing the reform programme in a more promising direction. Institutional support for the development of a competitive market is weak. Moreover, the initial steps of the programme repeat again the errors of the preceding reforms. An administrative reform of wholesale prices on a cost-plus pricing principle has been implemented, with all known negative effect. Also the first stage of restructuralisation of enterprises has been carried out. The outcome is again greater organisational concentration and the further strengthening of the monopoly structure of the market.

The issue of the diversification of property rights has mostly been avoided and remains a political and ideological taboo.

Adequate macroeconomic policies continue to be a critical and unsolved problem. An assumed tight monetary policy is not consistent with fiscal policy, which assumes a high degree of taxing enterprise profits, even under conditions of so-called self-financing. A special source of worry is the repeated mistake of the existing growth policy with its traditional priority to growth and investment drives. The central agency has not yet adopted equilibrium growth as a primary priority. It is even losing control over investments and states of disequilibrium on the consumer goods market have increased.

Thus in the Czechoslovak economy we are again experiencing a dilemma. So far inertia is prevailing. While the Czechoslovak economy is experiencing a number of crisis features similar to those of other economies of this type it also has a number of relatively positive features for bringing about a decisive turning point. The solution depends on the freeing of political constraints. But for the economist this also requires, last but not least, a critical re-examination of reform ideas and of the reform paradigm itself.

References

Bornstein, M. (1962) 'The Soviet Price System', *American Economic Review*, 52 (March).
Bornstein, M. (1985) 'The Industrial Price Revision', in Fink, G. (ed.), *Socialist Economy and Economic Policy*, Essays in Honour of F. Levcik (Vienna, New York: Springer Verlag).
Bornstein, M. (1987) 'Soviet Price Policies', *Soviet Economy*, 3(2) (April--June) pp. 96–134.
Brus, W. (1988) 'The East European Reforms: Lessons from Experience', Conference on Alternative Models of Socialist Economic Systems, Györ.
Dyba, K. and Kouba, K. (1988) 'Czechoslovak Attempts at Systemic Changes: 1958, 1968, 1988; Plan and/or Market' (Vienna)
Kouba, K. (ed.) (1968) *Náčrt základni koncepce rozvíjení ekonomické reformy* (Project of the Basic Concept of the Development of the Economic Reform) (EÚ ČSAV, Praha: Národohospodářská komise hospodářské rady).

Part IV

The Role of Commercial and National Banking in a Reformed Socialist Economy

8 The Role of Commercial and Central Banking: Yugoslavia

Ante Čičin-Šain *

INSTITUTE OF ECONOMICS, ZAGREB, YUGOSLAVIA

1 INTRODUCTION

In view of numerous programmes and attempts to reform the socialist economies, I feel compelled to start by stating my own understanding of the term 'reformed socialist economy' (RSE). (This term was chosen by the organisers of the Conference; I am accepting it as given.) In my interpretation of a RSE I will refer primarily to the recent developments in Yugoslavia, which are not only well-known to me but, in my opinion, quite indicative of possible further developments in other socialist countries.

My understanding of the reform proposals, recently elaborated and generally accepted in Yugoslavia,[1] is that the reformed socialist economy is to be regarded as a particular form of the mixed economy system. Such a system – towards which some other socialist countries, as well as Yugoslavia, seem to be moving – could be described as an open socialist market economy.

While the terms 'open' and 'market economy' are self-explanatory, the 'socialist' component of the envisaged mixed economy deserves some immediate clarification. I see the socialist features of the Yugoslav-type mixed economy to be characterised by:

1. The dominant position of the socially-owned production funds within the overall stock of productive capital
2. The outstanding position of the worker, whose role is conceived so that he should become a competent producer, an entrepreneur and a qualified decision maker in the major fields of social and political life
3. The explicit adherence to a set of social policy preferences,

159

defined on the basis of general socialist principles (this refers, in particular, to such issues as an implicit 'guarantee' of employment, health, education, culture, general solidarity, environment protection, etc.).

The system of a socialist market economy, like any other market economy, can be expected to function efficiently only if it is based on full decentralisation of basic economic decision making. This implies the explicit recognition of the full autonomy for the very numerous and quite heterogeneous independent economic units, not only for their 'current' economic transactions, but for their saving and investment decisions as well. The only known integrating and coordinating mechanism suitable for meeting the requirements of such an economic system is the market mechanism.

Evidently, the market mechanism cannot be expected to fulfil its functions if it is limited to domestic markets for goods and services only; as an indispensable precondition for the smooth and successful participation of independent economic agents in international exchanges, it also has to embrace the markets for factors of production and an appropriate foreign exchange market. It is clear that the realisation of these principles must have certain repercussions on the practical shaping of the specific socialist components of a reformed socialist economy mentioned above. Although a detailed discussion of these issues would lead to certain important conclusions, this question will not be further elaborated in the present paper.

The intention to adopt the appropriate market arrangements for factors of production is being stated in Yugoslavia under the term 'integrated market economy', although it might better be labelled a 'fully-fledged market economy'. The explicit recognition of the need to introduce markets for factors of production is the most outstanding feature of the present attempts at reform in Yugoslavia. In this context, it is to be added that there is general agreement on the need to have a well-functioning foreign exchange market; in fact, this market was successfully re-established in May 1988.

The intention to develop a fully-fledged socialist market economy necessarily implied a drastic change in the traditionally conceived role of the socialist government in current economic management and in 'long and medium term' planning.

Essentially, a considerable part of government activities has to be substituted by the autonomy of independent economic units. This is to be accompanied and supported by the development of an independent financial system and the appropriate macroeconomic policies. Within that framework, the planning mechanism has to be transformed into a mechanism for indicative planning and an auxiliary (subordinate) tool of macroeconomic policy. In fact, a considerable part of these changes has been taking place in Yugoslavia for quite some time, although it was not properly reflected in existing institutional arrangements.

It is within this context that the role of commercial and central banking in RSEs has to be seen. Since the financial institutions usually emerge as a reflection of the underlying needs of basic economic agents, and are supposed to be autonomous units similar to those in capitalist market economies, I can see no compelling reason for any fundamental dilemma concerning the main functions of the financial system within a full-size socialist market economy.

2 ROLE OF THE FINANCIAL SECTOR

The role of the financial sector in the overall process of economic development can be viewed as a two-way process, that is, both as a demand-following and a supply-leading process. Consequently, the main functions of commercial banks and other financial intermediaries on the one side, and those of the central banking system on the other, should be either similar or identical to the functions performed by the corresponding financial institutions in developed capitalist market economies.

This implies that the primary function of commercial banks and other financial intermediaries should be to provide for the efficient collection and mobilisation of financial surpluses, generated by those economic agents capable of financial saving, and their expedient transfer to other economic units, primarily enterprises, which are willing and capable of investing the available funds profitably. A developed capitalist environment is likely to offer a considerably wider variety of instruments for financial placements; their commercial banks can therefore be expected to remain much more sophisticated than their future counterparts in socialist countries. But in respect of the basic function of intermediation between the units with financial surpluses and the units with financial deficits, there can be no fundamental difference in the role of commercial banks in socialist market economies and their role in 'purely' capitalist economies. On the other hand, the main functions of the central bank or a central banking system in both groups of countries is the regulation of money supply, the maintenance of external liquidity and the management of foreign exchange reserves. As in the case of commercial banks, I can see no reason why there should be any decisive difference in the main functions performed by the central banks in full-size socialist market economies compared to contemporary developed capitalist market economies.

While there are no substantive dilemmas concerning the objective and the ultimate shape of financial institutions in fully developed socialist market economies, it is quite evident that there are many very complex and intricate problems related to the possibilities of implementing the principles on which an appropriate financial system has to be based. As the financial system cannot but be a reflection of the underlying basic arrangements in the real sector of the respective economy, it follows that the necessary changes in the financial sphere cannot be achieved without simultaneous changes in the 'real' economic sectors. The envisaged development of the financial sector in any socialist economy must therefore be viewed as a process parallel to changes in the non-financial sectors of the economy. Changes in the financial system do not represent ends in themselves but only a means of facilitating and promoting changes in the real sector. Thus, the transition from the existing systems of administrative and/or semi-governmentally run economies to the envisaged system of a socialist market economy with the appropriately developed financial system, is a process that will be confronted with formidable difficulties.

A considerable part of the evident deficiencies of present financial 'systems' in socialist countries, particularly in those which have made certain attempts to move away from the classical system of a centrally-planned (administrative) economy, has arisen as a result of an extended use and misuse of financial institutions for purposes for which the banking systems are not suited, and/or from various ill-conceived and therefore failed attempts to 'reform' the banking and other financial institutions. The outstanding examples of the former group of difficulties are the misuse of the banking system for fiscal or semi-fiscal purposes and soft-term financing of various 'priority projects' with the subsequent extention of 'rehabilitation loans' in order to salvage failed investments.

By failed 'reform' attempts in the second group I am referring to numerous institutional reforms mainly limited to purely organisational aspects of banking. Yugoslavia has an exceptionally rich experience with such reforms; a comprehensive analytical interpretation of the changing role of Yugoslav banks as financial intermediaries in different bank reforms is given by Mramor (1984).

It might be said that the evident difficulties and/or the inability of socialist countries to reform their financial systems is determined primarily by the unwillingness, reluctance and fear of accepting the appropriate changes in the real sectors of their economies. This unwillingness and fear are also reflected on the 'theoretical' and ideological level; they can be discerned from the very confused and distorted notions of the role of money and finance in socialism, and from the numerous inconsistencies in the attempted and failed reform projects.

Problems relating to possible transition processes from the inherited positions towards the ultimately envisaged solutions are very complex, and certainly quite different from country to country. In an attempt to contribute to the discussion of these issues, I will limit myself primarily to some of the most important problems of developing an appropriate system of commercial banks, which is currently seen in Yugoslavia as the crucial ingredient of an efficiently functioning socialist market economy.

2.1   The Role of Commercial Banks and Other Financial Intermediaries

The changing role of commercial banks and other financial intermediaries within the Yugoslav financial system has to be viewed together with the envisaged changes in the financial structure of the Yugoslav enterprise sector. The present financial structure of socially-owned enterprises is distorted in several respects. This can be attributed both to the rather vague notion of 'social ownership' and to the very intimate relationship between the socially-owned enterprises on the one side, and the banking system as a semi-governmental agency on the other. Without going into detailed analysis of the financing problems faced by the socially-owned enterprises in Yugoslavia, it must be pointed out that it was found necessary to re-examine the meaning of social ownership and to strengthen the financial base of the enterprise sector in such a way as to make the enterprises genuinely autonomous economic units, capable of acting under changing and competitive market conditions.

To this end it was found necessary to form a new base for the enterprises' own capital funds. This process is to be further strengthened by the current opening up towards other ownership forms.

Apart from the stock of socially-owned means of production, which are expected to be more efficiently used and reproduced on a larger scale in the future, additional resources and productive capacities are now expected to be included in the organised economic framework in Yugoslavia, belonging to and/or being managed by the private, cooperative and the mixed-enterprise sectors. This is becoming possible because of the recently adopted constitutional changes, which have provided for the recognition of different ownership forms, and for the dismantling of a major part of previously existing limitations on productive employment of hired labour and privately-owned resources.

The acceptance of different forms of ownership over the means of production also implies the acceptance of different enterprise and management forms for various types of companies. In order to meet the needs for greater flexibility of enterprise and financial sectors a whole range of different company forms has been devised.

The legal framework for the setting-up of new companies has been created after the adoption of the new Company Law. This Law represents a fundamental departure from the postulates on which the whole system of 'Associated Labour' was founded: all companies in the business sector of the economy, as well as commercial banks and other financial intermediaries to be founded under the new Company Law and the new Banking Law, have to be constituted as legal entities with their own property and, in particular, with an *equity capital which has to be provided, on a permanent basis, by the respective founders of the company*.

The decision to introduce the notion of equity capital and the corresponding equity financing is motivated by the intention of enabling the enterprises to bear the risks associated with the functioning of the market mechanism. This represents a fundamental departure from the long-lasting and unsuccessful attempts to strengthen 'self-financing' as the main vehicle to increase performance incentives and the 'independence' of socially-owned enterprises. A similar insistence still seems strongly present in several socialist countries. A comprehensive analysis of conditions necessary to implement such 'self-financing' principles has shown that they are incompatible with normal, non-inflationary, financial arrangements, which are based on the autonomous formation of genuine financial surpluses. Among the Yugoslav economists this point was particularly elaborated by I. Ribnikar (1981, 1984, 1985, 1986 and 1988.)

The introduction of equity capital, that is own risk-bearing capital, is also expected to play a decisive role in reducing the present excessively high dependence of Yugoslav firms on short-term credit financing. Consequently, all major decisions concerning current management, development and viability of each particular enterprise and/or commercial bank will have to be taken in accordance with their actual performance, as reflected in their financial results and synthetically shown in the development of their respective equity funds.

An additional impetus to changes in the functioning of commercial banks and other financial intermediaries comes from pressures to reform the financial structure of the enterprise sector. Profound changes in commercial banks and other financial intermediaries are needed primarily in order to organise and manage the banks as independent capital companies. This implies that their decision making procedures will primarily be determined by the logic of sound and safe capital placements. This logic is fundamentally different from the principle according to which banks act as a 'service to the associated labour', the principle which implied a widespread neglect of sound financial practices, and resulted in great misallocation of real resources, and the subsequent cumulation of very large losses, both in the banking and in the enterprise sectors.

Due to inherent systemic inconsistencies, the Yugoslav banking system was driven into a position of operating under a growing discrepancy between the actual costs it had to pay for the financial funds obtained, and the returns received on the placements of these funds. Since the largest number of basic decisions concerning the formation of financial savings in Yugoslavia has been made – since the mid-1960s – on an individual, decentralised basis, Yugoslav banks have been compelled to accept and mobilise an increasing portion of their funds by offering the depositors conditions which were attractive enough to draw these funds into the banking system. Evidently, this was being done without paying the appropriate attention to problems relating to the profitable placement of such funds.

In other words, Yugoslav banks were compelled – in fact, they were systematically passive and negligent – to operate under two mutually exclusive conditions: the funds obtained were increasingly paid the going market rates, whereas credits were granted in accordance with the 'needs' and paying capacities of the debtors. (A similar development is likely to be repeated in other socialist countries.)

The banks' deteriorating position was clearly reflected in the rapidly rising share of deposits denominated in foreign exchange. Since the actual cost of these funds was increasingly determined by the changes in the dinar exchange rate, commercial banks should have started long ago to charge the appropriate rates on loans granted, that is to act as independent financial intermediaries. This would have been in the interest of both groups of their business partners, the depositors and the credit users alike. It would have implied that the enterprise sector, as the dominant user of bank credits, had to pay the full cost for the use of external financial funds. Consequently, their decisions concerning the use of such funds and their general behaviour would have been substantially different.

This, however, did not occur, both for economic and for political reasons. The enterprise sector was steadily subject to some form of government interference. As a (tacit) compensation for that interference the government, supported by the Party, always stood ready to 'help' the enterprise sector by granting it access to cheap credit. The burden of these practices had to be carried by the banking system, for as long as such practices could be maintained.

Instead of developing its banking system in the direction of efficient intermediation between the increasingly autonomous savers and the ultimate borrowers, Yugoslavia tried to solve the problem by introducing one more of its original 'inventions', that is by creating a banking system that functions as a 'financial service to the associated labour'. Under this 'system' the primary scope of banks was to provide for an abundant and cheap credit supply to the socially-owned enterprise sector, without paying due attention to the actual structure and costs of bank deposits. This kind of arrangement was in a way a logical consequence of the proposition that banks had to be 'dominated by the associated labour', that is by their biggest and most heavily protected debtors. This provision, combined with other features of the 'associated labour economy', as well as the reversal of the country's balance of payments position after the second oil crisis, led ultimately to the outbreak of the deepest economic crisis since the Second World War, and a virtual collapse of the country's banking system.

The consequences of the prolonged economic mismanagement have ultimately become visible and generally known and this understanding played a decisive role in opening new alternatives for a comprehensive reform of the entire economic system. In the process, it was finally realised that the whole financial sphere has to get the role it deserves in a decentralised economic system. As far as commercial banks and other financial institutions are concerned, this implies that they have to be upgraded to the role of *independent* financial intermediaries, who have the right and the possibilities to *compete* for the available financial funds, and to place such funds with the borrowers who are able to offer the best security and the highest return on the funds received.

The main features of the imminent reform of the Yugoslav banking system, which will be implemented gradually, and which have to be viewed as the key factor of the whole reform concept, may be summarised in the following three points.

1. *An Entirely New Structure and New Functions of Bank Owners*
   Instead of the present bank 'founders', namely, the organisations of associated labour, the future owners of Yugoslav commercial banks will be shareholders, who may belong to any sector of the economy. The shares, representing the corresponding contribution towards bank equity, will be freely transferable among the old and the new shareholders. Certain limits, aimed at preventing the dominant position of any particular shareholder, are envisaged and defined by the Law.

   Banks will be liable only up to the value of their declared equity capital, including accumulated reserves. This will have some very far-reaching consequences with respect to the former system, in which the bank's founders were formally liable for the bank's obligations even with their own business funds. In fact, this regulation amounted to a provision that 'the society as a whole', in fact the government, was ultimately responsible for banks' liabilities. Consequently, neither the banks' external creditors, and bank managers, nor the borrowing enterprises were under pressure to be much concerned with the safety of banks' credit placements.

   The fundamentally new regulation of banks' liabilities is expected to result in the much more efficient management of banks, and a greatly increased responsibility for bank placements. This also would act as an efficient brake against any unsustainable expansion of bank credit, since it will have to be accompanied by the appropriate rise of the risk-bearing equity capital.

2. *The Structure of Assets and Liabilities and the Problem of Banks' Intermediation Costs*

Up till now, due to the dominant role of the banks' biggest client-debtors, appropriate attention was not paid either to the composition of banks' liabilities or to the quality of their assets, that is their credit claims. In such circumstances banks were willing both to accept quite expensive sources of funds – usually denominated in foreign exchange – and to apply rather soft policies with respect to the conditions of fund placements. The consequences were a very low degree of bank profitability and the cumulation of very large losses within the banking system, with the concomitant very high and increasingly rising intermediation costs.

The problems of banks' intermediation costs and their profitability have recently been analysed by a number of Yugoslav and foreign economists. E. Ermenc (1988) has devised a model aiming to determine banks' intermediation costs under conditions of strong external intervention ('financial repression') into banks activity, while M. Kos (1989) tried to estimate these costs for Yugoslav commercial banks, taken as a whole. His calculations indicate that the intermediation costs, defined as a mark-up on those loans which are not subject to preferential regulation, amounted to 28 and 40.5 per cent for 1987 and 1988 respectively. (These costs are expressed in respect to the annual average sum of banks' assets.)

According to that calculation, the biggest components of these costs in 1988 were related to: past business practices and non-performing loans (14.4 per cent); costs related to the imposed monetary regulation, that is, obligatory reserve requirements, etc. (9.2 per cent); costs related to credits extended at preferential interest rates (6.2 per cent); and costs related to foreign exchange losses (3.9 per cent). On the other hand, banks operating costs and their profits were estimated at 3.7 and 2.4 per cent respectively.

Although the relevance of the proposed model and the reliability of indicated intermediation costs may, perhaps, be questioned, as (implicitly) done by N. Mates (1987 and 1988),[2] the enumerated cost components and their relative shares can be regarded as highly indicative for the nature of problems faced by the Yugoslav banks. The high 'intermediation costs' are certainly not due to the inefficiencies of the banking system proper, but to some serious deficiencies of the entire economic system that result in very large misallocations and wastage of real resources.

Formally, these costs are mainly due to various components of past practices and to costs implied by the present regulations, which are again related to the practices that lead to large accumulation of losses within the banking system. The high intermediation costs of Yugoslav banks thus have to be interpreted as a particular form of tax, which has to be charged to all borrowers because of the prolonged neglect of sound financial practices. This also explains why banks started to charge 'exorbitant' positive real interest rates, occasionally amounting up to 50 or 60 per cent per annum when they were asked and allowed to shift to positive real interest rates.

Since the economic burden of such high positive real interest rates is pratically unbearable, these rates have, quite understandably, become the subject of very strong criticisms. Some of the critics were very quick to conclude that the positive real interest rates are not compatible with the 'present state' of the Yugoslav economy. However, it can be shown that there is no valid alternative to positive real interest rates within the contemporary decentralised economic systems. While there may be good reasons to look more closely into the actual banking practices in Yugoslavia, it must be understood that the behaviour of banks primarily is determined by the wider economic environment in which banks have been operating for such a long time.

In order to deal with the problem of unsustainable intermediation costs, some considerable changes in banks' assets and liabilities will have to be made. A part of the solution to this problem will most probably be the explicit recognition of the public debt, not only at the federal, but possibly at the republican and the communal levels as well.

3. *Changes in the Role of Bank Managers; Banks' Regional Presence; the Role of Other Financial Intermediaries and Qualified Supervision of Financial Activities*

In line with the envisaged changes, a reformed system of commercial banking also requires the training and selection of highly qualified and independent bank managers for different levels of banking activities.

Placed in a substantially different environment, the reformed commercial banks and other financial intermediaries will be expected to compete for the available financial funds throughout the country. On the credit side of their business, banks will be expected to compete against each other as well. This is much more likely to happen in the future, because the extension of new credits should result in better financial results for banks, their shareholders and managers.

Apart from commercial banks, that presently are the only group of financial intermediaries in Yugoslavia, other financial organisations – such as insurance companies, post-office savings banks and some similar institutions – also will have to be put in a position to act as full-size financial intermediaries. These institutions dispose of substantial financial funds, but up till now they were compelled to place them all with the commercial banks. Within a reformed financial system, there is both a need and a place for a much wider variety of financial instruments and financial intermediaries. It is within this context that the new, more active role of other financial organisations is to be seen. Commercial banks and other financial organisations also should be brought into a position to compete for particular groups of customers with different services offered.

A well developed and diversified financial system also needs to be supported by an appropriate prudential regulation and supervision. Since banks are the creators of money, the primary allocators of credit, the principal custodians of financial assets, and the managers of the payments system, their activities have to be carefully studied and supervised. Supervision of banks and other financial intermediaries, either by the central bank or by another specialised public agency, should be of a substantially different nature than it was up till now. Instead of the emphasis on issues relating to formal compliance with existing regulations, the main objective of a prudential financial supervision should be the analysis of the economic viability and soundness of all the relevant parts of an increasingly complex and highly interdependent financial system.

On the whole, we can conclude that the outcome of the ongoing reform of the commercial banking system in Yugoslavia primarily will depend on the ability and the willingness of all relevant actors to carry out the necessary changes in the real sector of the economy. The common denominator of these changes should be a general increase in the (physical) efficiency of all production and service activities.

Essentially the same holds true with respect to attempts to increase the efficiency of the Yugoslav central banking system. The main problem faced by this system in Yugoslavia is its excessive and permanently increasing reliance on inflationary financing. Monetary authorities will not be able to regain control over the monetary base and banks' credit activities for as long as there are forces in the economy that are able to maintain the positions allowing them to spend more than they produce. Once we recognise this fact, it becomes clear that the study of central banking in RSEs is an even more complex problem that, unfortunately, far exceeds the space available for this paper. It would, therefore, be very interesting and highly desirable to examine more closely the fate and possible developments of central banking in other socialist countries in light of the unfortunate Yugoslav monetary experience. The title of such a paper could very well read: 'Will the Yugoslav Mistakes be Repeated?'.

Notes

* I would like to acknowledge many helpful comments and linguistic corrections made by Dubravko Mihaljek, from the Ekonomski institut Zagreb and the Department of Economics, University of Pittsburgh. Any remaining shortcomings are my own.

1. The constitutional preconditions for the launching of the new reform were created by a set of Amendments to the Constitution of SFR Yugoslavia. The work on these amendments lasted for almost two years; they were finally adopted by the Parliament on 26 November 1988.

    The document containing a general outline of the present reform, entitled 'Osnove reforme privrednog sistema' (The Principles of the Economic System Reform) was elaborated by a special commission appointed by the Yugoslav Federal Government; it was adopted as the official Government document on 31 October 1988.

    A set of new systemic laws, amounting perhaps to some 40 new laws, is being presently prepared along the lines of the elaborated reform proposals. Some of the most important laws were passed in late December 1988, and several more are expected to follow during the first half of 1989.

2. In spite of the above mentioned elements of financial repression, N. Mates is drawing attention to the fact that the Yugoslav commercial banks performed exceptionally well during the last two years. Their successful performance was primarily determined by very low interest rates they were paying for sight and other short-term deposits and by certain provisions of the Yugoslav accounting system which provided for the split of interest rates into a 'revalorisation interest rate' and 'real interest rate'. Due to these features the banks were able not only to increase their profits, but also to write off an important part of their dubious claims.

172 *Commercial and National Banking*

References

Čičin-Šain, Ante *et al.* (eds) (1984) 'Poslovno bankarstvo SR Hrvatske', (Analysis of Commercial Banking in Croatia), published in *Prilog analizi tekućih privrednih kretanja i ekonomske politke u SR Hrvatskoj*, Ekonomski institut Zagreb, Zagreb.

Čirović, Milutin (1985) 'Inflacija i poslovne banke' (Inflation and Commercial Banks), *Jugoslavensko bankarstvo*, Beograd, 5.

Dimitrijević, Dimitrije (1981) *Monetarna analiza* (The Monetary Analysis), Centar za informativno izdavaćku delatnost, Niš.

Ermenc, Ernest (1988) 'Skupoća jeftinog novca' (The Expensiveness of Cheap Money), published in *Neki problemi sprovodjenja novćane, kreditne i devizne politike*; Analitsko Raziskovalni Center – Narodna banka Slovenije, Ljubljana.

Gaspari, Mitja (1988) 'Neki otvoreni problemi finansijskog i centralnobankarskog sistema i monetarne politike u Jugoslaviji' (Some Unresolved Issues of Financial and Central Banking System and Monetary Policies in Yugoslavia), *Jugoslovensko bankarstvo*, Beograd, 9.

Gup, Benton E. (1976) *Financial Intermediaries* (Boston: Houghton Mifflin).

Kos, M. (1989) 'Nekaj o stroških finančnega posredovanja' (A Note on Financial Intermediation Costs), *Bančni vestnik*, Ljubljana, 5.

Mates, Neven (1986) 'Gubici u financijskom sistemu SFRJ' (The Losses in the Yugoslav Financial System), *Naše teme*, Zagreb, 5–6.

Mates, Neven (1987) 'Značajne promjene u poziciji bankarskog sistema u 1986 god' (Important Changes in the Performance of the Banking System in 1986), published in *Aktualni problemi privrednih kretanja i ekonomske politike Jugoslavije*, Ekonomski institut Zagreb, Zagreb.

Mates, Neven (1988) 'Neki efekti obračunskog sistema iz 1987 i 1988 u bankama i privredi' (Some Effects of the Accounting Systems of 1987 and 1988 for Banks and the Enterprise Sector), published in *Aktualni problemi privrednih kretanja i ekonomske politike Jugoslavije*, Ekonomski institut Zagreb, Zagreb.

Mramor, Dušan (1984) 'Analiza banaka kao posrednika kod prenosa novčane akumulacije u Jugoslaviji u razdoblju 1945–1982 godina' (The Analysis of Banks' Intermediation Function for the Period 1945–1982), unpublished M. A. dissertation, Beograd.

Ribnikar, Ivan (1981) 'Novčani, kreditni i bankarski sistem' (The Monetary, Credit and Banking System, *Jugoslavensko bankarstvo*, Beograd, 4–5.

Ribnikar, Ivan (1984) 'Finansiranje privrede i inflacija' (Financing the Enterprise Sector and Inflation), *Socijalizam*, Beograd, 9.

Ribnikar, Ivan (1985) 'Finansiranje privrede i samoupravljanje' (Financing the Enterprise Sector and Selfmanagement), *Ekonomist*, Zagreb, 1.

Ribnikar, Ivan (1985) 'Inflacija, banke i planiranje u bankama' (The Inflation, Banks and Banks' Planning Mechanism), *Jugoslovensko bankarstvo*, Beograd, 12.

Ribnikar, Ivan (1986) 'Finance in denar ter neučinkovitost gospodarenja pri nas' (Finance and Money and the Inefficiency of Our Economy), published in Zbornik ekonomske fakultete Boris Kidrič Ljubljana, *Samoupravljanje in ekonomska učinkovitost*, Ljubljana, October.

Ribnikar, Ivan (1988) 'Financijski aspekt "društvene svojine"' (The Financial Aspect of Social Property), *Jugoslovensko bankarstvo*, Beograd, 7–8.

Službeni list SFR Jugoslavije (The Official Gazette). Beograd:
– 'Zakon o poduzećima' (The Company Law) Nr 77/1988
– 'Zakon o bankama i drugim financijskim organizacijama' (The Law on Banks and Other Financial Organisations) Nr 10/1989.

9 The Hungarian Banking Reform

Márton Tardos
FINANCIAL RESEARCH LTD, BUDAPEST

1 INTRODUCTION

In 1987 a reform of the banking system was introduced in Hungary. This reform means that now in Hungary, as in any developed economy, the most important institution of monetary intermediation is the system of competing banks, controlled by a central bank (the Hungarian National Bank (HNB) in our case).

This change had three interesting and general implications. First, the banking reform and the acceptance of the decisive role of money was introduced in a country where 40 years ago, when a socialist economy was made to develop, the idea of the gradual decease of money was accepted. Second, this change occurred in a socialist country which already, 20 years ago, had dismissed the system of Traditional Central Planning (TCP) based on mandatory planning and central allocation of products, and also had declared that the increased significance of the monetary processes was unavoidable. It regarded money, however, as a means of enforcement of the central will, that is an important economic force in helping the plan and the market to live together. Lastly, the Hungarian experience is very challenging because in Hungary it was already recognised in the mid 1980s that an efficient economy cannot succeed without a full-range market and without the organising role of money. It also became obvious what obstacles the creation of the market controlled by money must face in an economy where state enterprises and large cooperative firms are dominant and where private property and independent economic interests are weak.

174

2 THE ROLE OF MONEY IN HUNGARY

The statement that the circulation of money is the basis for a modern market economy is common sense, and those who dispose of considerable amounts of financial assets have command of the economy. Money is anything acceptable as a means of settling debt. Therefore in the modern economy money consists of liabilities of government (notes and coins) and of banks (bank accounts), i.e. money consists of claims held by individuals on banks and on the government, these claims being generally accepted as a legal tender. Money has no intrinsic value of its own in a modern economy; its use depends basically on the confidence that it will be universally acceptable in exchange for goods. The right to dispose of this medium lacking any intrinsic value constitutes, however, a source of enormous power. In the system of the TCP money should have died gradually, according to the claims of its best-known proponents. But in reality the role of money in the so-called real socialism of TCP has remained considerably significant. Even Lenin acknowledged that 'one must wait several years until there will be a state where the distribution of products can be organised in such a way that the role of money can be excluded' (Lenin, 1950). But the task of money is to be an instrument of the socialist economy and the economic planning in conformity with the interests of the masses of the people, as well as it is the means of the accountance and control of the social production and the circulation of products' (Politicheskaja Ekonomija, 1954). In Hungary, while preparing the reform – and similarly in other socialist reform economies – the fact that the TCP is an economy where resources are wasted and which is incapable of meeting consumer needs correctly was well realised (Péter, 1966; Kornai, 1980,). Therefore the so-called new economic mechanism was introduced, the Modified Central Planning (MCP). But this framework also treated money as the means of planning. Even the decrees determining the model of the new system stress the increasing role of money; its programme aims to secure 'a wider space of predominance . . . to the market and money . . . existing necessarily in the socialist economy . . .' What was meant was only an increasing role, still with subjection to the central macromanagerial authorities and no dominance. This was revealed in a statement claiming that 'this market cannot be left alone, cannot be a market of free competition, but it must be a market which regulates itself while being itself regulated and by so doing promotes the realisation of well-established economic plans'

(HSWP CC, 1966). The market and the money were allowed to play an independent role without constraints only in case their effect 'does not disturb the realisation of the main directions of the plan' or 'if the result of the market processes is preferable to what the fulfilment of the plan promises'. In these cases it was indicated that 'the realisation of the targets of the original plan need not be forced by regulatory means' (HSWP CC, 1966).

In fact, permanent state influence on and regulation of the economic processes is a characteristic feature of reform economies. So, for example, one is tempted to call the economic reform of 1968 in Hungary a change from direct central macromanagement to the system of indirect control using state monetary regulations (Antal, 1985).

In the MCP economy – although the central authorities do not rule the economy with directives but with unanimous monetary and thus indirect means – it was not money which was the source of power. The creation and redistribution of money among economic units maintained the discretional right of the central authorities. The reallocation of money and incomes meant mostly a technique for seizing levies on the efficient enterprises to bail out loss-making ones (Kornai and Matits, 1987). The central authorities used, and still use, price regulation, bank loans disregarding profitability considerations and the methods of tax exemptions and subsidies to arrange monetary and fiscal flows which contradict strikingly the requirements of efficiency.

As a consequence of this state of affairs, not money itself but the authorities redistributing money seize power in this system. This statement could be refined. In practice, the interventionary redistribution of money always comes into existence as an effect of attempts to handle disturbances. This technique can indeed cure the disturbances, and the redistributive authorities feel themselves justified in obeying the pressure to intervene if they want to satisfy the requirements of their primary task, being able to secure the smooth working of the economy. Nevertheless, the economic agents and the firms consciously use this pressure on the financial distributors to make their own situation better. A new phenomenon, bargaining about regulative measures, succeeds the bargaining about plan targets, and inescapably reinforces the contradictions and deepens the existent, quite chaotic, state of affairs which ridicules the envisaged ideal social harmony attributed to economic planning.[1]

The reform which can be considered as both market-oriented and limited in that sense, of the macro-management, only after a long time had the courage to face the contradiction that if it does not intend to achieve or even realise the dominant role of money, the representation of capital, the full-hearted organisation of both the capital and financial markets and, at the same time, a pluralistic social and political system, then it is not able to create an efficient market.[2] It was a long way from the recognition of this contradiction to the alteration of the aims of economic policy. But it was not this recognition which forced the Hungarian political leadership in the direction of a fully fledged market solution. On the contrary, it was that from the mid 1970s the economic situation had worsened because of the ambiguous reform and the rejection of the reform in some sense (hidden recentralisation), as well as the unfavourable changes in foreign markets. The decline at the end of the decade led to an acute crisis, highlighted primarily by the growing volume of debts to non-socialist countries. So from the mid 1980s on the leading strata of the party and the state hierarchy realised the necessity of not only a break with the policy of TCP but of being open to the possibility of a pluralistic parliamentarism and the creation of a fully fledged market as well.

Despite the above recognition, those in power wanted to defend the remainder of their position. So a strategy was created, brave in rhetoric and ambiguous in issues of actual transition: the so-called new wave of reform, which consisted of a) the encouragement of small entrepreneurship, including private activities; b) the separation of the enterprises of the state sector from the state hierarchy, first with steps towards self-management (1984) and then with the idea of property reform (denationalisation); and c) the qualified increase of the role of money in tax and banking reform, and with measures aiming at the liberalisation and deregulation of the economy.

It is this framework which provides the background for the strange story of the establishment of the commercial bank system – the theme of our study (1987–1988).

3 THE CREATION OF THE SYSTEM OF COMMERCIAL BANKS

On 1 January 1987 a new banking system was introduced in Hungary. The model of this banking system, as we have already mentioned, was the banking system in the Western market economies, which consists of commercial banks, the central bank and other financial intermediaries. The list of the financial institutions working in Hungary at the beginning of 1989 can be found in the Appendix.

The three main groups of these institutions are:

(i)   The commercial banks which open accounts for enterprises, collect deposits and give short- and long-term loans. In addition, they can invest a maximum of 20 per cent of their own capital.

(ii)   The financial intermediaries which have a limited opportunity for opening accounts and collecting deposits. They deal with specific financial tasks.

(iii) The central bank which is responsible for the whole monetary sphere and the stabilisation of the value of the currency.

The gravitational force of the past did not, obviously, facilitate the new institutional system to work in this purified form immediately. There are two types of transitional problems, which actually are dissolving now and can be characterised by the facts that (a) the Hungarian National Bank (HNB) had a total monopoly of the hard currency trade in the first two years of the banking reform, and (b) the majority of the banks were excluded from acceptance of private savings and giving loans.

A more serious problem was the situation inherited from the mono-bank system before 1987 and which resulted in such a messy monetary system that half of the enterprises did not use loans and a significant part of the other half were so much in debt that the new banks could not expect them to pay off the loans received in the earlier relationships. Furthermore, their actual liquidity could have been maintained only by giving loans to the non-creditworthy customers instead of stopping all connection with them.

Despite these difficulties, claimed to be transitory by the protagonists of reform, it was believed that simply because of the new banking system the centrally-determined money supply would circulate without substantial friction. It was expected that, on the one hand, money and the demand created by it could regulate the volume of trade with respect to the real capacities of the economy and thus make producers more efficient and, on the other hand and at the same time, that the efficient economic agents would be financed by loans for development and would be able to lead the economy into prosperity.

The effects of the transformation of the financial system after the banking reform cannot be evaluated by the evidence of only two years. But one could risk a proposition that during this short period the positive effects of the change in monetary policy on the Hungarian economy have not matched the earlier, perhaps too naive, expectations.

4 THE WORKING OF THE SYSTEM OF THE COMMERCIAL BANKS

4.1 Money Supply

When the new banking system was introduced, the monetary system, just as in earlier periods, had to overcome the contradictions arising from consequences of the parallel pursuit of the aims of both development and constantly adjusting equilibrium. In the 20 years after 1968 it was not the money supply which was responsible for the soft budget constraint of the enterprises. The mono-bank system was essentially successful in controlling the quantity of money present in the economy, and could keep it in tune with the supply targets and even with the planned level of inflation. The growth of the quantity of money never actually fitted the supply of goods and services (Portes, 1981). But the permanent shortages in goods and services appearing persistently, always accompanied by serious slacks, was, to my mind, not caused primarily by the over-supply of money but by the miniscule demand and supply elasticity of prices and by the discriminative income and money redistribution described above, which supported the survival of every enterprise and worked against efficiency (Mellár, 1988). The rigid adaptation of prices to the changes did not mean, however, that they would have remained as stable as is customary in a TCP, or would have been changing only insignificantly. The price system allowed pushes from the cost side to be effective, so after 1968 there was an inflation equalling the growth rate of the level of costs (Csori and Mohácsi, 1985). This cost-push inflation itself belonged to the mechanisms which reproduced the permanent failure to achieve a sufficient degree of income differentiation among enterprises, as has been hinted. The pricing authorities systematically hid enterprise losses by allowing price increases, while systematically obstructing attempts to increase the prices of those profitable products of which there was an acute shortage.

The new banking system was alleged to put an end to these practices. While fulfilling this it should also have cured the anomaly that because of the real capacities of the Hungarian economy and the misconceived developmental policy in 1985–1986, and, as a consequence of the anarchy caused by the reorganisation of the mono-bank system, the money supply exceeded the level required by the true capacity of the economy far more than the earlier prevailing norms have suggested. Secondly, the banking system was conceived as an instrument to create a prosperous economy by means of the banks financing and supporting efficient activities or industries. It is the contradiction between the simultaneous need for a restrictive monetary policy and ever-increasing money supply which character-ised the new banking system during its existence.

According to a quantitative analysis undertaken by a research group headed by the author, the money balances of the whole banking system, with respect to the adaptability of the markets at the end of 1986, not only exceed the customary level, but this even increased until the middle of 1987 while banks could arrange new financial assets through the channels of so-called refinanced credits.[3]

In the middle of 1987 the central authorities – above all the Planning Office – realised what was happening, and in cooperation with the HNB suspended the policy of expansion of the quantity of money through the monetary channels and tried to diminish the money balances. From the middle of 1987 until the end of 1988 there were permanent tensions in the economy due to this policy of decreasing the quantity of money. These tensions culminated in the first weeks of 1988. The HNB announced a policy of drastic with-drawal of money, but this attempt failed because of the opposition of the commercial banks. In February 1988 the Minister of Finance, the President of the HNB and the President-General Managers of two leading commercial banks (Hungarian Credit Bank (HCB) and National Commercial and Credit Bank (NCCB)) had agreed on a policy of perpetual monetary restriction. This policy determined the behav-iour of the banking system up to the end of 1988. As a result, at the end of 1988 the money supply exceeded the level of that at the end of 1986 by only 9 per cent, although the nominal transaction volume increased by 20 per cent and the GDP increased by 30 per cent during the same period.

Three remarks are necessary before a full discussion of the situation.

(i) The figures indicating the growth of nominal GDP can be

Table 9.1   Real economy, credit and financial flows (billions of forints)

	1986	1987	1988	Annual change per cent 1986/87	1987/88
Gross value of material activities: transactions (T)	2846	3119	3422	+ 9.6	+ 9.7
Consumption	779	905	1021	+16.2	12.8
Investment	293	328	352	+11.9	7.3
Domestic credit volume	982	1103	1144	+12.3	+ 3.7
at: Budget	103	145	154	+40.8	+ 6.2
Enterprises	584	619	612	+ 6.0	− 1.1
Public	235	272	300	+15.7	−10.3
Net foreign debt	459	629	707	+37.0	+12.4
M_1 Money[a]	275	308	300	+12.0	− 2.6
Quasi-money[a]	267	284	310	+ 6.4	+ 9.2
Total: M_2[a]	542	592	610	+ 9.2	+ 3.0
Securities and bonds	33,6	47,0	44,1	+39.9	− 6.2
Velocity of money (T)					
T/M_1	10,4	10,1	11,4	− 2.9	12.9
T/M_2	5,2	5,3	5,6	+ 1.9	5.9
Consumer price index				+ 8.6	+15.7
Domestic industrial price index				+ 5.4	+ 4.8

Note: [a]The Hungarian Statistical Office in 1989 started to publish new figures of money supply. These are not considered here because they are not comparable with earlier data.
Source: *Statistical Year Book 1988*, Central Statistical Office, Budapest; *Monthly Statistics of the Hungarian National Bank*.

regarded mainly as the consequence of a cost-push inflation since nominal growth of transaction volume was less than that of the money supply.

(ii) Those spheres of the economy which were decisively influenced by the market were much more upset by the monetary restriction than others, for the increase in the money balances of the state budget was higher than the overall increase in the money supply. In the years 1987–8 practically no bankruptcy cases occurred in the business sphere, contrary to widespread rumours. The couple of cases after 1985 induced no more than a warning effect. There are three possible reasons for this: first, the leading economic institutions feared the social impact of regular bankruptcy processes because there were so many enterprises near to bankruptcy due to liquidity problems and permanent losses. Second, the banks could not avoid rearranging terms with low creditworthy debtors and dared not ask for their bankruptcy, for in that case not only their profit would have been risked but they would themselves have come to the brink of bankruptcy. Third, neither the State Bank Supervisory Organisation nor the shareholders of the banks – who frequently turned out to be the uncreditworthy debtors – forced them to diminish the risk of maintaining their insane credit structure. So it is not by chance that the banks barely lent money from their limited balances to efficient customers.

(iii) Moreover, the commercial banks, although they were unable to meet the credit demand of their efficient customers, were eager to buy shares, mortgages, land and other assets out of their excess reserves, that is, to be involved in bigger, quicker and more secure investments outside the credit market.

4.2   The Working of the New Banking System 1987–8

The cornerstone of the revised system of income and monetary processes of 1987 was the attempt to keep the increase in the net domestic volume of debts below 20 billion forints in order to tame the foreign debt crisis. However, in the course of that the monetary flows of all three income recipient groups, the budget, the enterprises and the households, diverged from the targeted figures. The volume of net domestic debts increased by 121 billion forints which meant a 12 per cent growth instead of the intended 2 per cent. Enterprise incomes and profits exceeded the desired level, and with the boosted volume of short-term loans at the end of the last year, facilitated larger spending than was planned. What is more, private savings fell short of the targets because of the inflationary expectations due to the forthcoming taxation reform. The budget deficit was greater than in the previous year in spite of the 10 billion forint deficit decrease indicated in the modified yearly plan. The trade deficit in 1987 ($361 million) was only slightly smaller than in the very gloomy year of 1986.

The year 1988 turned out to be much more successful despite ill omens. The balance of trade turned out to be a $513 billion surplus. This positive change, was not a consequence of the improved production of exportables alone but was partly the result of the, for Hungary, favourable movements in world market prices and in cross exchange rates. Unfortunately the improved trade balance did not reduce the gross debt volume since the surplus on trade was consumed as a result of a politically important measure. The free opportunity for Hungarian citizens to travel to Western countries and change Hungarian Forints for convertible currency with the purpose of purchases abroad was offered. The increased freedom of Hungarian citizens offered by the World Passport, the document providing free opportunity for every citizen to travel abroad was not soundly prepared from the business point of view. The price distortion of the Hungarian consumer markets have remained too large, the forint has remained overvalued and the realisation of import tariffs were too significant to carry out liberalisation measures.

But even if we do not consider the Vienna 'shopping' of the Hungarian tourist we cannot regard the improvement of the trade balance as a break-through reached by the modified economic policy. The role of monetary restrictions seems to be minor even within the positive economic results. The two-digit inflation generated by the introduction of a VAT-type turnover tax and of a personal income tax (unmatched by the centrally-determined wages), as well as the import restriction and export growth attained through substantial managerial incentives, had more significant effects on the foreign trade achievements, than the restriction of the money supply.

I cannot, however, disagree with the statement that among others the restrictive monetary policy and administrative measures could keep inflation in 1988 around the planned level and that it could improve the efficiency of the market which had fallen into pieces after the consumption rush at the end of the previous year. The basic method of monetary restriction became the short-term credit cut. The commercial banks, threatened by illiquidity, could pass on the burden of the contracted money supply to enterprises with significant dependence on the credit market. Meanwhile the volume of the money balances in the enterprise sphere did not actually decrease. As is clear from Table 9.2, showing the contraction of the credit volume held by economic agents in terms relative to gross value of material activities in 1987 and in absolute terms too in 1988, the increased financial savings of the enterprises did not contribute primarily to the liquid reserves (checkable demand deposits).

4.3   The Working of the Commercial Banks and the Whole Banking System

Tables 9.1 and 9.2 suggest that in both 1987 and 1988 the monetary sphere had to solve the ambiguous task of counter-weighting the

Table 9.2 Credit and money balances of business enterprises and cooperatives in Hungary (billions of forints)

	1986	1987	1988	Annual change per cent 1986/87	1987/88
Gross value of material activities: transactions (T)	2846	3119	3422	+ 9.6	+ 9.7
Credit volume	351	363	320	+ 3.4	−11.5
Investment credits	103	116	120	+12.6	+ 3.4
Short-term credits	244	247	200	+ 1.2	−19.0
Deposit-volume	130	154	122	+18.5	−20.8
Demand deposit	80	87	70	+ 8.8	−19.5

Source: as Table 9.1.

liquidity improving excess balances arriving from the budget and bank channels, to correct *ex post* the monetary flows diverging from those indicated in the plan. Their money supply contraction was intended to be solved by financial institutions – according to declared principles – and with so-called fine measures including an active interest rate policy, the development of trade with bills and the issue of government securities. But these measures did not bring with them a general solution to the problem. The main obstacle was that while carrying out the monetary restriction with respect to the enterprises, the budget was used to make lossmaking firms creditworthy. At the same time the public withdrew its assets from the banks, because of the negative real interest rates. So the banking system had to diminish not only the short-term debt volume carried over from the previous year, but at the same time it was also supposed to match the demand generated by the increased liquidity from the extra budgetary expansion and from the growth of the liquidity by the consumers.

The main hindrance to the efficacy of the monetary restrictions via withdrawals of money from the enterprises was the fact that the excess outflow of money did not automatically manifest itself in an increase in the savings of the income recipients, but an increased amount of money was spread among other economic agents, offering a chance for the lossmakers' survival. Thus the administrative restrictions were paralysing partly the efficient enterprises but were not equilibrating the market. Secondly, as an extreme difficulty, the majority of the successful firms did not use credits at all, as mentioned earlier, and the most significant debtors were chiefly those enterprises for which the unavailability of new credits would have meant immediate bankruptcy. It is also a consideration that a bankruptcy process would have tragic social consequences if executed in the whole range of the enterprises and institutions concerned. Even a process against a narrower range of enterprises had to face several political and economic obstacles.

There is a third cause of the lack of effectiveness of monetary restraint, namely, the low degree of the economy's monetarisation. This is responsible for the failure of the discount rate (in Hungary it is called refinancing rate), the most sensitive policy instrument of the central bank sufficiently to influence the monetary processes. In the short run, the central bank could not dare to rely upon the dominance of the discount rate when choosing from regulatory measures, since the lack of cost sensitivity of firms could have induced a dangerous interest rate inflation.

A fourth constraint to central bank fine tuning is the limited amount of securities which the central bank is able to hold. This, of course, diminishes the role open market operations could have in regulating the level of liquidity in the economy. Only after issuing Treasury Bills regularly will the open market activities be gradually intelligible on the secondary market of securities.

Because of these weaknesses of the monetarisation of the economy, the central bank became inclined to apply a set of more direct methods of regulation. The most persuasive element of this set was apparently the central bank determination of credit quotas refinanced for the commercial banks. When the new banking system was established the credit quota determination was conceived as strictly dominated by transparent and standard central bank policy measures in controlling the prosperity of the economy.

But the differing asset structure of the commercial banks prevented a neutral application of central bank credit refinancing. In 1987 the two banks with the highest total balances (HCB and NCCB) started with a 23–30 per cent deposit rate and a 60–65 per cent refinanced credit rate. This structure was the opposite of the one in the Budapest Bank. And other banks, employing the full range of banking activities since 1987, did not even have any demand for refinanced credits. The random distribution of doubtful liabilities among the banks also hampered the creation of a competitive neutral credit refinancing scheme.

The tensions arising from the above problems peaked in the first quarter of 1988 as mentioned. Then the Planning Office and the HNB

Table 9.3   Bank credit in Hungary (billions of forints)

	1987 June	1987 December	1988 December
Credit refinanced by NBH	201,2	234,9	182,8
Matured credit volume	4,1	4,4	28,5
Rearrangement credit	–	6,4	15,4
Bills discounted by NBH		3,2	8,0
Outlays from non-existing accounts (queuing)	.	14,0	45,5
Prime rate of NBH	9,5	10,5	10,5

Source: *Monthly Statistics of the Hungarian National Bank.*

decided to launch a very strict monetary restriction by withdrawing refinanced credit outlays. This plan failed however. Only a compromise between the commercial banks and the HNB could succeed in releasing the tensions. The total volume of refinanced credits for the commercial banks has continuously decreased since the middle of 1987, and at the end of 1988 that total fell short of the one in June 1987 by 20 per cent.

The new commercial banks were obviously impeded in inducing economic development. But we must still answer the question: how could the monetary system keep the economy working amidst these phenomena which hindered any prosperity. The answer will point to the importance of trading with bills, the renewal of pay-off delays among enterprises (so-called queueing), the frequent neglect of credit regulations of the central bank, and other features. The wide range of interest rates and the unreasonably high lending rates in the productive sectors (the lending rate at the end of the period was more than double the discount rate in some cases) show the financial chaos.

5   SUGGESTIONS FOR FURTHER IMPROVEMENTS IN THE FINANCIAL SYSTEM; CREATION OF A UNIFIED FINANCIAL MARKET

The experiences of the two-year existence of the Hungarian commercial banking system show how hard it is to let the efficiency-promotive role of a commercial banking system work in an economy based on full-range nationalisation and collectivised agriculture. The only hope for achieving a powerful market and a money-compatible economy in a post-Stalinist structure is to produce the simultaneous existence of the following conditions (see McKinnon, 1983).

1. Strict control over the economic agents must be secured. This must avoid administrative rigidity and thus authoritative price control.

(a) The capital balances should be directly and thoroughly checked by the owner or by persons or authorities delegated by the owner, which means an immediate challenge to the competence and the mandate of the managers if the utilisation of some components of the capital are evaluated as contrary to the principle of profit maximisation (see Tardós, 1983 and Nuti, 1983).

(b) The market should require continuous ability to meet daily pay-off obligations from any firm. A different formulation of this idea would state that insolvent, illiquid enterprises should face automatic bankruptcy.

2. The money supply must be secured in accordance not only with the capacity of the economy but also with the requirement that any efficient, ready-for-expansion enterprise could receive credit even under restrictionary monetary policy.

(a) A high real interest rate is advisable on the financial markets.

(b) The prolongation or rearrangement of doubtful credits should be prevented.

(c) The investment activities of the banks should be constrained and compliance with the rules should be effectively controlled.

Only with the development of the institutions of economic and political enforcement of the different interest groups can these methods be efficient in promoting a successful market economy. Only this kind of decisive social, political and economic change can produce a state of affairs where liquidity and profit maximisation constraints could force enterprises to a permanent supervision of their production schedule. This also implies that the enterprise should not give up the maintenance of its 'traditional' production scheme just because it perceives chances for considerable modernisation through newly acquired capital but also because there are only such possibilities for the transformation of the non-profitable production schedule (in the case of capital shortage) which results in producing goods and services requiring a lower level of technology, or the decrease of the number of employees, as the only way to become profitable.

Preparations for the convertibility of the currency should be started only in accordance with the strengthening of the domestic currency and the market supporting it.

APPENDIX

Hungarian Banks

		Registered capital		
Central bank	National Bank of Hungary founded in 1924	10 000	million	HUF
Commercial banks	AGROBANK Agricultural Innovation Bank, Ltd. founded 1983	15 000	"	"
	Budapest Bank, Ltd	6 412	"	"
	Commercial and Credit Bank, Ltd	10 590	"	"
	Hungarian Credit Bank	13 983	"	"
	Hungarian Foreign Trade Bank, Ltd	6 003	"	"
	Innovation Bank for Construction Industry, Ltd	1 160	"	"
	Interbank, Credit Corporation for Development of Foreign Trade, Ltd 1988	2 176	"	"
	General Banking and Trust Company, Ltd	1 500	"	"
	General Bank for Venture Financing, Ltd	2 000	"	"
	National Savings Bank	1 300	"	"
	POSTABANK Corp. Post Bank and Savings Bank Corporation	2 229	"	"
	Savings Cooperatives	47 500	"	"
Development financial institutions	State Development Institution			
Specialised financial institutions	Bank for Investment and Transactions, Ltd	500	"	"
	Bank for Small Ventures	844	"	"
	Central Corporation of Banking Companies	1 000	"	"
	Industrial Bank			

Hungarian Banks *(continued)*

	Registered capital		
Industrial Cooperative Development Bank, Ltd	1 061	"	"
Industrial Development Bank, Ltd	3 200	"	"
INNOFINANCE General Finance Institution for Innovation, Ltd	500	million	HUF
INVESTBANK Bank of Technical Development, Ltd	1 233	"	"
INVESTRADE Corporation	100	"	USD
KONZUMBANK Consumer Cooperatives Bank, Ltd	1 042	"	HUF
MERKANTIL, LTD Affiliated Bank to Commercial and Creditbank	500	"	"
Central-European International Bank, Ltd	20	"	USD
Central European Creditbank, Ltd Középeurópai Hitelbank (KHB)	1 000	"	HUF
CITIBANK Budapest, Ltd	1 000	"	"
UNICBANK, Rt.	1 000	"	"

Notes

1. There was a fascinating debate on the role of money in the bargaining processes about output targets and regulations; see Gomulka 1985. Kornai 1985a,b; Soós 1985a,b.
2. I first contributed to this topic in 1969. It was published only in 1972 (Tardos, 1972).
3. We used the following function to calculate the interrelation between the quantity of money and the GDP:

$$\text{GDP} = 90\ 617.7 + 1.869\ M_2 \qquad R^2 = 0.9885$$
$$\qquad\quad (4.97) \qquad (34.7) \qquad\qquad F = 1203.7$$
(the t value is in parentheses)

To determine excess demand, a disequilibrium model was considered,

$$YD = 14\ 551\ 1.1 + 0.2727 \times PJOV + 1.5005 \times Ber + 0.6874\ Rexp.$$
$$\qquad (16.42) \quad (2.78) \qquad\qquad (8.24) \qquad\qquad (3.33)$$
$$R^2 = 0.998 \qquad\qquad\qquad \text{Durbin–Watson} = 1.734$$

$$YS = 0.0692 \times Rk + 22.6893 \times L - 0.8332 \times RIMP$$
$$\quad (7.35) \qquad\qquad (11.58) \qquad\qquad (-13.22)$$

YD = aggregate demand
YS = aggregate supply
$PJOV$ = income of the population
× Ber = investment
× $Rexp$ = real value of export
× Rk = real value of capital
× L = employees
× $RIMP$ = real value of import
(the t value is in parentheses)

References

Antal, L. (1985) *Gazdaságirányitási rendszerünk a reform után* (Economic Management after the Reform) (Budapest, KJK).

Csori, Klára and Mohácsi, Piroska (1985) 'Az infláció fö tényezöi 1980–84' (Main factors of inflation 1980–84) *Gazdaság*, No. 2.

Gomulka, S. (1985) 'Kornai's Soft Budget Constraint and the Shortage Phenomenon; *Economics of Planning*, No. 2.

Kornai, J. (1980) *The Economics of Shortage* (Amsterdam: North-Holland) p. 19.

Kornai, J. and Matits, A. (1987) *A vállalatok nyereségének bürokratikus újraelosztása* (Bureaucratic Reallocation of Enterprise Profits) (Budapest: KJK).

Kornai, J. (1985a) 'Gomulka on Soft Budget Constraint; A Reply', *Economics of Planning*, No. 1.

Kornai, J. (1985b) 'Hiány magyarázó elméletröl' (About the Theory Explaining Shortage) *Közgazdasági Szemle*, No. 2.

Lenin, V. I. (1950) *Collected Works* edition, vol. 29, 329, pp. 329–38 (in Russian) (Moscow Gospolitizdat).

McKinnon, R. (1983) *Money and Capital in Economic Development* (Brookings Institution, Washington, DC).

McKinnon, R. (1988) *Financial Liberalization and Economic Development* (International Center for Economic Growth, San Francisco).

Mellár, T. (1988) *Az egységes pénzpiac* (United Money Market) (mimeograph) (Financial Research Ltd, Budapest).

Nuti, D. M. (1988) 'Egy szövetkezeti pénzintézet terve' (Project for a Solidarity Fund), *Közgazdasági Szemle*, 12.

Péter, Gy. (1966) *Gazdaságosság és jövedelmezöség a tervgazdaságban* (Efficiency and Profitability in the Planned Economy) (Budapest: KJK).

Politicheskaja Ekonomija (1954) (Textbook of Political Economy in Russian) (Moscow, Gospolitizdat).

Portes, R. (1981) 'Macroeconomic Equilibrium and Disequilibrium in Centrally Planned Economies', *Economic Inquiry*.

Soós, K. A. (1985a) 'Hiányjelenségek magyarázatához' (To the Explanation of Shortage), *Közgazdasági Szemle*, No. 1.

Soós, K. A. (1985b) 'Hierarchikus gazdaságirányitás, a pénz restriktiv szerepe és a "hiány"' (Hierarchic Economic Control, Restrictive Role of Money and 'Shortage') *Közgazdasági Szemle*, 3.

Tardos, M. (1972) 'Economic Competition in Hungary', *Közgazdasági Szemie*, 7–8.

Tardos, M. (1988) 'A tulajdon' (Property Rights) *Közgazdasági Szemle*, 12.

Comment

Karl-Hans Hartwig
WESTFÄLISCHE WILHELMS – UNIVERSITÄT,
MÜNSTER, FRG

Provided that economic reforms succeed in diminishing the role of central planning and bureaucratic coordination on the one hand, and, on the other hand, will increase enterprise independence and market coordination, then the money and banking system has to differ considerably from its traditional structure. This is demonstrated obviously by the papers of Ante Čičin-Šain and Márton Tardos (Chapters 8 and 9 in this volume), dealing with the experiences of banking reform in Yugoslavia and Hungary, two of the most advanced countries on the road of reform.

Both papers are very stimulating and instructive. They provide information not only on banking reform, but also on the difficulties of reform in general. Although the conclusions drawn by the authors seem to be quite radical – for example Ante Čičin-Šain argues that there can be no decisive difference in the role and functions of banks in a reformed socialism compared to contemporary developed capitalist market economies – from a logical point of view they are right. The only solution is to establish a two-tiered banking structure which is characterised by a set of independent commercial banks and a widely autonomous central bank. In the papers this topic is hardly mentioned. There is no analytical foundation for such an institutional framework; moreover, its necessity is presupposed and the arguments are vague and general. Also the role of money seems to me overemphasised by Tardos. Money as such is just a commodity which saves transaction costs resulting from exchange and from storing values. Therefore the question is not to 'give money the power' or to 'realise the dominant role of money' but to establish markets, the efficiency of which depends on the monetisation of the economy.

These analytical gaps may be due either to the fact that the subject of the papers is practical experience, or because the authors regard the discussion of the basic arrangements as already completed. But in my view, one cannot analyse the role of commercial and central banking within the more general context of market forces in centrally-planned economies, without considering the fundamental structure of money and banking. The answer is obvious if one compares the functioning of money and banking in the traditionally centrally-planned economy with a reformed system.

1 MONEY AND BANKING IN A TRADITIONAL SETTING

The main features of the traditional money and banking system are its subordination to the central planning mechanism, and the separation of the types of money and of the types of monetary flows (Hartwig, 1987). The banking system acts as an arm of the central authorities. It is fully embedded in the central plan and has to secure the monetary alimentation of the planned activities and to control plan fulfilment. Organised as a state-owned single mono-bank with branches and subordinated special banks, the state bank plays the usual role of a central bank and of a commercial bank: besides being a bank of issue, it keeps the current accounts and deposits of enterprises and private households, and it is the creditor of the enterprise sector and the consumption sector. All parts of the state bank system have to check that the monetary funds are disbursed only for specific purposes.

In the traditional system money plays different roles (Dembinski, 1988). In the household sector money is a medium of choice. Anyone who possesses money is entitled to specify the period of time and the class of transactions in which he will spend it. Even if households are limited in their use of money by shortage and by the small range of assets available to them and if buyers may not influence the volume and assortment of goods, the freedom of choice granted by money in principle exists. Therefore money in the household sector is active, which means that money has influence on economic decisions. In the state productive sector money is 'passive' (Brus, 1963; Grossman, 1966). Changes in prices and quantities do not respond to changes in the stock of enterprises money for two reasons. On the one hand, the range of choice open to enterprises is strictly limited, resources are allocated centrally and all receipts are channelled in fixed proportions into a number of earmarked funds. On the other hand, there exist many ways for state enterprises to obtain money. Once a task is planned, the bank is bound to supply enough finance, even if the final transactions are more extensive and the final costs are higher than those originally estimated. Moreover, producers cannot go into bankruptcy, they do face a 'soft budget constraint' (Kornai, 1986).

These institutional arrangements result in separate spheres of monetary circulation. This is forced by the rule that in the productive sphere transactions have to be conducted with deposit money, while those between households and enterprises and within the household sector are conducted with cash. For the monetary authorities two distinct monetary problems exist. In the inter-enterprise sphere the state bank system has to perform the allocation of goods through the allocation of financial resources. In the consumption sphere, where households are free to use their money, the problem is to avoid global monetary disequilibrium, which depends on the quantity of money in circulation.

The easiest way to tackle the allocationary problem is to provide firms generously with liquidity. In this way plan fulfilment is not hindered by financial constraints, and hindrances to the economic performance are neglectable because of the institutional inactivity of enterprise money. To bring the monetary circulation in the consumption sphere into equilibrium, the state bank has to adjust the quantity of household money. While the money supply in the inter-enterprise sphere is endogenous, money supply in the consumption sphere is a control variable.

2 MONETARY POLICY AND BANKING STRUCTURE IN A REFORMED SYSTEM

Even if the traditional money and banking system works effectively – in fact it did not – its structure is incapable of solving the monetary problems emerging from economic reforms. As reforms increase enterprise independence, self-management, and self-financing the range of transactions into which money allows an enterprise to enter will expand, and the monetary problems will change. First, the problem of allocation of financial resources in the inter-enterprise sphere is no longer a task of the state bank system. Secondly, economic equilibrium in this sphere loses its immunity against an excess supply of money. Excess liquidity, being sterilised in the traditional system, now becomes highly dangerous for the overall economic performance. After the reform, the same lax monetary policy, which traditionally was the surest way to handle the problem of allocation of financial means in the socialised sector, leads directly to shortages, bottlenecks, and price increases. Moreover, because reforms remove almost all devices that traditionally kept the two spheres of monetary circulation independent of one another, excess liquidity in the socialised sector now easily spills over to the consumption sphere (Hartwig, 1987, and especially Dembinski, 1988).

The *de facto* unification of the monetary circulation and of the role of money entails two different, and to some extent conflicting, dimensions of the monetary problems: the control of the overall quantity of money, which is a purely macroeconomic problem, and the efficient allocation of financial resources within a large number of widely independent different economic units. No single institution, not even a state bank, is able to handle both problems simultaneously. For that very reason the monetary circulation in the traditional setting has been separated into two spheres.

There is only one way to control the overall quantity of money and to allocate the financial resources within the frame of a given quantity of money supplied: the creation of a two-level banking structure with a central bank at the top and a set of autonomous and competing commercial banks, supplemented by efficient capital markets. Contrary to the traditional planned economy, with its unified centralised banking structure and its two spheres of monetary circulation, in the reformed socialist economy a unified monetary circulation is connected with a separated banking structure.

3   SIGNIFICANT PROBLEMS OF A BANKING REFORM

To put into practice such a banking structure, as in Yugoslavia and in Hungary, is not easy. This is demonstrated with emphasis by Tardos and by Čičin-Šain; the latter argues that most of the problems are determined by the unwillingness to throw overboard the relics of the traditional system, and by the reluctance and fear of accepting the appropriate changes in the real sector of the economy. Outstanding examples, and the most important ones, are the problem of rights and incentives and the problem of money supply control. Both authors address these in detail.

Even in reformed socialist economies no clear responsibility mechanism exists, either for the enterprises or for the new commercial banks. Till now, lots of central interventions and bureaucratic interferences exempt managers from full responsibility for performance. According to paternalistic attitudes and for the sake of job security even insolvent firms normally get assistance to survive. Although bankruptcy procedures exist by law in the reformed socialist economies bankruptcies scarcely ever occur. To solve the incentive problem high emotional barriers concerning the property rights structure have to be overcome. Márton Tardos suggests the separation of management from a special institution representing 'ownership interests'. The latter would appoint and supervise the managers, whose competence and position is doubted in the case of critical situations. In Yugoslavia, fundamental changes have already taken place. By law, different forms of ownership are accepted now; equity capital has been introduced; and banks have to be organised as independent capital companies. Ante Čičin-Šain is right when he argues that the ultimate sanctions connected with these institutional changes will increase the efficiency of the financial system. But the result is a considerable shift in the property rights structure in favour of private ownership.

The other unresolved monetary problem confronting socialist systems is disequilibrium. Even if M1 decreased from 1987 to 1988 in Hungary, as Tardos shows, and even if the banking systems were essentially successful in controlling the money supply in different periods and different countries, these are exceptions. Normally the growth rate of the quantity of money never actually fitted the growth rate of real output. In an institutional setting, where prices are tightly controlled and fixed for longer periods, velocity declines, a situation which is characterised as repressed inflation. If prices are allowed to change to some extent, the price level increases. The latter will be the case in a reformed socialist economy, where repressed inflation is transmitted into open inflation, not only because of a lax monetary policy in the present times, but also as a result of enormous amounts of excess liquidity accumulated in the past. For the reform process this entails a great risk, because price inflation is perceived to be much easier than repressed inflation. After decades of price stability people are not willing to tolerate price increases. Reform reluctance grows, and for opponents this is a good excuse for recentralisation. It provides legitimation for suppressing market forces and reviving tight control and central interventions.

The only way to limit inflation in the long run is by a target-orientated control of the money stock by a widely independent central bank. While the first is accepted even by socialist economists, central bank autonomy seems to be regarded as too extreme. But as experience shows, dependence often provides the institutional basis for an economic policy, which might actually be destabilising. Governments normally tend to fulfil promises by a growth in the money stock, because of the low production costs of money. This process will continue as long as people do not realise that they cannot get more goods and services for their additional money, and that their real balances decline. If people lose their money illusion (or in the case of trade balance deficits) monetary policy becomes restrictive. Capitalist and development countries, as well as Hungary, Yugoslavia, and China, are examples of such a monetary stop and go. For that very reason, not only in a centrally-planned economy, as Richard Portes (1983) argues, but even in a reformed socialist system, socialism and monetarism have, in significant aspects, to be fellow travellers.

References

Brus, W. (1963) 'Pieniadz w gospodarce socjalistycznej', *Ekonomista*, 5, pp. 9–23.
Dembinski, P. H. (1988) 'Quantity versus Allocation of Money; Monetary Problems of the Centrally Planned Economies Reconsidered', *Kyklos*, 41, pp. 281–300.
Grossman, G. (1966) 'Gold and the Sword; Money in the Soviet Command Economy', in Roskovsky, H. (ed.), *Industrialization in Two Systems, Essays in Honor of Alexander Gerschenkron*, (London: J. Wiley) pp. 204–236.
Hartwig, K.-H. (1987) *Monetäre Steuerungsprobleme in sozialistischen Planwirtschaften* (Stuttgart: Gustav Fischer Verlag).
Kornai, J. (1986) 'The Soft Budget Constraint', *Kyklos*, 39, pp. 3–30.
Portes, R. (1983) 'Central Planning and Monetarism: Fellow Travelers?', in Desai, P. (ed.), *Marxism, Central Planning and the Soviet Economy* (Cambridge Mass: MIT Press).

Part V

Interconnection Between International Markets and Planned Economies

10 Market-oriented Reform of Foreign Trade in Planned Economies

Thomas A. Wolf*

INTERNATIONAL MONETARY FUND,
WASHINGTON DC, USA

1 INTRODUCTION

It has long been evident that greater integration of centrally planned economies (CPEs) into the world economy depends on fundamental reform of their foreign trade systems. In several CPEs, reforms designed to end their insulation from international markets, particularly for manufactures, have involved initiatives to dismantle the traditional institutional monopoly of foreign trade, to provide individual enterprises with both the autonomy and incentives to participate more actively in foreign markets, and to link the domestic price system more fully with the structure of prices prevailing abroad.[1] Planned economies undertaking particularly ambitious foreign trade reforms include China, Hungary, Poland and, relatively recently, the Soviet Union.

This paper reviews certain features of the foreign trade reforms undertaken in these economies. Its purpose is not to compare or to evaluate these reforms, but rather to examine some difficult issues that arise in the course of their implementation. The focus will mainly be on reforms aimed at stimulating expanded and more efficient trade with market economies; the complex mechanisms for trade with other planned economies, and in particular economic relations within the CMEA, are appropriately left for separate study. In several instances, however, the influence that the CMEA trading system may have on market-oriented foreign trade reforms is noted.

The paper emphasises the desirability of formulating a coherent reform strategy and complementary policies that take into account the inherent interdependencies of the different facets of market-oriented foreign trade reform. These elements, considered in turn in sections 2–4 below, include initiatives aimed at expanding enterprise autonomy and breaking up the institutional monopoly of foreign trade, adapting the exchange rate system, and reforming the domestic price structure and ultimately the price system. To the extent that reforms in these areas have proven to be less than complete in the transition, various policy and institutional adaptations have been made by policymakers which are nevertheless designed to promote increasing openness of the economy. These include the development of supplementary financial incentives for exports and institutional innovations aimed at partially decentralising the allocation of foreign exchange. Both of these facets of the reform process are briefly discussed in section 5. Some concluding remarks are contained in section 6.

2   EXPANDING ENTERPRISE AUTONOMY IN FOREIGN TRADE

It is not necessary here to rehearse the salient features of the state monopoly of foreign trade in the CPE. Suffice it to say that this institutional monopoly of foreign trade, comprised of essentially non-competing foreign trade organisations (FTOs) mainly subordinate to the Ministry of Foreign Trade and evaluated according to their fulfilment of detailed foreign trade plans, effectively separated and indeed isolated domestic producers and consumers in the CPE from foreign markets. The decentralisation of foreign trade decision making and the ending of the isolation of producing enterprises has therefore necessitated the breaking up of this particular type of foreign trade monopoly. Important initiatives in this regard have been taken by a number of CPEs, and have involved, *inter alia*, the easing of profile restrictions for FTOs (thereby promoting some competition among them), expanding the range of foreign trade intermediaries from which a producing enterprise could choose, and granting direct foreign trade rights to selected producing enterprises for a specified range of products. In some cases, a system of general licences has been established, meaning that enterprises with foreign trade rights can in principle now trade in any product not specified on a negative list. In at least one case enterprises are now in principle authorised to engage in foreign trade in any product not contained on a negative list merely by registering with the authorities and making a declaration to the effect that they have adequate infrastructure and personnel with which to conduct foreign trade operations.[2]

Enterprise autonomy in foreign trade, however, requires more than simply the dismantling of the institutional monopoly over foreign trade. More fundamentally, it is dependent on the extent to which enterprises have achieved greater autonomy generally within the domestic economy.[3] For example, the right to engage in foreign trade in any product not on a negative list may be of little value to an enterprise that is narrowly restricted in terms of what it can produce or sell on the domestic market. Moreover the right to export a given product will have limited meaning if one or more of the material inputs needed for its production are in excess demand in the domestic economy and subject to formal or informal rationing. In some cases, of course, the authorities may continue for balance of payments reasons to 'direct' that certain products be exported and in a certain quantity. In other cases, exports may effectively be restricted by the authorities so as not to exacerbate domestic imbalances in a general environment of excess demand. Export commitments to other planned economies under intergovernmental trade agreements, with attendant priority allocations of scarce material inputs and investment funds, may likewise have a constraining effect in practice on the freedom of enterprises to command resources in the market for export to the convertible currency area. The prevalence of soft-budget constraints for inefficient enterprises will also indirectly affect the autonomy of firms in foreign trade, as the subsidisation of such enterprises – whether directly by the budget, by intermediate level industrial associations, or by the banking system – will effectively limit the extent to which a profitable export-oriented enterprise can command increased investment and other resources through the market. Limitations on enterprise autonomy in importing are also likely to persist in the transition (see section 5 below).

It is indeed significant that successive reform programmes in planned economies have stressed the importance of expanded enterprise autonomy in general, and not just in foreign trade.[4] As participants in this conference know only too well, however, the struggle for expanded enterprise autonomy is a long one that has by no means been irrevocably decided in any planned economy. In addition to the obvious interest of the traditional bureaucracy in circumscribed enterprise independence, the domestic macroeconomic environment will also be a crucial determinant of the pace at which enterprise autonomy can develop. As long as the underlying rate of inflation in the economy exceeds the tolerable rate of open inflation, price controls will be employed and goods and services will at least partly be allocated through formal and informal rationing mechanisms. As noted above, this is bound to constrain the freedom of enterprises to engage in foreign trade solely in response to the prevailing set of price incentives. Moreover, price controls are likely to distort the incentives for engaging in foreign trade in the first place.

3   REFORM OF THE EXCHANGE RATE SYSTEM

Market-oriented reforms in planned economies seek to enhance the role of profits as the criterion of success for enterprises, whether socialised or private. This is believed to induce enterprise managers to become more competitive, improve product quality, and increase efficiency. To ensure that this profit incentive will lead enterprises to operate in ways that are also efficient from society's point of view, enterprise profits are intended to reflect a price structure that in turn mirrors the underlying pattern of relative scarcities. For policy makers who are truly serious about the efficiency of resource alloca-tion, the relevant pattern of scarcities will now be expanded to include world market opportunity costs as well as prevailing domestic cost and demand structures. The mechanisms that permit such a comprehensive evaluation of relative scarcities are of course the exchange rate and domestic price systems. In theory all such com-parisons could be made on the basis of shadow prices and shadow exchange rates, but the reform experience of most of the CPEs, particularly in the past decade, has been to move away from this approach toward the use of prices that directly affect the financial position of enterprises.

The classical CPE was characterised by strict separation of more or less fixed domestic prices and foreign currency prices for tradables. The latter were converted into so-called valuta or deviza values at *external* exchange rates typically based on obsolete gold parities. Profits and losses of the FTOs, determined by the differences be-tween the valuta or deviza prices in foreign trade and the structure of administered domestic producer prices, were effectively neutralised by the system of so-called price equalisation taxes and subsidies. With time, various *internal* exchange rates were formulated for different product groups in an attempt to provide a bridge between these valuta or deviza prices and those prevailing domestically, and to provide a basis for more efficient foreign trade decisions. For various reasons, however, including the fact that domestic prices frequently bore little relation to real domestic costs, these internal rates or coefficients were not notably successful in raising the efficiency of foreign trade decisions (Wolf, 1985). These internal exchange rates were typically also not used as the basis for settlements between the FTOs and domestic producers.

Fundamental reforms of this traditional system have tended to accompany attempts to broaden and make more direct the participation of producing enterprises in foreign trade (section 2).[5] One approach has been to fold together the external exchange rate and respective commodity-specific internal rates into so-called differentiated foreign trade multipliers (coefficients) that are actually used as the basis for domestic settlement of the foreign trade transactions of some enterprises.[6] A further step has been the combining of the external and internal exchange rates into a central foreign trade multiplier or commercial exchange rate to reflect, say, the average domestic cost of earning one unit of foreign exchange through exporting.[7] This new exchange rate would then be used to calculate the so-called transaction price for each traded product, which in principle would also be the price at which actual foreign trade transactions would be settled domestically. The system of price equalisation would also in principle be eliminated in foreign trade, although as a practical matter it might be perpetuated for some time as long as all foreign trade settlements were not made at these transaction prices. This commercial exchange rate might also be 'unified' with the non-commercial rate in settlements with the convertible currency area.[8]

Although reform of the exchange rate system in planned economies has usually been accompanied by a sizable *de facto* depreciation of the exchange rate,[9] it is nevertheless also the case that none of these economies has yet set its exchange rate at a level that would permit a substantial reduction of import restrictions and/or trade-related exchange controls.[10] One reason would appear to be that currency depreciation is viewed by the authorities in many of these countries as mainly inflationary. The extent to which an increase in the exchange rate is translated into an increase in the overall domestic price level depends, of course, on the degree to which the financial policies of the authorities 'accommodate' the price effects of the devaluation (Wolf, 1988c). But even more fundamentally, in a planned economy it depends on the extent to which the price system permits increases in transaction prices to be passed through to domestic prices in the first place, a point to which we return in the next section.

Other reasons for an overvalued exchange rate have included the aversion to marginalism inherited from the classical CPE, including the reluctance to reward intramarginal firms with abnormally high profits from foreign trade activities, but this aversion appears to carry progressively less weight in many planned economies. Another consideration may be the scope that an overvalued exchange rate gives for continued central intervention in foreign trade activities (Kozma, 1981). Moreover, various activities of high priority in the eyes of the authorities, including possibly some exports to CMEA countries based in part on inputs imported from the convertible currency area, are implicitly subsidised by central allocations of foreign currency at the overvalued official exchange rate (Török, 1988).

4   REFORM OF PRICES AND THE PRICE SYSTEM

Reform of the level and structure of domestic prices is no less important than reform of the exchange rate system, if a comprehensive and coherent mechanism is to be developed for the evaluation by enterprises of relative scarcities. Yet price reform, not to mention reform of the actual system for setting prices, has thus far proven to be far less tractable in planned economies than has reform of the exchange rate system. This is not surprising, however, for price reform directly threatens the traditional patterns of domestic production and (frequently subsidised) consumption, as well as the distribution of real income and, indirectly through the industrial dislocations it may induce, full employment and job security.

The well-known obstacles to price reform in planned economies are discussed in other papers, and it is also not the purpose of this study to describe and evaluate the fairly complex price systems prevailing in the different planned economies. Instead, this section will focus briefly on several issues that arise in connection with price reform and its relation to the foreign trade of these countries.

An important policy issue is the sequencing of price reform and the abolition of controls over trade and/or foreign exchange (hereafter: trade-exchange controls). CPEs embarking on reform typically – but not necessarily – are characterised by four types of price distortions:

(1) the equilibrium price level may exceed the official price level (aggregate excess demand for output of the socialised sector);[11] and (2) the structure of official domestic prices may differ from (a) the structure of domestic equilibrium prices, given the prevailing controls on trade and/or foreign exchange, (b) the structure of real domestic costs, and (c) the structure of world market prices.

If full price liberalisation were socially and politically feasible at the outset of the reform process, the sequencing problem might be rendered fairly insignificant. In so far as foreign trade is concerned, the optimal policy in this case would be also to abolish simultaneously all trade controls. Indeed, to delay acting on these controls in this case would mean achieving domestic equilibrium (at both the micro- and macro-levels) while domestic prices would in general continue to be distorted from world market price relatives. This is because the trade controls would block international commodity arbitrage, which is the mechanism by which domestic and world market relative prices are equalised.[12] As long as trade controls were maintained, the new structure of prices would encourage a reallocation of domestic production and consumption that would not in general correspond to the economy's true comparative advantage.

In reality, complete or even a moderate degree of price liberalisation has not accompanied the early phases of market-oriented reform in planned economies. Typically, in the early stages the authorities seek administratively to restructure prices for an important subset of economically strategic goods, such as energy and basic raw materials. Even with successive administered price reforms, both the overall price level and the different relative price relationships are likely to remain distorted for an extended period. In this event, the sequencing issue becomes more complicated. For example, if all relative price distortions were to disappear through an administered price reform but there were still excess demand for output of the socialised sector at the prevailing official price level (and exchange rate), there would be a possibly unacceptably high drain on the country's international reserves if trade exchange controls were eliminated.

On the other hand, if the administered price reform had absorbed all aggregate excess demand, but distortions remained at the micro-level, the elimination of trade controls might not constitute a major problem if combined with appropriate demand management and exchange rate policies.[13] They also might not lead to a pattern of trade flows that would remove the distortions, however, particularly if these distortions involved a structure of domestic prices different from that prevailing on world markets. (Observe that even if the authorities had managed through changes in official prices to equate the structures of domestic and border prices, this would presumably be only a transitory achievement as the structure of border prices would almost certainly change within a very short period.)

If changes in official domestic prices are to be the main vehicle for price alignment within some transition period, possibly the authorities should at least attempt to set out a general timetable for these modifications. The objective would not be to specify in advance what the exact level of each price would be at some future period because this level, which would be intended ultimately to equal the transaction price, would inherently be a moving target. Instead, a useful approach might be to announce the general goal of achieving a relative domestic price structure for tradables equal to that for border prices by some specified future date (at which time these prices would be liberalised),[14] and gradually moving official prices in that direction in the interim. If this transition period were not too long, enterprises and consumers would increasingly be induced to focus their attention on the likely future movements in these border prices, and investment would presumably be undertaken accordingly.

As long as domestic prices are largely administered (and here, for simplicity, we include in this category so-called contract prices that may be closely controlled), the question arises as to what extent the potential price effects of exchange rate changes designed to improve the balance of trade should be passed through to the domestic price level. There are basically two possibilities. One is not to allow these price effects to be passed through the system, presumably so as to avoid the inflationary consequences of a devaluation. In this case the devaluation could be expected in principle to have an *expenditure shifting* effect, as the higher transaction prices received by exporters induce them to shift production away from the home market toward exports and, to the extent they are not able to pass the higher cost of imports on to domestic customers, to reduce their demand for imports as well.[15]

Although the foregoing suggests that the trade balance impact of the devaluation may be positive, there will be other effects as well. The devaluation in this case could be expected to lead to increased excess demand pressures, for at least three reasons: (1) the devaluation would increase the profits of enterprises and thus the level of wages they could afford to pay, and the higher level of money incomes would not be offset by a higher price level; (2) excess demand for the goods actually exported would increase as supplies were diverted from the domestic market while their domestic relative price, the price level and hence their demand remained unchanged; and (3) to the extent that the heightened incentive to export led to a shift in output toward exports, the supply of other goods available to domestic users, at unchanged prices, would also decline.

There are reasons to believe that these excess demand pressures might lead to responses that would effectively nullify much of the trade balance effect intended by the devaluation. For example, there is the likelihood, in a planned economy, that the authorities will react to increased excess domestic demand by exerting various informal and formal pressures on exporters not to divert supplies from the domestic market (Kornai, 1982). Another factor is the phenomenon of forced substitution, by which consumers, faced with excess demand for non-traded goods caused by the shift in output toward exportables (point (3) above) would attempt to substitute the latter for the former. Whether they would be able to make this substitution would depend, of course, on the freedom enjoyed by enterprises to switch supplies away from domestic consumption.[16]

The other basic possibility is fully to pass through the exchange rate change into domestic prices. In this case the scope for expenditure shifting is different, and possibly less than in the case of nil or incomplete passing on of the effects of exchange rate changes. The prices of traded goods sold domestically and possibly those of other tradables will tend to be raised in this case *pari passu* with the transaction prices of products actually traded. The incentive for exporters in this case to switch supplies of these goods from domestic markets will therefore be diminished, and also the relative price change between traded goods and other goods (including non-tradables) that induces the shifting of production away from the latter will be lessened.

The passing through of the exchange rate change into the domestic prices of traded goods (tradables) will raise the domestic price level, however, and assuming non-accommodative financial policies by the authorities, this will have a demand-reducing effect. Whether it will also be *expenditure reducing* (and therefore, in this case, also expenditure shifting), which is essential to actually improving the trade balance, will depend on the size of the price level change relative to the initial level of excess demand in the economy (Wolf, 1988b, 1988c). Broadly speaking, the choice for the authorities in formulating their policy when following an active exchange rate policy in the transition is between aggravating excess demand pressures (without passing on its price effects), and inducing a higher level of domestic prices which in itself, assuming non-accommodative financial policies, will actually reduce excess demand in the economy (complete passing through of the effects).

In a target solution of domestic price liberalisation combined with the elimination of trade-exchange controls, both the level and structure of transaction prices would be consistent with external and internal balance and a domestic allocation of resources that is efficient from both a domestic and international point of view. During the transition, however, the question arises as to what should be the proper role for transaction prices. If used as a price ceiling for domestically traded goods, transaction prices roughly simulate the price effects of international commodity arbitrage. This would certainly be desirable from the standpoint of enhancing the use of prices to convey information about full opportunity costs. Transaction prices could also serve as effective price benchmarks for monopolistic producers selling on domestic markets.[17] In practice, however, the high degree of product differentiation that characterises markets for manufactured goods may make it difficult to administer such a price ceiling system.

It should also be recognised that the use of transaction price ceilings to simulate the price outcome of international commodity arbitrage does not, in the presence of still severe trade-exchange controls, ensure that domestic prices for tradables will be market clearing. The use of transaction price ceilings may therefore still have to be combined with continued central rationing of those products in excess demand during the transition.

5 SUPPLEMENTARY EXPORT INCENTIVES AND ALLOCATION OF FOREIGN EXCHANGE IN THE TRANSITION

As noted earlier, market-oriented foreign trade reforms in some planned economies have tended, at least for a transitional period, to be characterised by less than complete price reform and the setting of the official exchange rate at a level below that which would clear the market for foreign exchange. The authorities in these countries, seeking to accelerate the opening up of their economies, have in some cases developed a battery of supplementary export incentives consisting notably of tax reliefs, export subsidies, preferential credit terms, and foreign exchange retention accounts for exporters. The latter also serve, of course, as an important source of foreign currency for imports, and together with foreign currency auctions, retention accounts are playing an increasing role in some countries in the decentralised allocation of foreign exchange.

5.1 Supplementary Export Incentives

Central directives or informal pressures on enterprises to expand exports are of course still not unknown in planned economies embarked on market-oriented foreign trade reforms. Nevertheless, to the extent that the exchange rate has not always provided adequate incentives to enterprises to achieve the authorities' export goals, central directives of the traditional type have increasingly been replaced with a supplementary set of financial incentives. Their configuration and the relative importance of individual incentive arrangements differs considerably by country, and no attempt will be made to deal with them comprehensively. The issue addressed here is why these instruments appear to be preferred in some instances to bolder exchange rate action. Some general factors possibly explaining the reluctance of the authorities to depreciate further the exchange rate were noted in section 3. Here we will simply examine why a particular supplementary export incentive of considerable importance in some countries, tax relief, would appear to be so popular.

Systemic as well as *ad hoc* reliefs on account of exports are often provided from both enterprise income taxes and from taxes levied on firms for 'excessive' wage payments. Such reliefs are frequently said to be highly valued by exporting enterprises because of the direct effect they have on their after-tax profits and, in the case of wage-tax reliefs, on the amount that they can afford to pay in wages. At least two plausible reasons come to mind for why enterprises might prefer this type of export incentive to an equivalent currency devaluation. One reason might be the uncertainty of enterprise managers regarding the possible effective confiscation by the authorities of part or all of the increased profits due to the devaluation through, say, the loss of other fiscal exemptions already extended to these firms.[18] In an environment in which intensive bargaining with the authorities over financial exceptions is the rule, the authorities may view the most effective financial incentive on the margin to be yet another exemption which directly affects the post-tax rather than pre-tax profits of enterprises.

In the case of taxes on 'excessive' wages, an additional factor could also explain the preference for reliefs. If the tax-free ceiling on wage increases is defined by the centre independently of the growth in an enterprise's sales or profit, the firm's employees may not view the export supply response to a devaluation as ensuring an effective increase in their remuneration. In this case, only negotiating a direct relief from the excess wage tax would assure the enterprise's work-force of a tangible link between increased exports and higher individual earnings. In this way the widespread lack of financial discipline at the enterprise level, which in part necessitates the maintenance of an indirect mechanism for wage control from the centre in the first place, tends to subvert the effectiveness of uniform financial instruments such as the exchange rate.[19]

5.2   The Allocation of Foreign Exchange

Foreign exchange retention accounts for exporters to non-rouble markets have been established in several planned economies.[20] For many enterprises these accounts may only replace part or all of their previous central allocations of foreign exchange, but even so the accounts may actually expand these firms' range of choice with respect to the products they may import. In general there has been a tendency over time toward making the retention coefficients more uniform across enterprises. To the extent that differences in rates are maintained, they tend increasingly to be related to the degree of processing embodied in a firm's exports and less to the prevailing import intensity of these exports.[21] In some instances retention accounts are viewed by exporters as their single most important export incentive. While retention accounts with increasingly uniform coefficients represent a positive step away from pervasive 'addressed' central allocation of foreign exchange, it must also be recognised that in an economy with pervasive price distortions the existence of a partial retention system will be no guarantee of the efficiency of the structure of its foreign trade.[22]

In some planned economies foreign currency in retention accounts may be transferred by exporting enterprises to their suppliers. Recently, several countries have established various auction schemes which permit an even wider range of non-exporting enterprises to obtain access to foreign exchange. One type of auction provides the possibility for holders of retention accounts to sell their rights directly to other enterprises, and another involves auctions through which the banking system sells foreign currency to enterprises for the purchase of specified groups of products.[23] These auction schemes in effect provide that the average effective price of foreign exchange in the economy is closer to the underlying equilibrium rate than is the official rate. To the extent that domestic prices of imported goods are allowed to reflect transaction prices, transfers of foreign exchange among enterprises at negotiated rates or its sale in auctions or similar markets will tend to ensure the passing through of the higher exchange rate on these transactions. Moreover, in at least one case imports purchased directly from retention accounts are also permitted to be sold domestically at prices that reflect the exchange rate at which foreign currency is sold in an organised market setting (Dunaway *et al.*, 1989).

While the proliferation of such auctions, at which exchange rates may not always be determined freely, tends to complicate the exchange rate system, they may play a useful transitional role in providing the authorities as well as enterprises information regarding the true valuation of foreign currency in the domestic economy, and as a basis for eventual unification of exchange rates at a realistic level. The usefulness of such markets in determining an appropriate unified exchange rate will depend, however, on their size and the extent to which they are free to reflect market forces.

Beyond the foreign exchange made available to exporters and their suppliers directly through retention accounts, and by both exporters and the banking system through auctions, in some economies foreign currency continues to be allocated centrally for various priority programmes and investments. In some instances, however, the proportion of foreign exchange being allocated centrally is falling quite rapidly.

6 CONCLUDING REMARKS

This discussion of market-oriented foreign trade reforms in planned economies has sought to emphasise the inherent interconnectedness of the different reform elements, including the institutional changes that bear on the ability of producing enterprises to engage directly in foreign trade, modifications in the exchange rate system, and the reform of domestic prices and of the mechanism for setting these prices. The success of foreign trade reform, and therefore of a trade policy aimed at fundamental integration of planned economies into the world economic system, ultimately depends as well on the successful implementation of compatible reforms in the domestic economy as a whole. It is highly unlikely that a comprehensive, market-oriented foreign trade reform can be successfully grafted on to a basically traditional system of central planning. By the same token, it should be emphasised that the pace and even the extent of domestic economic reform, including the scope for expanded competition and price liberalisation, may depend as well on the pace and degree of reform of the foreign trade system.

Several planned economies have already initiated quite ambitious programmes of foreign trade reform. In some cases progress is being made in dismantling the institutional monopoly of foreign trade and in expanding the *de facto* freedom of enterprises to engage in foreign trade largely on the basis of market signals (section 2). In several countries these signals are now being conveyed much more clearly than under classical planning, as the exchange rate system is reformed and steps are taken progressively to link domestic with foreign prices (sections 3 and 4). Measures in these areas are frequently supplemented, however, by extensive use of other financial incentives for exporters and by transitional mechanisms for allocating foreign exchange on a more decentralised and in some cases more market-oriented basis (section 5).

The existing foreign trade and exchange arrangements of each of these economies must be viewed as transitional and as not yet representing totally internally consistent foreign trade systems. Nevertheless, in some cases these arrangements constitute a fundamental break with the system of foreign trade that characterised classical central planning. That this break has not yet been reflected in significantly deepened integration into the world economy is perhaps not too surprising given the relatively short history of most of these reform efforts. It probably also reflects, however, the need to push these reforms, as well as those in the domestic economy more generally, even more boldly so as to create more stable conditions for enterprises to have both the incentive and the ability to command resources through the market on the basis of more realistic price signals.

Notes

* The author has benefited from comments on an earlier version of this paper from J. Boorman, A. Boote, P. de Fontenay, J. Prust and G. Szapary, as well as discussion of this topic with C. Puckahtikom, H. Schmitt and J. Somogyi. The views expressed herein, however, are his own and do not necessarily reflect those of the institution with which he is affiliated.

1. For a survey of the institutional and policy factors that tend to insulate CPEs from world markets, particularly in manufactures, see Wolf (1988a) section 2.

2. Details on ongoing institutional reforms in the foreign trade of these countries appear, *inter alia*, in Dunaway *et al.* (1989), Ivanov (1987), Lavigne (1988), Płowiec (1988), Salgó (1986), Somogyi (1989) and Wolf (1989).

3. Also of growing significance in many planned economies is the liberalisation of restrictions on the operation of joint ventures with foreign participation. This is another topic that deserves treatment in a separate paper.

4. In theory, of course, it could be argued that trade liberalisation and greater integration into the world economy could be achieved by simply leaving the existing institutional structure intact but undertaking an administered price reform that removed price distortions *vis-à-vis* the world market and by subjecting enterprises to financial discipline. As argued elsewhere (Wolf, 1989), this is unlikely to work in real world CPEs because the authorities cannot possess sufficient information on which to set all prices efficiently; world market relative prices will in any event fluctuate constantly, and the imposition of financial discipline will be more difficult in an unreformed institutional environment.

5. It should be noted that no two planned economies have approached exchange rate reform in exactly the same way. On different exchange rate systems in some CMEA countries, see Wolf (1985).

6. This approach was experimented with in Poland in the late 1960s and has applied to part of Soviet foreign trade since the beginning of 1987. See Płowiec (1988) and Shagalov (1988).

7. In the Polish case, a 'submarginal' exchange rate concept has been employed in the 1980s (Płowiec, 1988).

8. Unification of commercial and non-commercial exchange rates for settlements with the convertible currency area was achieved by Hungary in 1981 and Poland in 1982.

9. The comparison being made is between the new commercial exchange rate and the previous implicit rate, equal to the product of the external rate and the average internal rate.

10. The issue of convertibility, in all its facets, is left for consideration in a future paper.

11. Portes (1983) has emphasised that of course what may appear as an aggregate excess demand problem may well be the perceived 'aggregate' of shortages at the micro-level that coexist with excess supplies in other markets.

12. International commodity arbitrage refers to the foreign trading activity that, in the absence of trade controls, would arbitrage price differences between domestic and foreign markets and tend to reduce these differences to a level no greater than the associated per unit transaction costs. Only by sheer coincidence would domestic price liberalisation lead to a domestic relative price structure identical to that on international markets, in the absence of free trade.

13. A trade deficit (and therefore a loss in reserves) could, however, exist in this case if there were net dissaving by the budget in the form of a net price equalisation subsidy that financed the existing level of trade at distorted prices. See Wolf (1980).

14. Although, see below, the problem raised by domestic monopolists, at least in the transition before trade is liberalised.

15. The sensitivity of firms to changes in relative prices is a hotly debated issue in planned economies; see Wolf (1988b, 1988c).

16. Forced substitution (Kornai, 1980) is a more plausible outcome in the event of the passing through of the exchange rate combined with fixed prices for non-tradables (Wolf, 1988b).

17. Transaction prices in convertible currency trade have played a major role in the Hungarian system of price regulation since 1980. A so-called producers' differential turnover tax is imposed on energy and raw material imports from the CMEA in order to raise their domestic prices to the level of corresponding transaction prices in convertible currency trade (Somogyi, 1989).

18. On the scope of such discretionary fiscal redistribution in at least one planned economy, see Kornai (1986).

19. Observe that tax reliefs designed to stimulate exports would, *ceteribus paribus*, tend to have the same type of impact on the domestic economy as a devaluation without the passing through of price effects, that is, they would tend to increase domestic excess demand pressures if price controls are pervasive. Marczewski (1988) also shows that even if an exporting enterprise does not actually receive the transaction price for its exports, but tax reliefs are made a function of exports valued in transaction prices (which has been the case in recent years in Poland), then the exchange rate in principle will still directly influence the firm's allocation of its output between the domestic and export market.

20. Such schemes exist in China, Poland (since 1982) and the Soviet Union (1987). In Poland a retention system for trade in transferable roubles has been experimented with since 1986. In Hungary, foreign exchange for importing is in principle assured to any enterprise that obtains an import licence.

21. Proponents of this shift in criteria view it as encouraging a reduction in import intensity, a change in the structure of imports, and an increase in the value added component of exports.

22. Also observe that, as in the case of export-related tax reliefs, but to a lesser extent, the successful use of retention accounts as an instrument to expand net exports is likely, *ceteris paribus*, to increase domestic excess demand pressures.

23. In the case of China, foreign exchange is bought and sold by market

participants in so-called foreign exchange adjustment centres which have been established in many cities.

References

Dunaway, S., Ishii, S. and Szapary, G. (1989) 'Economic Reform in China', (manuscript).

Ivanov, I. D. (1987) 'Restructuring the Mechanism of Foreign Economic Relations in the USSR', *Soviet Economy*, 3(3) pp. 192–218.

Kornai, J. (1980) *Economics of Shortage*, 2 vols (Amsterdam: North-Holland).

Kornai, J. (1982) 'Adjustment to Price and Quantity Signals in the Socialist Economy,' *Economie Appliquée*, 35(3), pp. 503–24.

Kornai, J. (1986) 'The Hungarian Reform Process: Visions, Hopes and Reality', *Journal of Economic Literature*, 24(4), pp. 1687–1737.

Kozma, G. (1981) 'The Role of the Exchange Rate in Hungary's Adjustment to External Economic Disturbances', in Hare, Paul *et al.*, *Hungary: A Decade of Economic Reform* (London: Allen & Unwin) pp. 205–220.

Lavigne, M. (1988) 'Comments on the Devaluation of the Rouble', (December) (manuscript).

Marczewski, K. (1988) 'Polityka realnego kursu walutowego w Polsce i Wegrzech w latach osiemdziesiatych', *Handel Zagraniczny*, 8, pp. 11–15, and 31.

Plowiec, U. (1988) 'Economic Reform and Foreign Trade in Poland', in Brada, J. C., Hewett, E. A. and Wolf, T. A. (eds), *Economic Adjustment and Reform in Eastern Europe and the Soviet Union: Essays in Honor of Franklyn D. Holzman* (Durham, N.C.: Duke University Press) pp. 340–69.

Portes, R. (1983) 'Central Planning and Monetarism: Fellow Travelers?', in Desai, P. (ed.), *Marxism, Central Planning, and the Soviet Economy* (Cambridge, Mass.: MIT Press) pp. 149–65.

Salgó, I. (1986) 'Economic Mechanism and Foreign Trade Organization in Hungary', *Acta Oeconomica*, 36(3–4) pp. 271–87.

Shagalov, G. (1988) 'Novy mekhanizm vneshneekonomicheskikh sviazei i mezhdunarodnogo sotrudnichestva', *Voprosy ekonomiki*, 5 pp. 138–48.

Somogyi, J. (1989) 'Hungary – Economic Reform' (manuscript).

Török, A. (1988) 'Stabilization and Reform in the Hungarian Economy of the Late 1980s' (manuscript).

Wolf, T. A. (1980) 'External Inflation, the Balance of Trade and Resource Allocation in Small Centrally Planned Economies', in Neuberger, E. and Tyson, L. D. (eds), *The Impact of International Economic Disturbances on the Soviet Union and Eastern Europe: Transmission and Response* (New York: Pergamon) pp. 63–87.

Wolf, T. A. (1985) 'Exchange Rate Systems and Adjustment in Planned Economies', International Monetary Fund, *Staff Papers*, 32(2) pp. 211–47.

Wolf, T. A. (1988a) *Foreign Trade in the Centrally Planned Economy*, vol. 27 in the series *Fundamentals of Pure and Applied Economics* (London: Harwood Academic Publishers).

Wolf, T. A. (1988b) 'Devaluation in Modified Planned Economies: A Preliminary Model for Hungary', in Brada, J. C., Hewett, E. A. and Wolf, T. A. (eds), *Economic Adjustment and Reform in Eastern Europe and the Soviet Union: Essays in Honor of Franklyn D. Holzman* (Durham, N.C.: Duke University Press) pp. 30–71.

Wolf, T. A. (1988c) 'The Simultaneity of the Effects of a Devaluation: Implications for Modified Planned Economies', *Acta Oeconomica*, 39(3–4) pp. 301–20.

Wolf, T. A. (1989) 'Economic Reform in Poland' (manuscript).

Note on Some Necessary Changes to Improve Trade of the USSR

Kazimierz Laski
UNIVERSITY OF LINZ AND VIENNA INSTITUTE OF
COMPARATIVE ECONOMIC STUDIES, AUSTRIA

The existing system of consumer goods prices is arbitrary and does not reflect scarcities. Even if increased imports could calm important sectors of the consumer goods market, the resulting equilibrium would not be adjusted to the expected reform of the wholesale prices. The latter, as we have learned from the paper of Professor Bornstein (Chapter 6 in this volume) and from the subsequent discussion, is in its present form not compatible with the idea of increasing the role of market forces in the economy; besides the implementation of the reform has been adjourned. The only reform of the price system which the Soviet economy indeed requires is to stop discussing price reforms and to introduce market-clearing prices, prices at which consumer as well as non-consumer goods are really available for the buyers instead of being more or less randomly distributed. The introduction of such prices would be a shock, first of all to the Soviet consumer. However, increased imports of western consumer goods could alleviate the shock caused by price liberalisation and would prove to the Soviet consumer that the reform means not only higher prices but the availability of goods too. This is preferable to increasing imports sooner, otherwise, the raised imports would mean only a short period of increased consumer satisfaction followed by a long and painful period of servicing the increased foreign indebtedness without improving the competitiveness of the country on the world market. This has been the case with the credit-financed short-lived consumption boom in Poland in the first half of the 1970s.

The USSR needs not only an additional supply of consumer goods but also a big shot of modern technology and know-how in many areas which are now underdeveloped. It needs at the same time an economic mechanism which is able to produce export goods, other than oil and some raw materials, which can be sold on western markets. The same applies to a still greater degree to other members of CMEA which are much more dependent on foreign trade and less rich in raw materials than the USSR. Indeed, foreign trade is the most important bottleneck in their further growth, especially for countries heavily indebted like Poland and Hungary.

This is perhaps the proper place to draw our attention to the poor performance of the CMEA countries in foreign trade. In a paper presented at a conference of the European Economic Association on 2–4 March 1988 in Hernstein (Austria) András Inotai compared manufactures exports of CMEA and developing countries, especially of the NICs, to the OECD countries. While total exports of manufactures to the OECD increased between 1975 and 1985 by 170 per cent, those of CMEA and of developing countries increased by 81 per cent and 394 per cent respectively. In the last group better than average results were achieved not only by such countries as Taiwan, South Korea, etc. but by Brazil (545 per cent) and Mexico (413 per cent), too. In 1985 total imports of manufactures of the OECD amounted to US\$ 829 bn. The corresponding exports of CMEA and developing countries represented US\$ 10 bn and 121 bn. South Korea alone (with US\$ 18 bn) exported almost twice as much as all CMEA countries together. Soviet exports (of US\$ 2.2 bn) were lower than those of the Philippines, and Czechoslovakia's exports (of US\$ 1.6 bn) were lower than those of Thailand.

Not only did the dynamics of manufactures exports of CMEA countries remain well behind that of developing countries, but the commodity pattern of their exports deteriorated too. Between 1975 and 1985 the share of chemicals and semi-manufactured goods in OECD imports declined from 39 per cent to 33 per cent, that is, by 6 percentage points. In the same period the corresponding share in exports of the CMEA increased from 48 per cent to 58 per cent, that is, by 10 percentage points while that of developing countries diminished from 39 per cent to 30 per cent, that is, by 9 percentage points. The same tendency manifested itself in the share of machinery and equipment. This share increased in the imports of OECD by 5 percentage points (from 44 to 49 per cent) and in the exports of developing countries by 10 percentage points (from 21 to 31 per cent) while it decreased in CMEA exports by 9 percentage points (from 28 to 19 per cent). Thus the developing countries were able not only to make better use of the opportunities offered by the growth of OECD demand but to adjust more efficiently to changes in the structure of demand. Inotai concludes that the socialist countries, as a group rated as the second industrialised world, have more and more become exporters of mass products of a low degree of processing and high material and energy intensity, of iron and steel instead of machines, of fertilisers instead of electronics and electrotechnical equipment (cf. Inotai, 1988, p. 190–5).

The different results of the CMEA on the one hand, and of developing countries, especially of the NICs, on the other, are the more remarkable because both groups pursued an active policy of strengthening their position in the world market, of imports of modern technology and of export promotion, of changes in the export structure toward manufactures, especially machines and equipment of an up-to-date technological standard. One of the reasons for the failure of this policy in the CMEA countries is the lack of initiative and creativity of individual firms, their inability to take risks, factors which are all present in the NICs basing their development on the existence of private ownership of means of production. The reforms in socialist countries consisting in the strengthening of market forces aim exactly at this weakness. It is not sure whether state-owned firms are able to achieve the same level of efficiency which is possible under private ownership, but only experience can give a definitive answer to this question.

There is still another conclusion to be drawn from the comparison between the achievements of the most successful NICs and the CMEA countries. The former did not simply follow the conclusions of the conventional theory of comparative advantage of the Ricardo and Heckscher–Ohlin type consisting in free trade policy. They rather concentrated on a factor which is missing in all these static theories, namely on technical progress. Luigi Pasinetti recently (1988) drew our attention to this factor. He gives an example of two countries: one developed, the other one underdeveloped, but both having exactly the same structure of prices. Under these conditions foreign trade in the pure form is not interesting for either country. Let us imagine, however, that labour productivity in the developed country is ten times higher than in the less-developed one. From the point of view of the latter country international trade linked with the process of learning from the former is an extremely interesting proposition. The main role of international interaction in this case lies not so much in the choice of an optimal point on the production possibility curve but predominantly in the shift of this curve outward from the origin of the coordinates system. Pasinetti concludes that the major and primary source of international gains is international learning, not international trade (cf. Pasinetti, 1988, p. 139–47). This is a rather fundamental proposition not only for less-developed countries but for socialist countries as well when they turn toward a more market-oriented economy.

Socialist countries are disappointed, and rightly so, by poor results of central planning. It seems, however, that sometimes they put too much hope on the healing forces of spontaneous market forces. The latter are important and absolutely necessary but a sound policy may and has to support (not replace) the market mechanism. It is said that Japan and the NICs follow two basic rules in their policy of choosing and supporting export-oriented industries: first, the chosen industries should be those which are the most promising from the point of view of expected rate of growth of labour productivity; as a rule these are young industries where the potential for further technical progress is still unexploited. Second, export promotion should concentrate on goods which are characterised by an expected high income elasticity of demand. These two rules have not much in common with the traditional theory of comparative advantage and with the postulate of state abstention from foreign trade. They seem, however, to deliver the results. Socialist market economies have to make a sound policy in several important respects. One of them (together with influencing the level of effective total demand) is export promotion (and import substitution) following the specified rules. The state support has to be strong enough to help the development of promising firms but not so strong as to let survive firms which cannot become after a while self-supporting. This is easier said than done. There exists, however, no other solution.

References

Inotai, Andras (1988) 'Competition Between the European CMEA and Rapidly Industrializing Countries on the OECD Market for Manufactured Goods,' *Empirica*, Austrian Economic Papers, 15 (1).

Pasinetti, Luigi (1988) 'Technical Progress and International Trade,' *Empirica*, Austrian Economic Papers, 15 (1).

Note on Poland

Urszula Płowiec
FOREIGN TRADE RESEARCH INSTITUTE, WARSAW,
POLAND

Professor Wolf has (in Chapter 10 in this volume) presented in a detailed manner the step-by-step evolution of centrally-planned economies into market-led economies, based on experience of east European countries. This deep analysis deserves to be attentively studied by countries which enter the way of transformation. In this analysis he stressed especially the link between the character of commodity prices and the devaluation of exchange rates.

As the changes in the Polish economy occur at present very fast, I would like to add some remarks on this subject, especially so since they lead to the growing interconnection between international markets and the Polish economy.

In the process of economic reform realised in Poland, one may distinguish three stages.

The first started in 1981–2 and included significant initial changes. Central directives in planning were abolished; enterprise concept was based on principles of self-dependence, self-financing and self-management; the autonomous price system was abolished and three categories of prices (official, regulated and freely determined between buyers and sellers) were introduced; uniform commercial exchange rates, one for the dollar area and one for CMEA, went into force; eleven branch ministries were merged into six; foreign trade rights could be already obtained by industrial enterprises, etc. But this stage proceeded more slowly than originally intended. The introduced changes were positive, but not numerous enough and too disjointed to have any visible impact on the functioning of the economy.

The second stage was initiated in 1986 (Xth Party Congress, July 1986) when it became obvious that it was necessary to accelerate the implementation of the reform programme and this time not only economically but also politically. Among these latter changes one should mention a more democratic election of members of parliament and, as a result, a more active role for parliament in the country's life; establishment of a State Tribunal and Constitutional Tribunal; formation of pluralistic advisory bodies (at the Sejm, at the State Council); establishment of the ombudsman's office and registration of many associations (about 2500).

The economic questions had two components: the acceleration of economic reform and the change of the plan for 1986–90. Initially the government was tending to treat economic reform instrumentally, that is as a process only of improving economic instruments, not linked to the provisions of the plan for 1986–90. Such an approach raised strong controversy.

The question of direction of economic reform was not so controversial. After some years of implementation of economic reform in Poland there was, in principle, consensus that the general idea was

- to liberalise enterprise and to stimulate entrepreneurship
- to increase the scope of market, and
- to aim at the convertibility of the Polish zloty.

This consensus emerged despite the fact that there is not – so far – any theory of economic reform in planned-economy countries. We think however, that rational pragmatism is quite a good idea and of sufficient compass.

In mid-1987 the detailed preliminary programme of sweeping reform was prepared. It aimed at the strengthening of strategic planning of the economy and at the evolutionary introduction of a product market as well as capital, foreign exchange and labour markets. After substantial discussion, the Sejm decided to push through a national referendum (29 November 1987) concerning the continuation of economic reform and the democratisation of political life. The moderately positive results of the referendum caused the revision of the economic reform programme, aiming at its slower implementation.

In February 1988 the massive regulation of wholesale and retail prices was accomplished in order to diminish subsidies and to improve relations between prices of foodstufs and other consumer goods. Large increases in prices (42–44 per cent was foreseen) and big automatic compensations (up to 36 per cent) by equivalent incomes caused a large spiral wave of wage increase. Some enterprises had no funds for this increase and in the beginning of May 1988 there were some strikes in Poland.

This situation was interpreted as need for accelerated realisation of large political and economic reform in Poland. This interpretation caused the change of government, a new Party approach to the problems of reforms and – in consequence – a new stage of reform.

From mid-1987 some important regulations and actions had already been undertaken and some others were in process.

By the end of 1987 branch ministries were merged into one Ministry of Industry. Besides, the Ministry of Internal Trade was joined with the Ministry of Material Supply and at present there is only one Ministry of Internal Market, dealing with consumer and producer goods. This change automatically increased the freedom of enterprises' activities.

At the same time other changes took place:

1. individual persons might already undertake, as agents, economic activity (except the sale of alcohol)
2. state enterprises might be transformed into companies with participation of the treasury and individuals; as a result workers can buy shares in the enterprises in which they work
3. a system of obligatory education of directors and their assistants was introduced; it is estimated that at least 15 per cent of directors in industrial enterprises should leave their posts
4. the initiation of activity by the Fund of Structural Changes in Industry, which can grant credits, subsidies or buy shares and bonds of enterprises producing modern, competitive commodities
5. substantial strengthening of regional councils; they have already become founding bodies for about half of all enterprises
6. the remuneration of directors includes constant (wage) and variable (bonus) parts; the latter depends on the relation of profit after taxation to the gross value of fixed capital plus stock; it is estimated that this bonus can as much as double wages
7. the liquidation of 33 enterprises, division of 284 enterprises and mergers of 10 economic units; besides during 1988 1596 companies were formed; the total number of socialised economic units grew in 1988 by 2800, while the number of private units (outside agriculture) increased by 45 000.

Many positive changes occurred in the field of foreign trade, which became the vanguard of economic reform. One should mention above all:

1. the active exchange rate policy; from mid-1987 a variable exchange rate policy was introduced and exchange rates are now changing every week in order to ensure the profitability of at least 75 per cent of exports both to convertible and non-convertible currency areas; so the exchange rate became the leading parameter in foreign trade decisions
2. the use of contractual prices based on export and import prices (except for oil, ores, cellulose and hides) in transactions between producers and exporters/ importers
3. a uniform subsidy to exported foodstuffs, separately settled in convertible (20 per cent) and non-convertible (50 per cent) currencies
4. establishment of more logical system of subsidies for industrial goods exported to free currency area
5. transformation of retention quota entitlements into retention quota accounts
6. establishment of the Export Development Bank on 1 January 1987; it actively promotes the development of current transactions as well as investment projects, in Polish zlotys and in hard currency.

Generally in 1986–88 the idea of export-oriented development of the country has gained large support.

The progressive inflation in 1988 (60 per cent, and still worsening the internal equilibrium) caused serious threat for the country's further development. In such a situation the Xth Party Plenum decided on deep reform of the party itself, the formation of a pluralistic society and the socialist market economy.

So the third stage of economic reform in Poland was initiated by the end of 1988. It is characterised by the fast, market-oriented changes and by the fast growth of inflation (76 per cent in January–February 1989 in comparison with the same period of 1988).

Among the most important economic changes introduced so far in this stage one should enumerate above all:

1. voting of the so-called economic constitution, that is, law equalising legal treatment of all sectors of the economy (state, cooperative, private) as regards taxes, subsidies, material supply, credits etc.; this law permits the undertaking of any economic activity by legal persons and individuals without being granted permission from any authorities (only registration is necessary);

private enterprises are allowed to employ unlimited numbers of workers; foreign trade activity also may be freely undertaken with some exceptions, which means the abolition of the foreign trade monopoly;

2. the amendment of the law on joint ventures with participation of foreign capital; it contains provisions on a three-year tax vacation period and then a 40 per cent rate of income tax; less than 51 per cent of state share in a company and even 100 per cent of foreign capital; and management by foreign partner;

3. the establishment since January 1989 of nine self-financing credit banks, making it possible for enterprises to choose credit banking;

4. the law on the financial system of state enterprises under which the enterprise pays dividend to the Treasury because of using state assets, which corresponds to the interest rate used in intra-bank relations;

5. a substantial change in the planning of imports from free currency areas; only 35 per cent of imports are paid from central funds and all the others are paid from retention quota accounts or due to purchases of currencies in auctions organised by three banks;

6. determination of basic interest rate of 44 per cent corresponding to a planned rate of inflation of 42–45 per cent;

7. the law on foreign exchange allowing free internal conversion of Polish zloty into dollars and vice versa, in banks and private counters (about 800 of such counters are foreseen);

8. the inclusion in the constitution of a new kind of property, that is, communal property;

9. the enactment of the law on bonds under which all enterprises (state, cooperative, mixed, private) are allowed to issue bonds, and legal persons as well as individuals are allowed to buy them;

So, as may be easily seen, the process of economic reform in Poland progresses from the concept of using market instruments to fulfil plan targets, through coexistence on equal footing of plan and market (hybrid system), to the socialist market economy, in which there is 'as much market as possible and as much plan as necessary'.

At present all kinds of markets are in the initial stage of development and are very imperfect, but it is largely admitted that Poland should aim at the introduction of commodities, foreign exchange, capital and labour markets. Ideological obstacles seem not to be the main barrier in this transformation. The problem is rather how to do it smoothly, that is, without hyperinflation and without a substantial decrease in the living standard of the population.

The transition from central management to the very large scope of market solutions in every economic sphere is inflationary and, as a result, the main problem is what kind of market should be pushed first, especially as the existing overindebtedness requires the maintenance of export surplus over imports, that is, it generates the permanent source of inflation. There is no experience in this field and there is not enough smart central regulation in this process. In consequence the reform is being realised in an assymetric way. Nevertheless, the preservation of an open economy policy is one of the characteristic features of this reform.

Part VI
Plan and Market in Developing Countries

11 Market Forces and Planning

Sukhamoy Chakravarty
DELHI SCHOOL OF ECONOMICS, UNIVERSITY OF
DELHI, INDIA

1 CHANGES IN THE ATTITUDE TO PLANNING

The role of market forces in the process of economic development
has been a central issue in development theory and planning for quite
a long time. However, the debate on market versus plan has gained
great contemporary interest because some of the earlier hopes enter-
tained about the efficiency of planning, especially centralised planning, as an instrument of social and economic transformation have
not been fulfilled by recent events. Clearly we have to learn from
experience and a rethinking on certain issues is called for. I have,
however, noticed that there is a great deal of impatience shown by
political authorities who would like to institute 'instant reforms' to
put an end to their current pressing difficulties, many of which result
from long-standing deficiencies of economic structure. When planning was recommended as a method of overcoming structural backwardness in countries such as India, emphasis was placed on the
ability of the planners to take a non-myopic view of the future, along
with ability to pool relevant information pertaining to different
sectors. In technical terms, the two major issues which planning was
expected to overcome were the sub-optimality of the savings rate and
the removal of 'secondary uncertainty'. Further, considerable importance was attached to the possibility that planning offers in mobilising
resources, such as surplus rural population or underemployed labour
in services. In principle, these putative advantages still remain relevant, especially in countries like India. Furthermore, considerable
improvements in information technology could have been expected
to strengthen the case of planning, as one of the major problems
facing the earlier generation of planners resulted from the fact that
costs of collecting information, processing them and subsequently

utilising them for policy making were often considerable. Earlier, the entire process was so time-consuming that certain aspects of economic reality which planners wanted to transform were liable to change, even before the corrective steps could be effectively implemented.

Things have improved on the range and availability of data yet the structural problems remain. How is it that we witness such widespread disenchantment with planning in many parts of the world? The issue deserves very serious consideration and the Conference on which this book is based was most welcome in focusing its attention on this crucial set of issues. It is interesting to note that the Conference was supposed to deal with market forces in planned economies. This implies an inversion of the normal terms of the debate which was generally described as the role of planning in enhancing the efficacy of the market mechanism and/or its ability to mitigate the adverse distributional implications of a market economy. There has been little doubt since the Second World War that many economies which were highly market-oriented, if not market dominated, adopted some form of planning. Keynesian economics demonstrated that the market may fail in a massive way. This recognition resulted in the acceptance of a full-employment norm in advanced capitalist countries along with certain correlated powers of implementation. In the 1980s, the move has been in the other direction. Centrally-planned economies have found virtues in the price mechanism which they have staunchly denied for a long time.

I believe that the present move is a healthy one provided we are trying to look at the issues from the angle of designing an economic system which combines the three basic desiderata of efficiency, equity and creativity. However, the present state of the debate is highly confused. It is not clear whether we are looking at what may be the allocative efficiency of the market or its creative role. Nor is it clear that, while criticising planning, we are not confusing excessive centralisation with 'planning'. All 'planning' has a systems orientation, but not all of them imply a very high degree of decentralisation. Further, there is little attempt to differentiate between historically specific and generic situations. Adam Smith is sometimes supposed to be making a wholly generic statement in favour of *laissez-faire*, when a closer reading would show that he was reacting against the mercantilist excesses which were such a prominent feature of many European economies in the eighteenth century. Similarly, Keynes (1946) talked in his posthumous essay on the US Balance of Payments about restoration of the vision of Adam Smith when countries would succeed in achieving and maintaining a high level of effective demand.

Thus, the dichotomy between Smith and Keynes may sometimes be overdrawn. Furthermore, questions of inequity are often connected with the exercise of effective economic power. While it is true that bureaucrats may often enjoy excessive amounts of power under certain systems of planning, the assumption that market economies are free from the contamination of 'power' is not warranted by any empirical evidence. Big monopolies and corporations can exercise enormous power with consequent effect on the distribution of incomes. Moreover, even under highly idealised conditions, the market outcomes cannot necessarily ensure even a reasonable distribution of incomes unless additional extraneous information is added. It appears to me that the present phase of disenchantment with planning and the corresponding enhancement of the allure of the market lie ultimately in a changed climate of opinion, being itself the product of certain specific historical experiences accumulated over the last forty years. It is necessary, therefore, that proper conceptualisation of what an economic system may be expected to perform in specific situations should be an essential component of contemporary research. This means that outcomes of specific intervention (or lack of them) should be studied in a time-dependent fashion, rather than in an extremely abstract setting. Such a procedure, however, does not negate the possibility of drawing certain general conclusions.

2   MEANING OF 'PLANNING' AND 'MARKET'

Basically I feel that much of the confusion that exists today in the on-going debate on market versus plan can be attributed to a lack of clarity in use of the terms. Taking the latter term first, I believe that the expression 'plan' should be understood primarily as a form of 'instrumental inference', an expression popularised by Adolph Lowe. It is similar to the concept of 'ratio duction' developed by Charles S. Pierce, the American philosopher of science. Lowe's use of the concept of planning as a system of inference is carefully distinct from the concept of planning as a command system, where the signalling function of prices is replaced by decisions taken in a hierarchical framework. While Lowe's primary purpose in his major book *On Economic Knowledge* (Lowe, 1977) was to put forward a concept of

'political economics' in place of 'traditional economics', his methodological ideas are, in my view, highly pertinent to the present discussions on economic reform. Much of the current debate revolves
around the idea that primacy ought to be given to the price mechanism over command systems. However, Lowe has critically examined
the postulational basis of supply–demand analysis which forms the
centrepiece of the price mechanism, whose operational limitations
are generally hidden in the axiomatics of general equilibrium
analysis.[1] His principal thesis has been that the replacement of the
supply–demand model is long overdue in an environment where
atomistic postulates along with extremum principles hold with severe
qualifications. However, Lowe's solution, to replace the traditional
model by 'political economics', raises several issues, which cannot be
discussed here in detail. It is, however, possible to suggest that
'political economics' serves as a useful vantage point from which one
can view planning as a form of instrumental inference. Let us first
define the term 'instrumental inference'. Such an inference, according to Lowe consists, first of 'derivation of one or more paths which
can transform the initial states into desired terminal states'. While the
derivation of the transition path is a necessary first step, based in
large part on structural requirements, it has to be supplemented by
establishing *behavioural* patterns which will set the system on 'goal-
adequate trajectories'. It can be maintained that while planners have
often paid some attention to the first task, that is, setting of terminal
goals, although often on a highly optimistic basis, relatively little
attention has been paid to the second. Furthermore, as in any
complex inference, certain mediate steps have to be carefully articu-
lated, including possible non-fulfilment of expectations, because of
various forms of uncertainty. However, it is possible to maintain that
in favourable political circumstances, planners can, in principle, do a
far better job of goal setting, including alternative scenarios than they
have generally done. While this failure on the part of the planners
may reflect both technical and political limitations, it is not at all clear
how the 'market' by itself can do a better job. I believe, however,
that extreme advocates of the market mechanisms will give up any
pretence of societal goal setting and treat 'equilibrium' as the immanent norm. This position is, however, highly questionable from the
philosophical point of view.

In my opinion, when one talks about greater reliance on the
'market mechanism', it would be more appropriate to talk about

specifying goal-adequate behaviour sustaining what can be called transitional paths, consistent with the terminal goals as envisaged by the policy makers and planners. This does not imply that one should abandon 'planning' as an instrument of inference. What is needed is a redefinition of its scope. I believe, that a return to '*laissez-faire*' will be a non-solution for big countries like China and India, or for that matter, Bangladesh, for the simple reason that demographic pressures in these countries threaten the continued viability of the system. The concept of 'viability' is a key notion that neoclassical theorists of market mechanism do not generally discuss. In fact, I believe than an over excessive preoccupation with short-term problems posed by demand–supply imbalances may lead attention to be deflected from the long-term structural determinants of a system of 'expanded reproduction'. While the latter notion needs extension to include ecological factors neglected in more classical formulations, attempts are being currently made to incorporate these dimensions. I can mention, in particular, the work by Charles Perrins (1987) and Bertram Schefold (1985), who approach the problem from a Sraffian perspective.

What are the components of goal-adequate behaviour? Turning back to Adam Smith, one can discern the relative emphasis on *directly productive* activities as against *rent-maximising* activities. There is an extensive literature on this class of issues in the context of developing economies, notably that of Krueger (1974) and Bhagwati (1982), whose argument is basically directed towards demonstrating that non-functional restrictions imposed by a regulatory state may end up in distorting the incentive patterns, especially through rigging prices, to the detriment of the process of capital accumulation. Sometimes, this approach has been applied in explaining the slow growth performance of the Indian economy as contrasted with that of South Korea. The basic point in many of these arguments is that state intervention invariably tends to alter the distribution of income in a manner which produces adverse effects on the growth of socially desired baskets of goods and services. No one can deny that some forms of state intervention do produce such effects. However, the basic question is whether a market system can always provide the needed set of signals. It is useful to recall that the main criticism of Frederick List against the free market system advocated by the classical school was that it attached too much importance to 'production' and too little to 'productive power' (List, 1966). List postulated protection to insulate the domestic manufacturing sector in order to provide time for learning. Even John Stuart Mill, an ardent proponent of classical thought, considered government intervention to promote 'learning by doing' as a good thing. It is, of course, true that the 'learning process' did not materialise to the desired extent in many developing countries even with protection. While government policies can and do help in promoting technical change, their impact in different regions or among different sectors could be uneven and this can lead to several undesirable consequences for the pattern of income distribution, some of which might not even have been anticipated. In short, the basic point is that when major structural changes are contemplated, goal-adequate behaviour may very well include scope for price as well as non-price mechanisms. What form the latter should take, that is, whether a regulatory framework or public ownership, is an issue which can be decided only in the light of the specific characteristics of a given situation.

I am also not fully convinced by the Krueger (1974) argument on rent-seeking, as it is not clear to me that 'without restriction, entrepreneurs would seek to achieve windfall gains by adopting new technology, anticipating market shifts correctly, and so on'. In other words, Krueger's argument seems to imply that all distortions are exogenous or policy-induced, and are not related to the structural properties of the particular economies. This argument also seems to suggest that resources can be shifted around costlessly or that non-distortionary forms of taxation can be pursued to the required extent by the governments. In the context of many developing countries, these are extravagant assumptions indeed. In short, while the planning process has to provide for incentive-adequate devices, the 'market' cannot be relied upon solely as an instrument for development in structurally backward economies. I may also point out in this context that Ishikawa (1985), in his recent analysis of Chinese economic reform, has also arrived at the same conclusion that the 'market adjustment process' cannot become a complete substitute for what he calls 'state economy', although his analysis runs on the lines of Hicks's distinction between a 'customary economy', 'state economy' and 'market economy' (Hicks, 1969).

I would also like to make some brief comments on the term 'market', which permits several interpretations. One can view it as a coordinating system, or in the language of cybernetics as a 'servomechanism'. It can also be perceived as an expression of an economic system based on 'consumer's sovereignty' judged as an ultimate value in itself. The first interpretation of the market can with some justification be regarded as an implementational one in the sense that it is not necessarily inconsistent with planning as a mode of 'instrumental inference'. In other words, it is perfectly possible to allow the macro-goals of a system and the principal action directives to flow from a properly formulated plan, while its micro-analogues can be left to be determined through the market. Some economists may not agree with this proposition, but I believe that the difference of opinion will disappear once a clear-cut distinction is made between the market mechanism as an efficiency promoting device and the 'market' as a process which has to be valued in itself. A large amount of literature has grown on this topic, but much of the discussion on this issue is, in my view, efficiency-oriented. This includes the contribution of Hayek, the most philosophically-minded of conservative economists. Hayek has been partly responsible for the recent revival of a market-oriented philosophy, although he does raise many epistemological issues as well in his Nobel lecture, 'The Pretence of Knowledge' (Hayek, 1974). However, it is not clear to me that 'planning' as a strategy can be easily dismissed on the grounds of efficiency, especially in the presence of non-convexities and uncertainty. It is true that market-led growth patterns have proved themselves efficient in some cases, but this has not been without certain significant side effects, besides being historically quite specific. On the other hand, if it is argued that 'planning' has exacerbated dualism in many developing countries, then such a situation is not always the inevitable result of planning, but it is rather the product of lack of *appropriate* planning.

3   THE CASE OF INDIA

It would be useful to give a certain degree of 'concreteness' by taking the case of India which I have tried to discuss elsewhere in somewhat greater detail (Chakravarty, 1987). Indian planning has been treated with a great deal of scepticism, if not downright hostility, by those who believe in the virtues of the market mechanism. In contrast, the so-called market-led economies of east Asia have been held up for general emulation. As I see it, there are certain major institutional differences, apart from the size of the countries, which cannot be ignored in carrying out these comparisons. We should not forget that political institutions prevalent in these countries have been very different from the ones prevailing in India, during the last forty or so years. Secondly, because of external interventions, certain changes were carried out in the areas of land reforms in these economies which have proved highly significant in determining the shape of subsequent course of economic events. Thirdly, the total real inflow of resources from the outside world into these smaller-sized countries has formed an extremely significant part of their recent experience, especially during the period when they switched their economic regime from an inward-looking to an export-oriented strategy.

These differences have resulted in the initial creation of a home market which allowed for certain product developments on an import substituting basis which could later be turned over towards export expansion when the subsequent circumstances so warranted. Furthermore, the relationship between wages and productivity was maintained in an authoritarian way to ensure competitiveness in the international markets. Thus, even if one were to rule out specific cultural and geographical characteristics of these countries, one can see that market mechanism was an instrument of ensuring the achievement of certain rational goals which the elite of these countries had set for themselves, or were perhaps obliged to accept.

In the Indian case, only the initial phase of land reform was carried out which resulted in removing non-functional intermediaries in rural societies but the Congress slogan 'land to the tiller' was not implemented. Rural inequality in the initial distribution of resources has affected adversely the efficiency of existing resource use as well as innovation proneness, with the exception of those areas which were institutionally dominated by a tradition of peasant proprietorship. Secondly, political democracy has allowed not merely for a full freedom of expression, assembly and party function, goals which are highly valuable in themselves, but it has also led to the fact that government has found it necessary to distance itself from management in the private corporate sector while at the same time serving as wage leader in the enterprises it has set up on its own. This has affected the process of generation of investible surplus in a manner already foreseen by Indian planners in their analysis of labour problems of a mixed economy. Thirdly, while for a relatively short period, India did receive a significant net inflow of resources from abroad, even though they were miniscule when adjusted for India's huge population, India had to manage its investment requirements very largely from domestic resources. The Indian economy has been constrained by foreign exchange for the most part. While some would maintain that planning itself has been largely responsible for such a situation, there has been little or no attempt to substantiate it on the basis of any worthwhile numerical analysis.

These days, proponents of the market have been arguing forcefully for a retreat of the state from major economic activities and allowing the private sector to assume the 'commanding heights', a reversal of the slogan of the mid-1950s. While there are no eminent proponents of the 'minimal state' argument in India and there is considerable evidence of inefficiency of some government-run industries, there is as yet little evidence that any public consensus exists on the extent to which India can reshape its agrarian institutions or would succeed in attracting foreign capital on relatively favourable terms. In fact, arguments put forward by leading political groups are highly contradictory, as even a cursory glance at the current Indian debates would show quite conclusively.

Meanwhile, there are certain objective facts as well as tendencies which no dispassionate observer can overlook. First of all, the growing demographic pressure poses serious problems for the future viability of the material reproductive basis, which requires provision as well as corrective action. Secondly, given the worldwide trend towards the adoption of a new generation of technology which is highly labour-saving, not only in manufacturing but also in services, and also the fact that there is nothing in the market economy to substantiate the point that there is an automatic and swift compensation mechanism, greater provision of employment opportunities either through new investment or through new training of labour are issues which loom large on the agenda of the State. Thirdly, development studies of recent years have shown very conclusively the great importance that human beings, if they are properly educated, nourished, housed and motivated, can play, not merely in promoting and in ensuring efficient utilisation of existing material resources, but also in expanding the resource base. Condemned to live a short and precarious existence, the same human beings can improve or worsen the situation and can bring about catastrophic changes.

Planning is necessary in this situation to take care of at least three sets of issues: (a) to ensure a sustainable natural environment; (b) to facilitate the rapid spread of education and technical knowledge along with access to basic health services; and (c) to adopt, adapt and innovate technological advances which can make effective use of the large resources of manpower. All this would imply that we have to map out an appropriate strategy of development. This obviously requires a coordinated societal response, of which classical forms of planning provide one example, but there can be scope for other forms of cooperative action. At the same time, given the argument about the dispersed character of information and also the high cost of collecting information which may become obsolete by the time it is available, we have to place greater emphasis on *market forces* in areas where quick adjustments are called for. Furthermore, we cannot ignore the fact that where 'quality' of information is more important than 'quantity', a consideration which seems to have been ignored in some of the earlier discussions on plan versus market, we must allow for greater creative initiatives to be assumed by individuals or sections of them. As Kaldor would have put it, for these purposes the creative role of the market is very important, a point of view which was fully appreciated by Joseph Schumpeter, but does not form a part of textbook versions of general equilibrium analysis.

We have to replace the earlier overdrawn distinction between plan and market by a notion of strategic planning with greater initiative for marketers, even if we do not share the Panglossian philosophy of some contemporary neo-liberal economists. It may be useful to recall in conclusion that Oscar Lange, who played a major part in the debate on the rationality of socialist planning during the famous debate in the 1930s took a somewhat similar position later in the 1940s when he wrote an important review of the book by H. D. Dickinson, *The Economics of Socialism* (Lange, 1942). Lange wrote that he found himself in complete agreement with Dickinson, who took the view that planning was not a rival but complementary to the price system. I believe that much useless controversy as well as unfruitful experimentation can be avoided if the full logic of this position can be comprehended.

To sum it up in systems theoretic language, we may need multiple feedbacks, positive as well as negative, in reaching our objectives of structural transformation in 'backward' countries. This is both an issue for future research as well as a conclusion of our experience.

Note

1. See also Kornai (1971) for a similar exercise.

References

Bhagwati, J. (1982) 'Directly Unproductive Profit-seeking Activities', *Journal of Political Economy*, 90, pp. 988–1002.

Chakravarty, S. (1987) *Development Planning: The Indian Experience* (Oxford: Oxford University Press).

Hayek, F. A. (1974) 'The Pretence of Knowledge', Nobel Memorial Lecture delivered at Stockholm (11 December 1974); reprinted in *New Studies* (London: Routledge & Kegan Paul, 1978).

Hicks, J. R. (1969) *A Theory of Economic History* (Oxford: Oxford University Press).

Ishikawa, S. (1985) 'Socialist Economy and the Experience of China – A Perspective on Economic Reform', A. Eckstein Memorial Lecture, Ann Arbor: University of Michigan (mimeo).

Keynes, J. M. (1946) 'The Balance of Payments of the United States', *Economic Journal*, LVI (222) (June).

Kornai, J. (1971) *Anti-Equilibrium: on Economic Systems Theory and the Tasks of Research* (Amsterdam: North-Holland).

Krueger, A. O. (1974) 'The Political Economy of Rent Seeking Activities', *American Economic Review*, 64, pp. 291–303.

Lange, Oscar, (1942) 'Review of H. D. Dickinson "The Economics of Socialism"', *Journal of Political Economy*, pp. 209–303.

List, F. (1966) 'The National System of Political Economy', (published in German in 1841) (New York: Augustus M. Kelley) Reprints of Economic Classics.

Lowe, A. (1977) *On Economic Knowledge* (New York: M. E. Sharpe) 2nd edn.

Perrins, Charles, (1987) *Economy and Environment* (Cambridge: Cambridge University Press).

Schefold, B. (1985) 'Ecological problems as a challenge to Classical and Keynesian Economics', *Metroeconomica*, 37, pp. 21–61.

12 Market Development in Chinese Economic Reform

Dong Fureng

INSTITUTE OF ECONOMICS, CHINESE ACADEMY
OF SOCIAL SCIENCES, BEIJING

China is a socialist developing country. As a socialist country, China is faced with the task of reforming the traditional socialist economic system; as a developing country, she is confronted with the task of economic development (including the development of the political system, culture, science and technology, and social structures). These two task are interrelated. The past decade has witnessed important achievements in China's economic systems reform, but complex problems remain to be solved. This paper reflects on some of these problems in China's economic reform in which a developing socialist country is in a period of transition from a product economy which rejects the market mechanism to a commodity (or market) economy.

1 NEW OPERATIONAL ECONOMIC MODELS

The traditional socialist economic system is a highly centralised one which rejects the market mechanism. Although it might claim some achievements during the initial stage of China's industrialisation, the development of the economy, higher and diversified needs of the people, new industrial and technological revolutions elsewhere and closer economic relations between nations thereafter made the defects of the system more conspicuous and serious. These defects were highlighted by the extravagant use of resources, poor economic efficiency, slow progress of science and technology, commodity shortages, inadequate provision of services, unsatisfactory improvement in living standards and the increasing incapability to meet the higher needs of the people. Consequently, Chinese economists eventually

240

abandoned traditional socialist economic theories which maintained that socialism was incompatible with the market mechanism. Instead, there emerged the concept that the socialist economy is a planned commodity economy. Despite wide differences on various details, there is a consensus that the socialist economy cannot (or cannot completely) exclude markets. Based on this recognition, three economic models have been proposed.

The model of planning supported by market regulation

In this model, the economy is essentially subject to mandatory planning. The market, as an auxiliary instrument, would play a limited regulatory role in less important economic activities, such as exchanges of residual products between farmers after their own household consumption is met, and production and exchange of certain less important industrial consumer goods which are of lower value but which exist in hundreds of thousands of varieties. Some people believe that this model is not a solution to current problems since there are no fundamental changes in the mechanism through which a country regulates its economy. At present, few people still cling to this model.

The model of the dual-track system (parallel regulation through the mandatory plan and the market)

According to this model, economic activities would be grouped into three parts. The first group of activities would be regulated by the mandatory plan, covering the most important activities such as key state construction projects as well as the production and distribution of major producer and consumer goods. Mandatory planning of these activities would be retained although appropriate reduction in scope would be needed. The second part would be subject to indicative planning. That is to say, plan targets are referential or for guidance, with their implementation effected through the use of economic levers by the state. The market mechanism would play a regulatory role *but* under state control. This group of activities should be expanded to an appropriate extent. The third part would be completely under market regulation and would include residual products of farmers, less important industrial consumer goods and some services. Actually, the Chinese economy is presently operating under this dual-track system. Some economists (including the author) are of the view that this system is of a transitional nature and should not be regarded as the target model in the reform of economic mechanisms, although others believe that it should. An economy operating on a dual track is bound to run into frictions and chaos. Enterprise behaviour in such an economy is also characterised by duality: enterprises are eager to get inputs allocated by the state at low controlled prices while ready to sell more products at the market at higher market prices. The dual track system can only be transitional.

The model of the regulated market (state regulation of market and market guidance of enterprises) as described in the decision of the Thirteenth Congress of the Chinese Communist Party

In this model, the mandatory planning would eventually be phased out. Indirect control by the state would be realised through regulation of the market through economic parameters. The effects of such regulation would be transmitted through the market to enterprises. The market in turn would act as the belt to link enterprises with the state, with other enterprises and with other members of society. This model has been adopted as the policy target for China's reform of the economic mechanism. The Chinese economy should move in this direction from the present dual-track system. Many economists are in favour of this model, but opinions diverge widely about methods of its implementation.

Three sets of reforms are needed in order to move the economy towards the model of state regulation of the market and the market guidance of enterprises: first, a shift from direct control and regulation by the state to indirect instruments; second, establishment and improvement of markets; and third, transformation of state enterprises into independent and self-sustaining actors in the market, which accept the rules and regulations of the market.

These reform requirements were set forth in the Seventh Five Year Plan (1986–90) which also called for the foundation of the new economic system to be laid down during the plan period. However, in practice reforms since then have encountered countless difficulties.

2   GENERAL FEATURES OF MARKET DEVELOPMENT

To realise 'state regulation of the market and market guidance of enterprises', the establishment and development of markets are indispensible. Without the market, and without developed and properly organised markets in particular, there can be neither effective regulation of the economy through the market mechanism nor effective indirect control of enterprises through market intermediation by the state. Thanks to the reforms of the past decade, the market is taking shape and is playing a bigger role in regulating the economy. In 1987, the number of goods under the mandatory plan of the State Planning Commission dropped from over 120 in 1984 to about 60, and their share in the gross industrial output value of the nation decreased from 40 per cent to about 20 per cent. In the same year, the number of materials allocated by the state materials supply authorities dropped from 256 (in 1984) to 20, and commodities under the plan of the Ministry of Commerce were reduced from 180 to 22. The share of steel products under central allocation decreased to 47.1 per cent while that of cement, timber and coal dropped to 15.6, 27.6 and 47.2 per cent respectively. As the scope of mandatory planning in the spheres of production, distribution and supply has become smaller, the commodity economy is developing and expanding. In price reform, the share of products subject to floating and market-determined prices has also increased; for agricultural products, it is 65 per cent, for industrial consumer goods, 55 per cent, and for producers' goods, 40 per cent.

Along with the expanding role of the market in price formation, price is becoming an effective instrument in market regulation of the economy and in resource allocation. The embryonic markets for capital, labour, technology and housing are growing. Securities exchanges, foreign exchange regulatory centres and markets for enterprise mergers have been set up in some cities such as Shanghai (securities exchange) and Wuhan (mergers). Economic activities of rural households and urban industrial firms are increasingly market-oriented. The share in the national economy of collectives, private and individual firms, the wholly foreign-owned and foreign joint ventures – all firms subject to the market direction – is increasing. In 1987, their share in the total value of social retail sales reached 61.5 per cent, and that of industrial output value rose to 40.3 per cent. Even the state sector has seen more and more of its activities become market-oriented. The market is clearly playing an increasingly important role in regulating the Chinese economy.

The market, however, cannot become fully developed within a short span of time in an economically backward country such as China. It is bound to be a long-term process. The market in China is still in a rudimentary stage. This is evident in the following features:

1. At present, the major market is primarily a product market, especially for consumer goods. A large proportion of producer goods is not traded in the market, although there is progress in this direction. The author has the impression that about 50 per cent of agricultural products are not transacted on the market. Factor markets for capital and labour are just beginning to take form.

2. The product market is essentially a spot market. There is no futures market, although efforts are being made to experiment with it.

3. Cheques and bills are hardly used in market transactions. The use of bank credit, while progressing, is still at the elementary stage and commercial and consumer credit remain untapped.

4. The market is operating on a limited scale only. Small and isolated markets predominate. It is far from a unified national market.

5. The organisational structure of the market is crude, with rules yet to be established. Although the number of economic contracts rose from 300 million in 1983 to 1 billion in 1987, default cases showed an even faster increase. For instance, defaults as proportional to the number of contracts signed in 1987 were 14 per cent by state enterprises, 55 per cent by collectives, 2 per cent by foreign joint ventures, and 22 per cent by individual-run firms (including rural households) (*World Economic Herald*, 1988). Of bank loans, 10 per cent cannot be paid back or be repaid on time. Since the rules of the game are yet to be established in the market, the deregulation of administrative control leads to serious chaos. Some institutions, firms and individuals have thus made windfall profits. The development of the market for producers' goods is an example. Some have capitalised on the immature nature of the wholesale market for these goods in short supply with prices skyrocketing. For example, the state price for urea was RMB 410 per ton but its market price was as high as RMB 1300 per ton. Similar examples can be found in the price movements of steel and other products.

6. Serious imbalances exist in the regional development of markets. A few markets in the coastal areas (e.g., Pearl River Delta) already show certain features of a developed modern market. The majority, however, is still crude and undeveloped. Markets are either non-existent or assume medieval forms in the economic

backwaters (most of the rural areas in China have only regular country fairs).

7. Mechanisms through which the market functions, such as competition and pricing, remain to be developed. As obstacles on factor mobility between sectors and regions exist, it is difficult for competition to develop.

8. The domestic market is loosely linked with the international market. There are huge discrepancies between domestic and international prices. This has adverse effects on domestic production and external trade. Petroleum products which would be highly profitable in international price terms can hardly recover their costs because of domestic price distortions.

These defects and the slow pace of market development in China may be attributed to the underdevelopment of the economy and systemic problems. The next section discusses these problems.

3   CONSTRAINTS OF UNDER-DEVELOPMENT

The constraints imposed by economic underdevelopment on market development have been underestimated and even neglected in the reform process. This is reflected in the requirement to establish a sound market system during the Seventh Five Year Plan period. People used to believe that the removal of institutional barriers to the development of a commodity economy could automatically lead to the formation and development of the market. Some Chinese economists have rightly pointed out that without price deregulation, that is, if administrative and arbitrary pricing do not give way to market determination of prices, there will be no market formation. However, they believe that once prices are deregulated, the market can grow on its own account. Reform practices tell us that the world is not as simple as that.

Their assumption has proved valid in some relatively economically advanced coastal areas (such as the Pearl River and Yangtze River deltas) which have a buoyant commodity economy and closer ties with the international market. Since market-oriented reforms began, these areas have undergone rapid market development although many problems remain. In other and much larger areas, market growth has been restricted by economic underdevelopment.

In these regions, particularly West China (both the Northwest and the Southwest), the mountainous areas and rural areas generally, the predominant characteristic is that of a natural or semi-natural economy. Social division of labour is yet to develop. The inevitable journey from a natural economy to a commodity economy still lies ahead. People are ready to exchange their products only when there are surpluses. In the past decade, some regions, especially the coastal areas, have experienced rapid expansion of non-agricultural industries which serve as the driving force of market development there. In comparison, the development of such industries has been particularly difficult in other areas. Economic backwardness obstructs market development, while the absence of the latter in turn poses obstacles to economic development. Market formation and development in China will be a long process. It will be completed when the natural or semi-natural economy is transformed into the commodity economy. Economic systems reform can remove institutional obstacles to the transformation and hence accelerate the process, but they can by no means replace it. The journey to a well-developed and modern market system is even longer. Furthermore, it cannot be completed without the economic and social modernisation of the country.

Another major constraint to market development in China is the backward transport and communications systems. In 1986, railway physical density and traffic physical density were 54.7 km per 10 000 sq km and 0.10 km per 1000 sq km respectively, compared with the United States level of railway density of 268 km per 10 000 sq km in 1984 and traffic density of 0.68 km per 1000 sq km in 1983. In this regard, India, another large developing country has a more extensive transport system than China: India's railway density was 206 km per 10 000 sq km in 1984 while its traffic density was 0.55 km per 1000 sq km in 1979 (*China Statistics Abstracts*, 1987).

In China, products cannot flow between regions because of poor transport facilities and services. For example, citrus products rot away in Sichuan because there is no means to transport them out of the province. In 1988, many places suffered serious pork shortages, yet the meat was piling up in Sichuan. Similarly, while others were waiting anxiously for coal, Shanxi, the coal mine of China, felt itself unable to expand capacity because of the same problem. The incapability of some areas to develop a commodity economy is due to the underdevelopment of the transport sector. Even in Wenzhou, Zhejiang province, one of China's most advanced regional commodity economies, there are places (mainly mountainous areas) where only processing industries that produce locally consumed goods (e.g., bean curds) can develop because of the limited size of the market due to transport constraints. The poorly developed communications system has played an equally negative role. The fragmentation of markets is closely linked with the underdevelopment of these systems. It takes time for a uniform national market to emerge and develop.

Old values embedded in underdeveloped economies are another set of obstacles to market development. Life in a self-sufficient natural economy several thousand years old has taught many Chinese to look down on commercial activities. Wenzhou and Jinhua are neighbours in south Zhejiang province, yet farmers in the two areas are worlds apart in their attitude towards commercial activities and non-agricultural industries. Wenzhou farmers have historically been known as adventurous and imaginative. They go out in large groups when there is not much to do in the fields. Almost everywhere, people can see Wenzhou farmers around, working as carpenters or fluffing cotton with a bow. Some have even gone abroad to try their luck. This entrepreneurship was stifled under the old planning system but rekindled once reforms started. Soon, specialised markets that are among the largest in China emerged in some Wenzhou towns, such as markets for garment buttons, low voltage appliances, clothes made of synthetic fabrics and badges. Buttons sold in Qiao Tou market meet 50 per cent of the total demand of the national apparel industry. Every day, about 4000 to 5000 people flock to the market, buying and selling buttons. Just next door to Wenzhou, Jinhua farmers looks down at doing such business. Their objective is a stable life, having enough to eat and wear. They stick to the land. They are afraid of being seen as rich as this might invite gossip and jealousy. In a county in Xinjiang (autonomous region), apples rot in orchards. No one dares travel the 2 km to the county town market for fear of loosing face. To them, street peddlers and market traders are dishonest species. Their philosophy is 'as long as one can survive, one should not downgrade himself to industrial or commercial activities' (*People's Daily*, 1988). This attitude towards commercial activities, indeed the concept and values of thousands of years, has seriously obstructed the development of a commodity economy and the market and can be gradually discarded only through economic development.

A poorly developed social structure is a third obstacle to market development. The adaptation of the social structure to a market economy cannot be achieved overnight.

To sum up, in a developing country like China, it is imperative to remember the obstacles to marketisation posed by economic as well as political, social and cultural underdevelopment. Market development is a historical process that can be completed only over time. The market will grow and mature in the transition from a natural economy to a commodity economy and in the expansion of the latter. The development of a modern market has to be realised in tandem with economic, political, scientific and technological and cultural modernisation in China.

4   OWNERSHIP AND THE PROPER FUNCTIONING OF THE MARKET

In China, market development and the adoption of an indirect macromanagement mechanism in which the state regulates the market and the market guides enterprises have encountered unexpectedly formidable obstacles which this paper can describe only in broad terms.

Market development is directly linked to the transformation of the government's function, that is, a shift from mainly direct control over the economy by the government to mainly indirect regulation by the market. As mentioned above, over the past decade of reforms government functions have changed to certain extent, with a reduction in the scope of central mandatory planning and in the number of products under central allocation. Thanks to reforms which decentralised the central government's fiscal power, enterprises now have retained profits. In 1987, the retention rate of state enterprises was 17.5 per cent of their gross profits, and 33.7 per cent of net profits (*China Economic Yearbook*, 1988). Some authority has been delegated to enterprises, such as autonomy in production planning and sales.

Despite all these, state enterprises still remain subordinate to government agencies and are subject to government interference. Ministries are still responsible for the allocation of 300 different categories of materials, the production of 900 products under mandatory plans and 1200 products under indicative planning. Decentralisation has brought about less interference from the centre. But there is no corresponding change in the behaviour of local authorities. Mandatory plans of local authorities have become larger, and some indicative targets have become mandatory. Investigations reveal that of mandatory targets given to enterprises, 38 per cent came from provincial governments. A level lower, municipal authorities add their own mandatory targets. Although mandatory targets from the centre to Shanghai account for 18 per cent of the city's industrial output value, major products of Shanghai, particularly those of the metallurgical, textile and machinery sectors, are without exception under the mandatory plan. Even their 'above-plan' output is subject to the mandatory plan (*People's Daily*, 1987).

This situation has gravely impeded market development. As enterprises cannot solve their problems through the market, they turn to the government. According to a survey of 170 enterprise managers in Liaoning province, 63 managers, that is, 37 per cent of the interviewees, complained about too few mandatory targets (*Statistics*, 1987). This is because mandatory targets bring with them mandatory allocations for low-priced inputs. Why it is so difficult for the government to change its function? Apart from state enterprise behaviour and performance (to be dealt with later in this paper), there are several other factors.

China's political system reform has lagged behind its economic reform. As executives at lower level of the government hierarchy, enterprise managers have to listen to their supervisors, and their organisations are yet to be separated from the government. This political relationship between leaders and subordinates has to be rooted out. Otherwise, it is hard to foresee any fundamental change in government functions. No authorities would like to have their authority weakened as power always brings with it privileges.

Under the present system of central–local fiscal relationships, local authorities have their own fixed incomes and proportions of central revenues. This system has intensified local government interests in securing higher incomes through tightened control over local enterprises.

As the market is growing only slowly, its constraints on enterprise behaviour are ineffective. State enterprises remain insensitive to the rules and signals of the market. Chaos is commonplace. The government is reluctant to slacken its interference in economic activities on the pretext of avoiding a regulation vacuum. It is only natural for government agencies to go back to direct controls that have often proved efficient after chaos. This is a vicious circle in the Chinese reform: there is no formation and development of the market when the government still relies on direct control; but without the market, the government is unable or unwilling to give up direct control and interference. This explains why the past decade has seen the recurrence of cycles of deregulation and retrenchment. China has yet to break up this circle.

Market development is also related to whether state enterprises can gear their activities to market movements. An enterprise in a market environment is at the same time an actor and a recipient of regulation. Therefore, it has to be autonomous and self-sustaining. Complete autonomy in management has not been realised, as illustrated above. Self-sustainability has been realised to an even lesser extent. Actually, it is difficult for state enterprises to become self-sustaining under the ambiguous property relations of state ownership.

State enterprises as they now stand are not actors and recipients of market regulation. They, especially those under mandatory planning, cannot make their own decisions in accordance with market movements. They are not motivated to compete. They cannot make appropriate responses to market signals. Nor can the market impose hard constraints on their activities. As state enterprises in such a status account for a significant proportion of the economy, it is difficult for the market to grow and operate properly. Therefore, indirect regulation and control by the government in the past fell short of the expected objectives. The government has had to return to some direct control measures when indirect control failed. Government authorities tried to control the excess demand of enterprises for funds through interest rates, but in the end inflation cropped up. This is because enterprises were not at all concerned about interest repayments and local authorities could hardly suppress their impulse for economic expansion. As indirect control proved ineffective, the government resorted to administrative cutbacks in fixed investment and credit. This is also true with attempted changes in pricing and management of commercial activities. This is the situation that besets China at the moment.

The enterprise reform which enables enterprises to become autonomous and self-sustaining is a key factor for the Chinese economy to move into a market system. In other words, this is what the author has termed as an issue of how to make public ownership compatible with the market mechanism. It is a difficult question of historic significance for any socialist country undergoing reforms. If no answer is found, efforts to establish a new economic system operated by a regulated or guided market mechanism will be abortive. In the absence of an answer, socialist countries undergoing reforms are afflicted with numerous difficulties, such as loss of control on investment and consumption, price spirals and economic disorder. The issue is particularly difficult for a developing country like China, as the country is faced not only with the aforementioned problems in state enterprise reform, but also with barriers to market development.

To facilitate a solution to the problem, the author believes that there is a scheme that could be functional.

First, except for political and social justifications or in strategic sectors and natural monopolies where state ownership should be maintained, enterprises in other sectors should be turned to private ownership (in the case of some small state enterprises) or collective ownership. More enterprises may be put under the joint-stock system of mixed ownership.

Second, a multiple ownership structure should be developed. Public ownership should assume more than one form, including collective ownership, cooperative ownership and various forms of mixed ownership as well as state ownership. Apart from the predominance of public ownership, there should be individual ownership of the self-employed, private ownership that employs workers other than family members, and public–private mixed ownership.

Such reforms would help the formation and development of the market. Except for those wholly state-owned, it is easier for enterprises under various forms of ownership to become autonomous and self-sustaining, responsive to market direction. The proposed scheme would be conducive to the compatibility of public ownership and the market mechanism, as wholly state-owned enterprises would account for a significant share while enterprises under other types of public, mixed, individual, and private ownership can become actors and recipients of market regulation to varying degrees. Hence, the compatibility of public ownership with the market mechanism. At the same time, the introduction of the indirect mechanism through which 'the state regulates the market, and the market guides enterprises' would be facilitated, because retained in the economy (especially in strategic economic sectors) are wholly state-owned enterprises, enterprises under other types of the public ownership and public/private mixed ownership. They would support state regulation of the market and the economy at large via the market mechanism.

To conclude, as a socialist developing country, China is bound to encounter problems peculiar to her, as well as difficulties common to all socialist countries in the transition to a market economy and in market development.

References

China Economic Yearbook 1988   (Publishing House of Economic Management), pp. xi–47
China Statistics Abstracts 1949–86 (1987)   (State Statistical Bureau) pp. 206.
People's Daily (1987)   May 14.
People's Daily (1988)   Nov 21.
Statistics (1987)   no. 3.
World Economic Herald (1988)   Economic Contract and Economic Order, May 30.

Comment

Tsuneaki Sato
FACULTY OF ECONOMICS, NIHON UNIVERSITY,
TOKYO, JAPAN

1 INTRODUCTION

The so-called 'third wave' of economic reforms in socialist countries started roughly at the turn of 1970s and 1980s, with Hungarian and Chinese reforms playing the top-runner's role at the beginning and later joined by Polish and Soviet ones in the mid-1980s. The fact that two big countries like the USSR and China joined the reform movement is itself a sign that this 'third wave' has a *potentiality* of becoming, over several decades to come, a big tide of changes, transforming *eventually* the socialist economic system into one capable of coping with the requirements of a rapidly changing world environment. The single fact that China did not join the 'second wave' of reforms, while condemning it as 'revisionism' and a 'retreat to capitalism', and the Soviet Union was playing a negative role in the reform trials from the late 1960s until the mid-1980s suffices to explain the scope of changes now taking place. Needless to say that in order to turn this 'potentiality' into reality these countries will have to go a long way, the more so, as we see now a lot of signs that these reform efforts are encountering tremendous difficulties which, in turn, are calling for the adoption of 'adjustment policy' (China) or a 'programme for recovering economic health' (*programma ekonomicheskogo ozdrovleniya*, Soviet Union).

However, what does give a special weight to the reform movement of the 1980s is not, of course, its 'quantitative' aspect, that it is now joined by two big countries, but its 'qualitative' aspect. The new 'qualitative' aspect of the economic reforms now going on in these countries can be summarised as follows:

1. Extension of the market to producer goods sector (abolition of Material–Technical Supply System which was done in the 1960s

253

by the Hungarian reform only), while in the 1960s the market was confined mainly to consumer goods sector.

2. Hardening the 'budget constraint' (J. Kornai) of enterprises, which raises the problem of their 'life and death' if it is brought to the logical consequence, coupled with a heavy emphasis on free market pricing.

3. Efforts aimed at the introduction of labour, financial, capital as well as foreign exchange markets, which entails the 'pluralisation' of the sources of income (recognition of the income on capital and of unearned income).

4. Gradual marketisation of the social service sector through the extension of the share of paid services. And as a well-functioning market is most unlikely to be compatible with monopolism of state ownership.

5. 'Pluralisation' of ownership and of enterprise management: coexistence of state, collective, private and mixed (all kinds of contract and lease system) forms of ownerships, while the first is supposed to play the leading role.

6. Separation of 'management' from 'state ownership' by delegating strategic decision making to the enterprise level (or self-management council) or by transforming enterprises into joint-stock companies.

7. Clearly expressed orientation toward integration into the world economy: opening up the economy in various forms (setting-up of joint ventures and 'special economic zones').

8. Initial efforts aimed at the 'pluralisation' of the political system, though the terms used are different in the countries in question.

Taken together, there is a clear tendency toward a 'mixed economic system' (of 'a socialist type', as Kornai put it), based on the recognition of the 'universality' of the market economy common to all modern economic systems, capitalist or socialist.[1] Here lies, perhaps, one of the fundamental differences between the reform concepts of 1980s and 1960s, when the economic reform was understood usually in terms of the 'combination of plan and market', the latter playing rather a supplementary role.

In this connection, the problem of effective macroeconomic policy (regulation) is gaining utmost importance. This idea was expressed in the beautiful phrase adopted at the Thirteenth Congress of the Communist Party of China 'the state regulates the market, while the market directs enterprises', a phrase always quoted in the writings of Chinese reform-minded economists.

If the phrase is taken literally, the difference between capitalist and socialist economic systems *might* be interpreted eventually not so much in terms of ownership and relations of plan and market, but in terms of effective macropolicy (regulation) exercised over the market with due attention to such values traditionally associated with socialist ideas, as security, stability, equality and solidarity, as some east European and even Soviet reform-minded scholars have already begun to discuss.

What precipitated these changes is undoubtedly the 'pre-crisis situation' (M. S. Gorbachev) experienced, though to a different degree, by socialist countries in the late 1970s and early 1980s, a sense of crisis brought about by the widening economic and technological gap with advanced market economies and the threat coming from NIEs (Newly Industrialising Economies) whose dynamics of development far surpassed any predictions we made in the early 1970s. In this sense, there could be an analogy between the crisis of capitalism in the 1930s when capitalism tried to overcome it by means of state regulation of the economy, transforming it into a 'capitalist type' of mixed economic system (contemporary capitalism), and the crisis of socialism in the 1980s when it is trying to overcome the crisis by means of deregulation and, in some respects, '*re*privatisation' of the economy.

It goes without saying that, though the idea expressed in the phrase 'the state regulates the market, while the market directs enterprises' is not only beautiful, but also correct, it does not automatically ensure the practical realisation of macroeconomic regulation, which presupposes not only the modern institutional set-up of the market, but also the mastery of policy techniques and know-how related to financial, monetary and credit policies, in particular. The discussions now going on in China on how to overcome the overheatedness of the economy seem to illustrate this point.

Having said the above, I shall now turn to the very interesting paper presented by Professor Dong Fureng (Chapter 12 in this volume) which, if roughly divided, deals with two main problems: one related to the specific features of market development in China, and another, closely connected with the former, to the economic reforms.

2 SPECIFIC FEATURES OF MARKET DEVELOPMENT IN CHINA

Professor Dong Fureng approaches the problem using two measuring rods: one is the underdevelopment of a domestic economy which has not yet succeeded in forming a unified domestic market, coupled with big differences in the development of different regions, and another the centralised economic system established in the early 1950s after the Soviet model, which contributed, to a greater degree, to preserve the 'natural' ('material', as the Chinese economists used to say) character of the national economy, or even intensified it.

I found this argumentation quite correct. Market development in China is a long 'historical process', in the course of which dual tasks will have to be solved: first, the transition from a predominantly 'natural economy' to a commodity one, and second, the development of a 'modern market' which can proceed only in parallel with the modernisation of the whole country. Economic systems reform can remove institutional obstacles to the transformation and hence accelerate the process, but can by no means replace it'. (Dong)

This cannot but give a very strong imprint on the process of economic reforms in China. In some sense, it is not merely a transition from the traditional economic system of socialism (TES) to a market-oriented one, as is it is usually understood. It also faces dual tasks: curing the illness inherent in TES, on the one hand, and overcoming the 'natural economic thought' associated with the semi-natural economic character of the national economy, which, however, was intensified at first by the 'War Communist Supply System' established during the liberation war, and later by TES introduced after the Soviet model as well. 'Socialism with a Chinese face', a phrase Chinese leaders are very fond of quoting, should be understood to mean solving the above dual tasks. The problem is not so simple after all.

In this connection, the present writer has to recall the peculiar development process of Chinese revolution. In pre-war times, well aware of the 'semi-colonial-and-semi-feudal' character of Chinese society, the CPC had set out with the theory of a 'revolution in two stages', that of 'new democratic', as a result of which a 'new democratic society' and 'new democratic economy' (a kind of NEP) was to be established together with a 'coalition dictatorship' as a political superstructure, and then socialist stage of revolution.

However, soon after the People's Republic of China was proclaimed the CPC preferred a course of 'premature' construction of socialism to further development of this 'new democratic society [economy] which was supposed to make full use of a mixed economic system. So, the 'revolution in two stages' was compressed into 'one', leaving the task of the first unsolved. Moreover, the 'natural economic thought', intensified by the introduction of TES, was further strengthened during the course of 'Great Leap Forward' (1958) and 'Cultural Revolution' (1966). It should be noted here that TES, which is operated mainly in physical terms, and autarchic 'natural economic thought' yet fit easily with each other.

So, it seems to the present writer that the economic reforms in China have in some sense an implication of a return to the unsolved tasks. What Professor Dong Fureng points out correctly should be seen in such a broad historical perspective. What economic reforms in China will have to deal with is not quite the same as in European socialist countries.

3 PROBLEMS OF THE 'DUAL-TRACK SYSTEM' IN CHINA

Next comes the problem of how to characterise the economic system now operating in China (so to say a 'typology' problem). As Professor Dong writes in his paper, there seems to exist a consensus among Chinese economists that it could best be characterised as a 'dual-track system', which relies on three different tools of control: mandatory plan, indicative plan and market regulation, while the target model to be attained in the future is defined as 'the model of a regulated market', just as expressed in the famous phrase 'the state regulates the market, while the market guides the enterprises' (Thirteenth Congress of CPC, October 1987). The latter target model is, of course, a step forward from the decision adopted at the CPC, CC Plenum in October 1984, in which a socialist economy was defined rather vaguely as a 'Planned commodity economy'.

In the present writer's view, the theory of 'dual-track system' could be extended to apply to the actually functioning economic systems in the USSR (after the adoption of the law on state enterprises in June 1987) and several east European countries, and to some extent, to Hungary too, though with several rather strong reservations.

Take, for example, the Soviet reform scheme as exemplified in the law on state enterprises and related documents. Though the intention was proclaimed as a target in the future to abolish the system of mandatory plan indices, it has in fact been preserved in the guise of 'state [?commercial] orders', and control figures which were supposed to play the role of guidelines only. According to the provisions of law, the share of state orders was to account for roughly 60–70 per cent of output in the case of manufacturing industries, but in actual practice it turned out to be well over 90 per cent and in some cases even more, nearly 100 per cent. So, there is little difference between the obligatory plans and state orders. What did actually come out of the much publicised 'law on state enterprises' was just like 'Viel Lärm um nichts – nur eine Maus' (A lot of noise for nothing – only a mouse), as Germans say.

The history of economic reforms in socialist countries has shown quite unequivocally that even the official abolition of the system of mandatory plan targets does not necessarily lead to the formation of a decentralised, regulated market model. It is now widely recognised that, thanks to the contribution by Hungarian reformers, even in the widely renowned Hungarian NEM, which had formally abolished both the system of obligatory plan indices with their breakdown to the micro-levels and that of material–technical supply, thus giving a much wider scope to market forces, what actually did come into being was a kind of 'third model', namely 'indirectly centralised system' (L. Antal) or 'not plan, not market' (T. Bauer) system, as Hungarian reformers criticise it.

Though, of course, there is no place whatsoever officially reserved for such *de facto* plan targets binding enterprises as 'state orders' (*Goszakazy*) in the Soviet reform scheme, it is recognised as well that in the Hungarian case the same system is preserved in an *invisible* form of the so-called 'expression of expectations' by the central authorities (it is called in Japan 'administrative guidance').

It seems to the present writer that the Soviet reform scheme is so far trying to establish this third, intermediate model within a much more centralised framework of control figures, state orders as well as a retained system of material–technical supply and still unreformed system of pricing. What existed in the Hungarian system until quite recently in an *invisible* form does appear in the Soviet case quite explicitly, in a *visible* form, making it little better than the old one. Therefore, a clear difference between the Soviet and Hungarian reforms could not be denied: it gives the latter good reason to classify it as a system of 'indirect bureaucratic coordination', Variant 1B as J. Kornai put it.

What I wish to stress here is that there exists rather a striking similarity, not between the Hungarian and Chinese reforms as usually accepted, but between the Soviet and Chinese ones, *if* we exclude from our consideration such sectors as agriculture, trade and service, small-sized village industries and foreign economic relations (opening up to the outside world), where Chinese reform made undoubtedly a large score, while focusing our attention on the reformability of large-scale state industries. They have in common that they are best characterised as 'dual-track systems'.

Hungarians are now trying to make a breakaway from the halfway, half-boiled 'not plan, not market system', while the task is raised before the Soviet and Chinese reformers how to make headway from a position which falls far behind that of the Hungarians.

However, to get rid of such a dual system is a very difficult task, far more difficult than it is usually supposed to be, even though the defects inherent in the system are widely recognised: it is to blame, at least to a considerable extent, for the loss of macroeconomic control which gave rise to the grave economic difficulties both countries, China and the USSR, are now facing. Much depends on whether they will be able to stabilise the situation, however, keeping in sight the 'logic' of the reform.

We cannot but entertain deep apprehensions about the fact that market-oriented reforms in socialist countries, Yugoslavia, Hungary, China and then the USSR, seem to have fallen into the same trap of inflation after several years of initial, sometimes remarkable, success. The Soviet case is, however, quite different in that the reform there is now meeting its 'hard days', without the people having enjoyed the first 'happy days' of reform; especially in the day-to-day life of consumers. To devise an effective 'adjustment [*ozdrovlenie*] programme, which is consistent with the logic of reform, is not an easy matter, to say the least. Discussing the 'Market Forces in Planned Economies' here should serve to help find a way out of the present situation, and not the other way round.

Note

1. The writer has discussed this problem elsewhere (Sato, 1983).

Reference

Sato, T. (1983) 'Possibilities for and Limitations to a [Mixed Economy] in Socialist Planned Economies', a paper presented at the international conference held in Sapporo, 23–25 August; *Acta Slavica*, 2 (1984) Slavic Research Center, Hokkaido University.

Comment

Cyril Lin
ST ANTONY'S COLLEGE, OXFORD, UK

Two basic sets of issues are addressed in the papers by Professors Dong Fureng and Professor Sukhamoy Chakravarty (Chapters 12 and 11 in this volume). The first is essentially a conceptual one: namely, what is the most appropriate economic mechanism (plan versus market) for developing countries seeking to industrialise? The second concerns the operational or practical question of the lessons of the Chinese experience with market-oriented reforms: reforms in the context of a less developed socialist economy and whether this experience tells us anything about the possibility of designing a mixed plan-cum-market system in hitherto centrally planned economies. Let me begin first with the second issue – the Chinese reform experience as summarised in Professor Dong's paper.

In looking at China, we have to make a distinction between problems in the Chinese reforms which might be generic to other Soviet-type systems – given similarities in systemic departure points – and the *sui generis* problems which are peculiar or unique to China as a less developed country (LDC). Professor Dong's paper offers excellent insights into the latter type of problems, so I shall focus on the more generic aspects.

China in 1978, at the commencement of the reforms, was in certain respects even more primitive than the prototype Soviet-type system in that it contained elements of War Communism. The absence of labour markets, and extensive reliance on rationing, are examples of this fact. Nevertheless, it displayed many of the classic symptoms of a Soviet-type command economy: shortages, declining growth rates and economic efficiency, slow technological progress, soft-budget constraints in state enterprises, investment hunger, repressed inflation, etc. Consequently, a number of problems which emerged in the course of reform derived from these systemic 'initial conditions'. Reforms over the past decade in China allowed repressed inflation, deriving from conditions of shortage, to be transformed into open inflation attendant upon partial price decontrol. Reforms have also generated considerable economic, social and political tensions because they have redistributed costs and benefits not only across sectors, but also across regions and various interest groups. (These kinds of tensions in China have previously never reached the proportions of those in east Europe.) The process of partial reform has also led to soft-budget constraints getting softer rather than harder, given the increased diversity of sources of working and investment capital while enterprise autonomy remains marginal and while the system of state ownership remains intact. At the same time, the failure to overhaul the price system meant a complex and unmanageable system of compensatory adjustments in the fiscal system which only exacerbated the 'bargaining' features in the system.

In particular, it has been the local governments, and not the primary economic units, which have been the major beneficiaries of market decentralisation. Local governments in China have usurped most of the decision making powers that were formally accorded to enterprises. This interpretation is supported by Dong Fureng's assertion that despite the narrowing of the scope of command planning (that is, reductions in the number of products subject to obligatory plans and allocated through the state materials supply system) at the central level, there has been a concomitant and inverse growth in the scope and details of direct and indirect local government controls over enterprises within their jurisdiction. This suggests that in certain respects decentralisation and even marketisation have actually resulted in greater *indirect centralisation*. The reasons for this must be (a) the failure to enforce the intended separation of state and party; and (b) more importantly, the partial nature of reforms where insufficiently developed product and factor markets have forced enterprises to continue to depend on local government and local party authorities for supplies of scarce materials, funds (usually in breach of centrally-determined credit norms) and marketing of output (in protected local markets). These problems relate to (lack of) changes in the system of state ownership (which I shall discuss later).

The growth of the economic powers of local governments is, as mentioned earlier, inversely related to the loss of the central government's ability to enforce macroeconomic regulation. This is most evident in the progressive loss of central control over investments since 1978. In 1977, about 80 per cent of total capital construction investments in China were financed through the central state budget with extra-budgetary investments (financed by local governments and enterprises) accounting for the remaining 20 per cent. In 1988, the ratios were approximately reversed. Thus, on the one hand the decentralisation of economic decision making powers to local authorities have moved far ahead of the state's ability to establish new institutions and instruments for indirect macro control; on the other hand, it is questionable whether such controls, even if they were in place, would be effective when enterprise behaviour and soft-budget constraints remain unaltered.

Here, in talking about generic problems of marketisation in Soviet-type systems, I think we need to recognise that there is a special sub-category of problems peculiar to very large economies such as China and the Soviet Union. In these large economies, unlike the smaller east European countries, there is the additional issue of intermediaries between the state and the primary economic units – intermediaries such as the provincial governments in China and the republican governments in the Soviet Union. In China, there was a deliberate and conscious attempt to have the local governments perform an intermediary function for two reasons. First, command planning in China was reduced in scope but was not totally disbanded, and thus the traditional function of local governments as an executive agency remained; with decentralisation, these functions were enhanced. Secondly, there was the belief that local governments could play a positive role in the development of markets since state enterprises on their own lacked the expertise or resources to engage directly in market transactions. But this was a vicious circle: with enterprises continuing to be protected from market forces, the process of 'learning by doing' in a new (market) environment was retarded and the 'godfather' role of local governments became increasingly essential and institutionalised. Consequently, the result was the development of highly imperfect, segmented and monopolistic (regional) markets where local governments pursue beggar-thy-neighbour policies and erected inter-provincial trade barriers.

It may well be the case that Soviet reforms would not assign a similar role to the local governments, but nevertheless it seems reasonable to expect that republican governments there will in any case arrogate such powers during the process of marketisation. This is because these outcomes result from the nature of the political system, that is, the monopoly of power by one agency. It also depends on the design of the budgetary and fiscal systems: local governments will always want to retain control over enterprises as revenue (even if unprofitable) generating centres.

Brief mention should also be made here of the importance of

regional policy in large economies. To my knowledge, no market economy has ever succeeded in alleviating regional disparities through a total or primary reliance on the market mechanism alone. In very large countries where there are significant ethnic minorities, and where natural resources tend to be located in minorities' regions (as in the Soviet Union and China), redistribution is especially important yet redistribution or regional development of backward areas through Hirschman-type 'trickle down' effects operating through market forces have never really worked successfully.

I would argue that the most important lesson so far of the Chinese experience with market reforms is this: the devolution of income rights, and even property rights, through greater enterprise autonomy, in the absence of fundamental changes in both the political and ownership system leads to a perverse form of the classic Soviet-type system which I have elsewhere characterised as 'market Stalinism' – a system where the *fundamentals* of command planning are not disbanded but market processes are simply grafted on to existing structures. Moreover, *cultural* (broadly defined to encompass economic) attitudes, values and behaviour associated with the old system remain and thus distort the objectives of marketisation. Thus, even with some changes in income and property rights, it is primarily the local government and other state agencies that enjoy *transaction rights*, or the right to engage in market transactions. It is state administrative organs, and not primary economic units, that have become the main actors in the incipient market economy by virtue of an unreformed political system. This feature is also a cause as well as result of the highly partial nature of factor and product markets on China.

Let me turn now to problems in the Chinese reforms which are perhaps more specific to China as an LDC. Professor Dong's paper, in Section 3, identifies four specific problems of marketisation arising out of China's low level of economic development. These are: (1) a 'natural' or 'semi-natural' product economy (this refers to the underdevelopment of commodity production and exchange and the associated low level of functional specialisation); (2) inadequate infrastructure, as exemplified by backward transport and communications networks, which contribute to market fragmentation or immobility of factors and products: (3) traditional values ('feudal') characterised by the low esteem in which commerce and 'business' are held; and poorly developed social structures.

These are without doubt features of underdevelopment (in fact, they define it) and are usually seen as obstacles to the proper functioning of markets. But I would suggest that they are at the same time products of the Soviet-type system, and as such are relevant and applicable to other more developed socialist economies. Consider, for example, the first point concerning China's low level of commodity production. During the Cultural Revolution period (1966–76), there was a deliberate attempt in China to negate commodity production and the Law of Value. This policy ('small yet comprehensive, large yet comprehensive' was then the slogan) led to the creation of self-reliant, self-contained, comprehensive and autarchic economic sub-systems or what has been called a 'cellular' economy. This policy was a motivated by defence considerations, and (b) a response to the difficulty of centralised planning and balancing, such that the Chinese sought to resolve the planning problem by decomposing the national economy into self-sufficient local economies with minimal interregional and intersectoral flows of materials and products. From this point of view, the low level of commodity production was as much a feature of Soviet-type systems as it was of underdevelopment: the Philippines, with a much lower level of development than the Soviet Union or Hungary, has a more developed commodity production and exchange system.

I would also question whether the problems of 'traditional [feudal] values', and of underdeveloped social structures, are specific to LDCs. Are they not problems in the Soviet Union and most east European countries as well? Markets, or the experience with markets, in China is certainly much more recent than in the Soviet Union: how many people alive today in the Soviet Union have direct experience of markets, seven decades after the October Revolution? The disdain of commerce in China may be traditional, but it is also common to other socialist countries and is as much an ideological legacy of Marxism (or at least some interpretations of it) as it is a pre-modern characteristic. Similarly, weak legal systems – a vital aspect of underdeveloped social structures – are common to communist countries and cannot be regarded as unique to economic underdevelopment.

Yet these features characteristic of underdevelopment might well be a double-edged sword where market reforms in socialist countries are concerned. They pose obstacles to developing efficient markets, but they might also offer what I would call – to borrow a concept from development economics – 'advantages of backwardness'. For example, the predominance of agriculture in socialist developing economies makes the task of reforms relatively easier because production processes and relationships within the sector are simpler. The lower level of interindustrial interdependence, or what Marx called 'socialised production', should also make it easier to contain the disequilibrating effects during the transition from one economic system to another. In this sense, a less mature and hence less complex economy reduces Koopmans-type 'secondary uncertainty' which is as present in a reforming Soviet-type system as it is in market economies. These advantages of backwardness, however, are greater in China than in the more developed Soviet and east European countries.[1]

A key point raised by Professor Dong with which I agree entirely concerns the question of whether markets would develop 'naturally', of their own accord and automatically, once man-made constraints on its development were lifted. Dong's paper suggests not, on the basis of the Chinese experience. In this respect, I wonder whether socialist governments have not overestimated the natural propensity of marketisation. This overestimation is perhaps yet another legacy of ideology: for a long time, communist leaders have tended to exaggerate the dangers of 'capitalist restoration' – that class enemies and economism (in other words, markets) lurk under every bed and floorboard. Yet when controls against such alleged tendencies are lifted, markets fail to develop of their own accord. The record of reform in China demonstrates that lifting ideological, political, legal and other institutional constraints to marketisation may not be sufficient.

My final comments concern a point implicit in Professor Dong's paper but explicit in Professor Chakravarty's. This is the basic question of the merits and demerits of planning and market in developing countries. Professor Dong clearly believes that a market system (or at least a larger role for it) is essential to China's modernisation, and his conclusion is based on China's development experience. Professor Chakravarty, on the other hand, believes that developing countries cannot dispense with planning, and his conclusions are also based on experience – that of India. This is a strange juxtaposition of experiences and conclusions indeed! China under central planning has recorded one of the world's most impressive long-term economic growth rates, alleviated the worst aspects of poverty, and ensured basic needs for the overwhelming majority of the population. Yet this record has led Professor Dong and many other Chinese to conclude that China needs more market forces and less (direct) planning. India, on the other hand, a market-based economy albeit with

extensive state intervention, has had a less successful overall economic record despite important economic achievements (which these
days tend to be underestimated): it has failed to eliminate widespread
poverty or achieve high growth rates. Yet Professor Chakravarty's
conclusion is that planning is critical in LDCs and needs to be
retained!

To be sure, both authors do not pose the problem in mutually
exclusive terms of either plan *or* market, and both argue for a
mixture of both. For example, Dong advocates a system in which the
'state regulates the market, the market regulates the enterprises'.
Chakravarty is less specific and his argument for planning is, as I read
it, a refreshing (and indeed timely) reminder that one should not go
from one extreme (Soviet-type command planning) to another (a
total *laissez-faire* market system). But his arguments for planning do
not seem to take account of the experiences of planning in both
western and socialist countries: it is too much of a rehearsal of
previous arguments without explaining why planning has worked in
some form and countries and not in others. I cannot but feel that
general, commonsensical solutions which advocate elements of both
planning and market too often prove to be convenient conceptual
compromises which in many cases are either operationally unfeasible
or obscure fundamental and unresolved issues. Some of these issues,
to my mind, are as follows.

First, the question is not one of whether LDCs (or any economy,
for that matter) should have elements of both plan and market, but
rather one of which (plan or market) should be the predominant and
fundamental economic mechanism. In other words, it is not a question of degrees of mix between plan and market, but one of choosing
between two different animals altogether. We ought here to recall the
interwar debate on planning. Carl Landauer, Jan Tinbergen, amongst
others, believed in the premises of a market mechanism but argued
for planning as a supplement or corrective in cases of market failures,
externalities, public goods, etc. Marxist and socialist advocates of
planning, in contrast, regarded planning as a superior alternative to
the market mechanism and called for the replacement of the latter by
the former. These are two fundamentally different positions which
socialist reformers have to recognise: either you have an essentially
market system with 'corrections' through planning only in cases of
possible market failure, or you have an essentially planned system
where markets operate at the margin in instances where you have
'planning failure'. But a clear choice as to what basic economic

mechanism should predominate has to be made, and general principles which opt for a 'bit of both' are neither here nor there and only evade the issue. This point can be illustrated by considering the title of our Conference: 'Market Forces in Planned Economies': such a title and the issues involved are altogether different from one concerned with 'Planning in Market Economies'.

Secondly, we need to recognise from experience that plan and market actually cohabit uncomfortably and generate considerable tensions and frictions. If this assertion is true, then a number of questions and implications follow. Is it possible to devise forms of planning in market economies (or conversely, market processes in planned economies) which are effective yet at the same time do not militate against or undermine the efficient functioning of the market mechanism? Is there an optimal mix between plan and market where such frictions are minimised and where the advantages of both systems are realised? Professor Brus, for example, has expressed scepticism about the possibility of market systems accommodating any 'formal' planning. But even if the answer to these questions is yes, then the redesign of economic institutions and control mechanisms still has to take account of potential conflicts between plan and market – in other words, there is a need to devise new types of institutions and instruments addressed explicitly to this problem. It may be insufficient to simply take, off the shelf, bits of market and plan and throw them together: aspects of market and plan may have to be adapted and recombined in new variants.

Finally, it seems to me that there is a strong asymmetry in economic reforms depending on departure points. Market economies are perhaps more able to introduce and accommodate elements of planning in the form of state regulation of economic parameters where the state acts as a 'facilitator' of desired outcomes. But in centrally planned economies, the introduction of market forces confront, and require changes in, far too many social, political and economic fundamentals. The underlying premise in these economies is that the state is the principal producer of goods and services. Without a change in this basic premise, it is difficult to foresee any possibility for substantive progress towards ownership reform, development of capital markets and other systemic changes that market reform presupposes.

These are the basic issues which, I believe, all reforming socialist economies have to confront, whether they be developed or underdeveloped.

Note

1. The case in point is agricultural reforms. China's agricultural reforms were able to succeed in the initial stages without concomitant reforms in the non-agricultural sectors partly because of the relatively self-contained and self-sufficient nature of Chinese agriculture in which a significant proportion of inputs was internally produced. Agriculture in the Soviet Union is much more mechanised and dependent on the state–industrial sector for inputs. This suggests that it would be more difficult for agricultural reforms in the Soviet Union to succeed without simultaneous reforms in the industrial and commercial sectors, rendering the whole reform process more complex.

Part VII
International Consequences

13 *Perestroika* of the Soviet Economy in the Light of East–West Relations

Oleg Bogomolov
INSTITUTE OF ECONOMICS OF WORLD
SOCIALIST SYSTEM, USSR ACADEMY OF
SCIENCES, MOSCOW, USSR

1 *PERESTROIKA*

According to one witty remark, the main result of *perestroika* in the USSR resides in the fact that it is still under way. Particular results in different areas are not assessed unambiguously. In 1988 the situation on the consumer market deteriorated noticeably. But the feeling that the country is in the process of change is becoming stronger. If the situation in the USSR is looked at from the viewpoint of the shifts occurring in China, Hungary, Poland and some other socialist countries, one comes to the conclusion that the search is ongoing for a new model of socialist societal organisation adequate for the modern epoch with its revolutionary changes in technology, culture and information. The need is for democratisation of public life and international relations and for a new political thinking. The Stalinist model proved to have no prospects for ensuring social progress under the changed conditions.

The new model still does not enjoy a full unity of opinion. The actual experience of individual countries is diverse, but it is clear that the changes already under way will have far-reaching domestic and international consequences. The image of socialism will be radically changed. The gulf between countries of the two systems will be bridged to a considerable extent.

Perestroika in the USSR has already continued for four years. Changes have covered political concepts, including foreign policy, mass media, public consciousness, culture, legislation, cadre policy. Economic practice is increasingly being involved in these changes.

The political climate in the country is being improved. The task of democratisation of society and the party has been put on the agenda and an acute struggle for its practical realisation is going on. Up to now, however, this is more liberalisation than democratisation of society in the full sense of the word. The most radical shifts have taken place, perhaps, in the public consciousness, in society's understanding of its past and of those problems that it still has to solve. *Perestroika* is supported by the majority of the population, since they understand that there is no other alternative but stagnation and creeping into a deep social and economic crisis.

The people are full of expectation; there is live interest in the press, TV, broadcasting, but no real improvement in their life has come yet. As one of our humorists says: 'Today it is more interesting to read than to live'.

2   THE RECENT ECONOMIC SITUATION

The national product increased in 1988 by 4.4 per cent, compared with 3.2 per cent annual average over the two preceding years. The 1988 results point to acceleration in rates of economic growth but, due to the aggravation of inflationary trends, growing difficulties in supply and in external economic relations, this positive result is not realised by the population. Moreover, the national income actually used for accumulation and consumption is less than production since losses took place, including those from the worsening terms of external trade. The situation is improving in agriculture and housing. Over 1986–7 the gross agricultural output increased by 18 per cent as compared to the average annual level of the preceding five-year period; the grain yield gain was about 30 million tons, that of meat 2.1 million tons. However, these results are insufficient and do not eliminate the necessity for a large-scale import of grain and other foodstuffs. Over the last three years these imports have amounted to nearly $50 billion (30 billion roubles). The year 1988 was one of crop failure and evidently will give but a very modest gain in agricultural output with a certain decline in the grain yield to 19.5 million tons. The state budget funds are being rearranged to satisfy urgent social needs of the population, among which a special emphasis is placed on health care, education and housing. The number of completed flats increased from 2.1 million in 1986 to 2.3 million in 1987 and about the same figure in 1988. Wages of teachers and medical personnel are being increased; a pension reform and higher pensions are expected.

3 PROBLEMS AND IMPROVEMENTS IN THE DOMESTIC ECONOMY

The reform of the Soviet economy is burdened with problems accumulated over the previous period. Among them the most serious implications are associated with significant disturbances in the structure of social production: the low quality and technical level of many products; high production costs; insufficient skills; and the culture and discipline of workers. The lagging behind of agriculture and the manufacture of consumer goods in conjunction with a hypertrophied development of heavy industry is one of the fundamental defects of our economy. However, heavy industry itself developed erratically; machine building, fine chemistry and electronics are still underdeveloped. The production infrastructure is another weak point. Building industry capacity is concentrated on the construction of new projects and is poorly adapted to jobs associated with modernisation and re-equipment.

The structure of the economy is subject to great inertia. This explains to a large extent the fact that aspirations for a greater dynamism in our development have not yet been realised. Another reason is the inertia of the existing mechanism of economic management, that is, bureaucratic resistance. That is why the economic independence of enterprises can be only partially ensured, likewise their transition to self-financing, though this is required by the law on state enterprise that came into effect in 1988. The reason for this is the still prevailing strict control by the ministries, the lack of a wholesale trade market and imperfections in the price and tax systems. The situation can be improved through a price reform and replacement of the state system of distribution with wholesale trade. This will take several years.

Market methods of economic management still do not play their proper role and hence have not provided tangible results in reducing production costs, increasing the productivity of labour, improving the quality of goods or accelerating technological progress. The planned regulation of production is effected through a state order which is compulsory. In 1988 it covered 85 to 100 per cent of the industrial output. In 1989 it will spread, for example, over only 25 per cent of machine tools, 60 per cent of the products of fuel and raw material industries, and 30 per cent of light industry output. The output beyond the state order is intended to be commercialised through the wholesale trade at prices which will be formed, to a greater extent, on the basis of a contract between seller and buyer.

State planning in future will take on a more indicative character. It is intended to cease elaboration of annual plans centrally and to limit the central function to preparing five-year plans only. The influence of the state of the economy for the accomplishment of the planned targets will be effected in several ways:

(a)   through the allocation of financial and material resources still remaining at its disposal (their share will be considerably reduced)
(b)   through the levers of taxation, credit and price policies
(c)   through state orders.

The success of *perestroika* is dependent today to a great extent on the cure of two harmful diseases. These are inflation and the shadow economy which nourishes corruption. For a long time the state budget has suffered from a deficit. This year it is expected to amount to 100 billion roubles, or 11 per cent of the gross domestic product (GDP) which is a consequence of rapid growth of expenditure and considerable reduction of budget revenues. The latter declined as a result of the drop in prices of Soviet exports and cuts in the state production of alcohol. The budget deficit is compensated by money and credit emission not backed by goods. The state debt is growing. The money in the hands of the population seeks goods and does not find them. Despite the state control, retail prices grow by 4 to 5 per cent a year. But the growing inflation is revealed first of all in the disappearance of one commodity after another from the consumer market. TV sets, refrigerators, washing powders, electric lamps, etc. have all become items in short supply.

Similar difficulties are experienced by industrial and agricultural enterprises in the acquisition, with their own money, of construction materials, metal, transport and building machinery and many other kinds of equipment. The commodity hunger becomes more acute despite an increasing output of goods which are in deficit.

The cure of the money-credit system and hence of the domestic market (both the consumer market and the wholesale trade market being newly created) is intended to be effected by way of cutting budget expenditures (military ones for some major investment projects, subsidies to losing enterprises, management expenses), sales and leasing of some kinds of state property (small- and medium-scale enterprises, flats, land plots), a stricter control of the growth of cash payments to the population, and the growth of tax revenues as a result of the higher efficiency of operation of enterprises. But the main hopes are for a higher output of foodstuffs and manufactured goods for the population.

The progress of *perestroika* envisages correction of its original concept with a change of certain priorities in economic policy. The general course remains unchanged: rejection of command-administrative methods of management and incorporation of market mechanisms into the planned economy. There is a greater understanding of the fact that *perestroika* can provide the quickest results in agriculture and in industries producing goods and services for consumers and that in these very sectors the appropriate measures should be taken first. This is evidenced also by the experience of Hungary and China.

In agriculture the task is to liberate the producer from administrative intervention and control on the part of the party and state authorities, to shift over to market leverage by management. The principles of independence, self-financing and self-repayment of collective and family farms are to be more persistently put into practice. In addition to collective and state farms, or within their framework, true non-étatised cooperatives originate. A greater scale of operations requires leasing of land, implements, livestock and other property to family collectives or small cooperatives. The lease-holding contract, as numerous examples show, gives an increase in the product output and in labour productivity of up to 1.5–2.0 times.

The enhancement of market regulators in agriculture in 1988 resulted in the situation where the demand for agricultural machines, especially tractors and grain harvesters, fell by one-third. The recent meeting of the CPSU Central Committee dealing with agrarian matters should become a landmark in the emancipation of agriculture from administrative–bureaucratic control and in transition to new forms of agrarian relations. The law on lease-holding is being prepared. Steps are being taken to shape a market for agricultural produce and to abandon gradually the administrative system of its distribution.

The easing of leasing relations encourages collectives of industrial enterprises to take advantage of them. In this case loss making enterprises quickly become efficient. There are already several dozen small enterprises leased by the state.

The law on cooperatives enabled the rise of a strong cooperation movement in towns. About 100 000 cooperatives have been formed in construction, servicing, manufacture of consumer goods and in other spheres. They satisfy numerous needs of consumers, although their total sales do not exceed 1 per cent of the retail turnover of this country. The activities of cooperatives, bearing in mind the imperfection of their legal and tax regulation and absence of true fiscal control, have engendered acute contradictions in society. The state refused to provide cooperatives with many kinds of raw material, components and machinery which they badly needed, at state prices. In the absence of a wholesale trade market, cooperatives were bound to resort to unlawful sources of provision through bribes. Enjoying substantially unlimited freedom in setting prices, they laid all their expenses on the consumer. State enterprises, deprived of this freedom and likewise the freedom to increase wages, became impotent to compete and bring down the prices set by cooperators. The unsatisfied economic demand of the population for numerous goods and services enabled cooperators to inflate prices and incomes, frequently without any care about the quality of their products. Up to now, unfortunately, cooperatives give an additional impetus to inflation and corruption and enhance an unjust differentiation in incomes. Under the pressure of public opinion, efforts are being made to restrict and, in some cases, even prohibit the activity of cooperatives.

In the series of measures for the healing of the Soviet economy a special emphasis is given today to expansion and a radical re-equipment of the food industry and light industry and a rapid building up of capacity in the manufacture of cars and other durable goods. In the allocation of investment and foreign exchange funds by the state the interests of the food industry and light industry generally were usually neglected. As a result, their equipment was kept obsolete for decades. Now an accelerated modernisation is planned along with the erection of new plants, especially small and medium-sized ones. The state assigns big investments for these purposes, intending, for example, to double the production capacity of light industry within six to seven years. More than 100 enterprises and R & D boards of the military industry have been engaged in the design and manufacture of equipment for these industries.

All other production assets of the economy need renovation on a modern technological basis. *Perestroika* also envisages the solution of the problems of scientific and technological progress as the most important component. We still have no great opportunities for increasing investment in technical reconstruction. Our resources are very limited, which forces us to give priority to modernisation of the on-stream enterprises with a view to ensuring fast repayment of the expenditure. For similar reasons, a greater number of small-scale projects is being implemented; the scope of capital construction is being narrowed. The construction industry itself is undergoing *perestroika* and rearrangement to improve its efficiency, to reduce time limits and costs of construction.

Machine building ranks first in the programme of modernisation since it defines technological progress. The forms of integration of science and production are being improved. There are intentions to establish research-and-production concerns which would incorporate enterprises of different ministries. A strong need for that is felt in the new areas of technology.

The reform of economic relations between the central and local power aiming at greater independence for territorial bodies of management in the republics, areas and regions has become especially urgent. The share of individual territories in covering federal spending should be defined on the basis of more definite and just criteria. The principle of equivalence should be more strictly observed in the inter-regional exchange. The budget of a region and the supply of the regional market should be put into a direct relationship against the results of the local economic activities.

4 CHANGE IN INTERNATIONAL AFFAIRS

The aims of *perestroika* of the Soviet economy also cover the activation of trade and cooperation with other countries. Despite recent measures to make the Soviet economy more open to the outside world, real shifts to the better will take time. Foreign trade turnover is still stagnating, mainly due to the drop in oil prices. This unfavourable trend should, of course, be counteracted.

The export potential of Soviet industry and science should first be enhanced. It is not utilised to its full capacity because of bureaucratic centralisation of management and insufficient information about its achievements in other countries. This situation will apparently be improved after 1 April 1989 when all enterprises, associations and production cooperatives start to exercise their right of direct export–import transactions.

An important source of expanding Soviet exports is the vast stock of scientific and technological achievements accumulated by the Soviet Union in basic and applied research. Its commercial use would make it possible to export principally new articles. This is one of the promising areas of joint enterprise with Western companies.

The expansion of imports of machinery and equipment from the west on credit cannot be regarded as a promising way to promote external relations. The cost of these credits today is very high. Taking into consideration the ineffectiveness in starting up imported equipment and in ensuring its profitable operation (which, unfortunately, is characteristic), the growth of foreign indebtedness will lay a heavy burden on the Soviet economy. Therefore it is likely that preference will be given to other forms of collaboration: industrial cooperation, joint ventures, free zones of joint enterprise organised on Soviet territory.

In our country scores of joint enterprises with western companies have been formed. The economic, financial and legal conditions of their establishment and functioning are being improved. The western approach to investments of this kind is rather cautious. The restraining factor in the progress of this form of business relations is the requirement of foreign trade self-repayment. Certain contradictions between the interests of the partners are also observed, since western firms intend to expand their sales on the Soviet market, while we want to increase our incomes in freely convertible currency by means of such ventures. Difficulties also include insufficient information about the available possibilities for organising joint enterprises and demands for this or that kind of product. Their activity is hindered by the lack of a free market for raw materials, difficulties in ensuring a trouble-free provision of enterprises, and insufficient quality and technological level of components, parts and materials. However, the greatest difficulty lies in the poor adaptability of the internal economic mechanism of the USSR to the incorporation of joint ventures, as well as the non-convertibility of the Soviet rouble and its unrealistic exchange rate.

Evidently the obstacles in the way of the formation and functioning of such enterprises can be overcome to a great extent through the provision of special tax-free zones which would have a preferential legal and economic regime. The enterprises operating in these zones would be given the opportunity to carry out their transactions in freely convertible currencies and at the prices of western markets (except for wages, land renting, etc.) which might eliminate the problem of the poor adaptability of their operational activity to the internal economic mechanism. The possibilities for the creation of such zones on the Baltic and Black Sea coasts, at the Soviet–Finnish frontier, in the Far East, as well as the mechanism of their functioning and self-management, are being studied now by the Soviet government.

In assessing the prospects for a greater involvement of the Soviet Union in the world economy one more significant circumstance should be taken into consideration. An important role in the integration processes occurring in the world economy is played by transnational corporations. Despite all the controversies about their activity from the perspective of the national interests of the countries where they have their affiliates, these corporations do contribute to the proliferation of technological progress and enhance interdependence of different countries. They have an ever-growing influence on the dynamism and geographic flows of world trade. The Soviet Union has no large transnational companies with affiliates in various countries of the world, nor has it divisions of western transnationals on its territory. Joint ventures will evidently contribute to the transnationalisation of production in the Soviet Union as well. But at what time and in what forms it will take place is difficult to foresee now.

An impulse for the revival of the world economy and expansion of world trade, including that between east and west, could be generated, in my opinion, by the practical implementation of the proposals for the control of nuclear and conventional arms and their reduction. Only limited progress in this area is observed now. Nevertheless, the conversion of the military industry is ever more becoming a practical task. In the west it is associated with the search for new markets; in the east with expansion of import opportunities. Through cuts in its enormous counterproductive military expenditure, the USSR will become an even more promising partner for western companies.

It is evident that finding the balance of interests in the political sphere, settling actual political controversies, becomes the main factor today in activating business cooperation. Its expansion, in turn, can promote interest in political détente as well.

The trends in the development of world trade during recent decades are displayed in the intensification of trade exchanges within each of the three worlds: North–North, South–South, East–East. To some extent, this is an objective of the external economic policy of developing and socialist states. For this reason it is quite possible that in the future the socialist countries will give priority to the development of mutual economic relations. The urge of the CMEA member countries for a substantial intensification of their integration is well known, especially in solving major scientific and technological problems and in advancing industrial cooperation. In the field of modern technology, this is the subject of CoCom's embargoes by which the CMEA member countries are endeavouring to ensure their independence and limit their vulnerability on the basis of mutual cooperation. But the general principal motto of their external economic strategy can be formulated as the intensification of their mutual cooperation in the interests of strengthening competitive positions in relations with the rest of the world, and first of all with the leading industrialised countries.

5 THE FUTURE

The turning point in the Soviet Union in its internal development and in external economic relations makes us think of the course of events in the future. The main reserves for improving the economic situation of the USSR which should be unleashed by *perestroika* are, of course, domestic and primarily in the sphere of politics rather than in the economic sphere. Democratisation of society, emancipation of the people's consciousness, awakening of talents and a moral uplifting of society are capable of giving a strong impetus to further development. The hopes for acceleration of social and economic progress are also associated with importing a more open character to our society and economy in respect of the rest of the world.

The changes observed in politics and in the mechanisms of societal organisation, though in the initial stage and not yet a widespread phenomenon, point to development for the better. This process will apparently take ten to fifteen years and be accompanied by an acute struggle of opinions and conflicts between the old and new modes of action. As regards relations between different social systems, a weakening of many contradictions can be expected here, as well as a greater compatibility of economic interests and approaches. The east–west interaction will hardly be an exception in the process of strengthening interdependence and the interweaving of economic development of the countries of the world.

14 International Consequences of the Economic Reforms in Planned Economies

Marie Lavigne

CENTRE D'ECONOMIE INTERNATIONALE DES
PAYS SOCIALISTES AND UNIVERSITY OF PARIS I,
PANTHEON-SORBONNE, PARIS, FRANCE

1 THREE APPROACHES TO THE SUBJECT

It is very difficult to forecast the consequences of events in the making. Seen from a 'capitalist' point of view, the 'reformed socialist economy' is certainly a puzzling object, to which the classical, or standard, centrally-planned economy might be preferred. On the micro-level, reforms have as a first consequence a disorganising effect. Instead of trading (exceptionally cooperating) with state trading entities (the well-known FTOs, foreign trade organisations), the businessman has now to find his way among all sorts of potential partners who themselves know little about their own rights and about foreign trade in general. On the macro-level, the governments of the reform-ed or reform-ing socialist economies claim to be treated according to the usual practice applying to market economies, and the past (and future) negotiations between the EEC and the eastern European countries are a demonstration of this. When shifting from the strictly economic to the political perspective, there is the feeling that the west 'should' help the east so as to be logical with a past policy which promised more flexibility on the part of the west if only the 'collectivist' regimes were to abandon the principles of directive planning, overwhelming domination of state ownership, and a single-party political system. But how, and to achieve what?

It is generally felt, without knowing how, that the reforms should induce a higher rate of participation in the world economy. If they

283

do, what are the consequences? In this paper I would like to suggest three possible approaches:

1. *The relational, or participative approach*
   This suggests that there is a 'world international system' to which the socialist countries did not belong up to now, or did belong but only marginally. The basic problem is then to include them in the world economy. This in turn raises a number of questions:

(a) How are we to *measure* this process?
(b) What *conditions* might be required for that?
(c) What *advantages* would derive from such an involvement?
(d) Is it possible to expect a greater participation of socialist countries in *international economic organisations*?

2. *The comparative approach*
   This leads to a discussion of the convergence issue. By the way, we should not speak of convergence, because there is no sign of it in the 'capitalist' world. On the contrary, when comparing the present situation with the one existing at the time when Jan Tinbergen launched the concept, we see that market economy regimes are consistently removing what still remains of planning or state regulation. Neither should one speak of 'submergence' as did Grossman debating with Tinbergen. At present the reformed economies are not 'converging' along with capitalist economies towards something common, nor are they submerged by capitalism. They are rather verging on a new system which they call market socialism, without having yet defined it.

3. *The feedback approach*
   This is my paradoxical point. We have always (in the west) assumed that the changes occurring in the socialist economies were bound to affect them more or less strongly, without affecting the west. This applies to the developing as well as the developed economies. But is it really so? If successful, the changes which occur in the socialist 'reformed' world might have some impact on the west as well.

I shall focus on the first approach, although it seems to me that the other two points might be relevant, and I shall revert to them in my conclusion.

2 PARTICIPATION IN THE WORLD ECONOMY

It is commonplace to say that the standard centrally-planned economy behaves in an autarkic way. The 'classics' in this field (Pryor,
1963, Wiles, 1968; Holzman, 1974, 1976, 1986) have evidenced and
analysed that (for the most recent treatment, see Wolf, 1988). For
the sake of brevity, one may use the distinction drawn by Holzman
between block autarky and functional autarky. This allows explanation of how, through the very characteristics of their system, the
CPEs tend both to insulate their economies from the outside world
and, as a regional grouping, to achieve 'trade destruction' in addition
to trade diversion. When it became obvious that the insulation from
international economic disturbances could not be achieved, another
group of analysts explained how the CPEs managed to control (or
not) these adverse effects (Neuberger and Tyson, 1980).

Having during quite a long time strongly opposed this description
of their 'system-autarkic' economies, the economists of the socialist
countries now insist on the need to 'open up' to trade and cooperation with the outside world.

2.1 Analysis of 'Openness', or 'Opening Up'

This is not easy, as acknowledged by Wolf (1988) in terms to which
any of us would be ready to suscribe: 'Because of its hybrid character,
the modified planned economy is much more difficult to 'stylize' than
either the CPE or the market economy' (p. 52).

The 'system-determined' *statistical problems*, as Wolf (1988) calls
them are not so easy to solve. The *participation ratio* measuring the
share of foreign trade in national income (product) is certainly better
approached in a reformed economy (hereafter RE) when there is a
significant exchange rate and better national account statistics. But
new discrepancies emerge because the various REs apply different
methods – and because there remain 'non-REs'! As for the measure
of the 'block autarky' (or, if preferred, of the centrifugal/centripetal
trends within the CMEA) nothing is improved; on the contrary.
When all the CMEA members were standard CPEs there was a
coherent cross-rate rouble:dollar for all the currencies. This might
occur again if and when the CMEA becomes a real 'unified market'.
Right now, I claim that nobody can answer the question: What is the
share of trade conducted within the CMEA in total trade of the
socialist countries? Should anyone here convincingly answer that

question, I would consider it as a great achievement of this conference! Let me just quote my favourite example: in their own calculations, Hungary and GDR make 50 per cent and two-thirds respectively of their foreign trade with other socialist countries. Should Hungary apply the cross-rate rouble:dollar derived from the rates of exchange of the mark and reciprocally, Hungary would be seen as trading for over 70 per cent of its total trade with the socialist countries, and for GDR the ratio would be around 40 per cent.

These are not only technicalities. The difficulties mentioned have an impact on the measurement of Eastern competitivity, a standard, if any, type of indicator in foreign trade theory. Here I refer to an article by Winiecki (1988), which discusses Western measurement methods for assessing competitivity and sorts out the 'methods to be used without, or with only small, modifications' (such as the CMS indicator), from methods which require great caution or are misleading if not outright inadequate.

We are thus left with very simplified indicators which do not show much. Are the REs more open than the standard CPEs? Yes, they have to be just because they are REs, which means that they have a more 'realistic' rate of exchange which immediately makes them *look* more open. Are they competitive? No, they are not: the only meaningful measures revolve around indicators of the CMS type, which show that the eastern European countries are losing ground to the NIEs (newly industrialised economies) on the western developed markets, as Poznanski (1986) has shown.

This leaves us with few conclusions about the ways to increase openness, or to improve competitivity. Moreover, it amounts to considering only part of the international activities of the REs, as openness, in these approaches, makes sense only toward the West, and competitivity is measured only on the western market. True, it is probably impossible to do more, because the REs, as well as the 'non-REs' (a group in which I have to include both GDR and Romania, although for quite different arguments) belong to a 'non-RE' integration grouping. But then it is really dramatic because we leave such a large field aside: could one imagine discussing how the EEC countries participate in the world economy but leaving the EEC itself aside?

2.2 The Conditions to be Met by the REs to be Considered as Fully-fledged Members of the International Economic System

Most of the conditions under discussion have already been set by the various bodies which were entitled to express them. For instance:

- Indicative planning at most, autonomy of decision of firms at the lower level, meaningful prices linked with world prices, meaningful rates of exchange: these are the conditions which Hungary has (successfully) met in negotiating with GATT (1973) and the EEC (1988). (As we know, these conditions were not exactly met in 1973 but the admission to GATT was also a political move; as for the negotiation with the EEC, it was very difficult for Hungary to get rid of the 'reciprocity' argument, according to which a state-trading country has to make 'reciprocal', and not just 'equivalent' concessions in trade negotiations.
- The same as above, plus a meaningful domestic interest rate, allowing the standard package of adjustment measures recommended by the IMF as a condition for loans to work effectively. These were the conditions asked from Romania (1981), Hungary (1982), and later on Poland. The conditions were 'met' in the sense that the adjustment measures were effective (in the case of Romania and Hungary) – but not because market instruments were used; because the central planning methods were put to work, and we know how harshly in the case of Romania.

The west should feel bothered at such a display of 'conditions'. What if the REs 'meet' them indeed? The USSR is acting very cleverly in this sense. A new tariff code is to be introduced and a new tariff to be applied from 1 January 1990. The decree of 2 December 1988, providing for that very candidly states that among other reasons this is done to strengthen 'the basis of the international commercial negotiations, namely with the GATT and the EEC'. Likewise, to counteract the objections according to which the demands of the socialist countries do not always match the competence of the market-economy institutions to which they address themselves, the USSR has carefully studied the Treaty of Rome and has written in a demand for virtually all the areas of competence of the Community.

Moving to a much more political field, what about the CoCom restrictions on exports to the 'communist' countries? What conditions are to be met so that they be eliminated? Should these countries cease to be 'communist' and might this be identified with moves towards a multiparty system? What if some of them move in this direction, and the others not? If CoCom restrictions are justified by the need to reduce the military potential, or to limit the military build-up of these countries, what will happen if disarmament – not to speak of the possible neutralisation of some countries – goes on?

I leave all these points open for discussion. Among the economic issues, there is of course the big question of convertibility. Has the national currency to be convertible so as to facilitate, or determine, a successful participation in the world economic system? I belong to those who consider that internal convertibility (for residents) has indeed to be achieved as soon as possible. As for the external convertibility (for non-residents), it is not such urgent a task, and it is altogether impossible to achieve without a commodity convertibility of the domestic currency.

2.3 The Advantages From a Growing Involvement in the World Economy

The REs' governments, who believe in competition, expect a greater efficiency of their domestic enterprises from the competition with the external world, and also a 'learning' effect which is particularly sought through the operation of joint ventures, special economic zones, etc. They know, of course, that competition from outside is beneficial and effective only when there is competition inside. This has also been discussed here. They have also to get better acquainted with all the non-trade, non-commodity aspects in the operation of the international economic system.

By 'non-trade' aspects or restrictions (which is quite different from the protectionist restrictions in trade) I mean the operation of the multinational enterprises. Should the movement of joint ventures expand, the REs should become more familiar with these practices, which they do not know and which will not be readily disclosed to them by their partners.

By 'non-commodity' aspects I mean the operation of the world financial markets. The socialist countries are not ready to enter that world. The 'financial innovations' now practised (auctions, capital markets, etc.) are fascinating in their developments, but have little to do with what we witness in the 'capitalist' world. I would even say that a standard CPE, with a monobank system and clever, well-trained people having a monopoly access to the foreign currency reserves of the countries, has probably greater opportunities to take advantage of the capitalist financial markets than have the half-decentralised REs. I would stress that since the beginning of the 1980s the usual financial instruments to which the CPEs were accustomed – government-guaranteed loans and eurocurrency bank loans – have shrunk to less than 20 per cent of the capital movements. The CPEs are almost the last borrowers in these forms. They are not, and it is difficult to imagine how they might be, involved in the restructuring of financial instruments which was induced by the soaring Third World debt.

One may ask, in this connexion, whether the reforms are going to have an impact on the management of external debt. They should not add to the creditworthiness of these economies; they might affect it negatively if it felt by the central authorities that borrowing is going out of control. Not a single RE has reached such a degree of decentralisation. As seen from the case of the USSR, the reform process allows a discussion on the amounts and aims of borrowing to develop, which may lead to some uncertainty. If such discussions lead to more rational choices as to objects which should be financed by foreign borrowing, this might be seen as a positive outcome, not yet to be observed.

What about the west? The western businessmen look for markets, and second for profits. They see a contradiction between their drive for markets and the east's desire to increase exports, and they fear the solution lies only in increased compensation deals. This might be avoided by a larger and more successful industrial cooperation (which would also generate profits, if only by reduced transport costs by comparison with Third World ventures). Again we are brought to the joint ventures, not so successful up to now. The USSR seems to head toward an experimental format: to set joint ventures in special zones which would act as laboratories for experimental management or industrial techniques. Hungary has already followed this path. This would mean integrating the conditions of the world economy by first growing them in greenhouses. Again a point for discussion.

2.4 Would the Reforms Allow the REs to Play a More Active Role in International Organisations?

Discussion on GATT or the IMF is clearly a political issue, to be discussed between the USA and the USSR – or else among Western countries, which is not the aim of this paper.

A more relevant topic is the relations between the socialist countries and the EEC. The outcome of the negotiations in progress as well as of the agreements already concluded in 1988 (with Hungary and Czechoslovakia) is certainly crucial, much more than the politically symbolic EEC–CMEA agreement. Here the socialist countries are – rightly – focusing on the elimination of the non-tariff barriers which they hit in their exports to the EEC. They should also follow the negotiations in progress with the Third World, and the fierce conflicts in the Uruguay round (especially for those of them which belong to GATT), because these will determine how their competitors will be treated. As for the consequences of the Single Market: yes, it may have protectionist consequences, but it will also provide a Single market, and here it will be interesting to see how the EEC will tackle the question of the national quotas – a question not yet settled.

I would end this section with pleading the cause of the CMEA. The scepticism which the *perestroika* of the CMEA arouses when mentioned, the powerful centrifugal tendencies expressed in almost all the European CMEA members (for different reasons), seem to me quite worrying from the point of view of a successful openness. I am perfectly aware of all the obstacles to a real change within the CMEA, be it from the point of view of trade arrangements, of price-fixing or of currency mechanisms. But the west should not be so happy in witnessing these centrifugal tendencies. A strong and market-oriented eastern European community would serve the interests of the west more than an ineffective plan-regulated integration falling into pieces. The whole world is now organised in a network of regional integrations, the variety and usefulness of which is not enough called to attention.

3 CONCLUDING REMARKS

A few words on the *comparative approach*. Generally it is discussed in terms of 'plan–market' (as in the present Conference) or of 'state–private ownership' opposition. In a period when everybody (with very few exceptions) believes in the market instruments and (almost) nobody believes in direct planning (another question is how to get rid of it) a field to explore is that of economic policy. I do not believe that in the REs anyone has a clear view of economic policy because to achieve that there would already need to be a market; otherwise economic policy is identified with residual direct planning correcting what goes wrong during the painful process of creating a market (for goods, labour or capital). Also, I would like to draw attention to the concepts of deregulation and privatisation. Deregulation was first mentioned, as far as I know, in a book edited by Zaslavskaia's Institute in Novosibirsk in 1985 (Kutyrev, 1985). I fear that here again, it is confused in the east with 'deplanification'. As for 'privatisation', the reform economists in the socialist countries have a very straightforward view: privatisation is the devolution of state ownership to private owners (leasing included), whereas in the capitalist world, it is something quite different. In the developed market economies, privatisation (apart from its political context, as in Great Britain or France) is essentially a means to get additional finance for the government. In the developing market economies, it amounts to selling national assets to foreign owners from developed countries. This should be borne in mind when discussing 'privatisation' in the socialist countries.

About the *feedback effects*. Is the reform movement in the east to have any impact on the western economies, other than through trade and cooperation flows? Even for the communist parties in the west, Soviet-type socialism, even (or more than ever!) in its reformed format is not seen as a model for domestic political changes, not to speak of the economic field now that inflation and unemployment are a feature of the RE. The same might be said, even more dramatically, for the developing world. It is probably too early to formulate such a question. We all know what a counter-productive centrally-planned economy may be; we have plenty of textbooks for that. We have yet to learn what a workable reformed economy may be. Up to now, it has not solved the problems pertaining to the 'non-market' sector (environmental, social, cultural) much better than the market economies, and sometimes much worse (health). Should it succeed in doing so, the international impact might be great.

References

Holzman, Franklyn D. (1986)   *The Economics of Soviet Bloc Trade and Finance* (Boulder, Col.: Westview Press, Praeger Publishers).
Holzman, Franklyn D. (1974)   *Foreign Trade under Central Planning* (Cambridge, Mass.: Harvard University Press).
Holzman, Franklyn D. (1976)   *International Trade under Communism, Politics and Economics*, (New York: Basic Books).

Kutyrev, B. P. (1985) 'Reglamentatsia i Deglamentatsia v Upravlenii' (Regulation and Deregulation in Management), in Ryvkina, R. V. (ed.), *Puti Sovershenstvovaniia Sotsial'nogo Mekhanizma Razvitiia Sovetskoi Ekonomiki* (Novosibirsk: Institute of Economics and Industrial Organisation, Siberian Branch of the Academy of Sciences) pp. 41–8.

Lavigne, Marie (1986) 'Eastern European Countries and the IMF', in Béla Csikós-Nagy and David G. Young (eds), *East–West Economic Relations in the Changing Global Environment*, Proceeding of an IEA Conference (London: Macmillan) pp. 287–97.

Marer, Paul (1985), *Dollar GNPs and Growth Rates of the USSR and Eastern Europe* (Baltimore and London: The Johns Hopkins Press for the World Bank, 1985).

Neuberger, Egon and Tyson, Laura d'Andrea (eds) (1980) *The Impact of International Economic Disturbances on the Soviet Union and Eastern Europe, Transmission and Response* (New York: Pergamon Press).

Poznanski, Kazimierz (1986) 'Competition Between Eastern Europe and Developing Countries in the Western Market for Manufactured Goods', in Joint Economic Committee, Congress of the United States, *East European Slow Growth in the 1980's*, vol. 2, pp. 62–90.

Pryor, Frederic L. (1963) *The Communist Foreign Trade System* (London, Allen & Unwin).

Wiles, P. (1968) *Communist International Economics* (Oxford, Basil Blackwell).

Winiecki, Wojciech (1988) 'The Applicability of Western Measurement Methods to Assess East European Competitiveness', *Comparative Economic Studies*, 30 (3) (Fall) pp. 33–50.

Wolf, Thomas A. (1988) *Foreign Trade in the Centrally Planned Economy*, International Monetary Fund (Chur, Harwood Academic Publishers).

Comment

John P. Hardt
LIBRARY OF CONGRESS, WASHINGTON, DC, USA

Several observations on *perestroika* as discussed by Academician Bogomolov (*Chapter 13 in this volume*) are in order:

- *Perestroika* is comprehensive and synergistic.
  The political economic costs of transition – the implementation of *perestroika* – are likely to be greater in the short run, the benefits in the longer term.
- Time sequencing to balance the competing requirements of economic efficiency and political acceptability are difficult to programme and assess.

1   *PERESTROIKA*: COMPREHENSIVE AND SYNERGISTIC

Restructuring   Technological restructuring centres around increasing factor productivity and the quality of outputs through the rationalisation of inefficient sectors. In order to achieve economic growth, and particularly growth of hard currency exports, Soviet policymakers must modernise their economies. By focusing investment on increasing both the efficiency and quality of exports, Soviet's limited resources might be put to maximum long-term advantage.

Economic reform   The process of reform, of putting the economy on a basis of objective criteria, involves first the decentralisation of management in the enterprises. Indeed, most economists believe that economic equilibrium can be achieved only through the combined effects of restructuring and reform: the development of market forces through the monetisation and decentralisation of the economy, application of principles of self-management and self financing, and accountability and adherence of western standards of statistical reporting. In addition, high commitment is required to the active implementation of the newly established market principles, with the contingent costs, among others, of bankruptcy and structural or functional unemployment. The decentralisation requires reduction in responsibility and staffing of the central economic bureaucracy and the regional party.

Political reform   Participation and sharing in economic decisions are required so that society's willingness to accept and support changes that may be individually onerous reaches adequate levels. A reconsideration of ideology is essential, especially regarding citizens' rights to ownership of private property and the establishment of independent and cooperative associations for production and consumption and tolerance for unequal income distribution based on productivity.

Renewal   This implies a return to old principles of central strategic or guidance planning without destroying the Leninist or socialist stability. Effective leadership or guidance in implementing and coordinating comprehensive reform is likely to come from the top leadership in the government and party. In the short run, they may be strengthened by a perception that indigenous roots precedent for change are being drawn on and that the success of change does not necessarily assure the 'euthanasia of the ruling class' (the Party *nomenklatura*).

Interdependence   This would involve an effective interrelationship of domestic markets to foreign prices and markets to the comparative advantage of both. The new commercial policy, should include the objectives of increased merchandise trade with the developed west; more balanced hard goods trade with CMEA countries, and more commercial trade – and less aid – to the developing countries. Just as the key to domestic modernisation success centres on production of more goods of world quality, obtaining more hard goods imports may be seen as the key to success in foreign commerce. Many countries have preferred the non-competitive comfort of the CMEA market. As the Soviet Union presses for more hard goods imports this protected enclave may disappear.

2   THE POLITICAL AND ECONOMIC COSTS AND BENEFITS OF TRANSITION

The political and economic costs of transition in order to implement *perestroika* are likely to be high in the short run. Benefits will come in the longer term.

Restructuring   Some initial movement toward the levels of energy, metals and other material input conservation as compared with levels of Western industrial economies as well as improvement in factor productivity would be concrete indicators of success. Increasing hard goods output and export would also be success indicators.

Closing plants and renovating capacity will lead to interruptions in output to be followed only in time by installation and effective operation of new capacity. Workers in the Soviet Union are fearful of unemployment and the prospect of job mobility. In part, this viewpoint has developed as a result of generations of state emphasis on the evils of capitalism, in particular regarding worker unemployment and inflation.

Economic reform   Establishment of a monetary balance strengthening the value of the indigenous currency and some adjustment of relative prices related to world market forces might be early indicators. A credible monetisation basis for assessing bankruptcy would perhaps be another evidence of accomplishment that would yield benefits in economic performance. Publication of statistical measures using internationally accepted methods would constitute a significant indicator of commitment to economic reform.

Decentralised management operating on an effective price system is likely to be effective only after a series of steps involving development of an internal monetary equilibrium with elimination of subsidies, retraining of personnel and development of profits and incomes policy based on newly developed market forces. In the past, consumer goods, including food, transportation, and housing have been heavily subsidised and incomes kept basically even. Establishment of an effective price system and an incomes policy based on market forces would lower standards of living for many and raise it for some – in direct contradiction to long-standing party egalitarian philosophies.

Political reform   Introduction of a competitive electoral process, both within the party and later between the party and outside groups and the establishment of a multi-party government would be considered a further development. Another sign of progress would be a substantial reduction of the number of bureaucrats in ministries, reduced share of those employed to 'direct the economy' by micromanaging the enterprises from the centre instead of working directly in enterprises in industry and on the farm. Effective re-employment of those governmental and party cadres made redundant by diminution of the management role of the central bureaucracy and party units would re-emphasise a governmental move in favour of mobility of labour toward its most efficient market use. Appropriate progressive tax structures would indicate a certain degree of political commitment to reasonable inequality of income distribution.

Failure of the government to win popular support for restructuring, economic reform, and interdependence would further delegitimise the government and increase social unrest and political instability. Popular acceptance and support for government reform policies, however, will require the participation of all of the affected parties (say the whole adult population) to cushion the adverse effects of transition. This could, for example, translate into demands for 'competition in the political sphere' – a direct challenge to the domination or 'leading role' of the party in favour of a multiparty state.

Renewal   Participation of workers, managers and citizens as a whole in the economic and political decision making process might, however, lead to serious setbacks in the development of a rational new economic system. New systems may emerge from the process of democratisation and renewal whereby national and socialist roots which better approximate the diverse histories and interests of various regions other than Great Russia may bring to light many historic sources of friction within the USSR.

Opening up for discussion traumatic political events, such as events of collectivisation and the Great Purges of the 1930s, the Second World War and Soviet interventions abroad, until now either ignored or reinterpreted to suit both Moscow and the indigenous party leadership is very important. Equally important as an indicator of progress is the development of an indigenous model for comprehensive reform responsive to the unique historical roots of each ethnic group and relevant to resource endowments, stages of development, and other differentiation factors.

Interdependence   A positive change is desirable in the level, structure, and quality of exports to the west. Increasing, or at least maintaining, the current market share in the global economy would also suggest substantial positive progress in developing a viable internal and external economic strategy. Penetrating the world market, obtaining market shares and effectively absorbing advanced technology imports will require time, skill and good fortune. Moreover, interdependence implies a decision strongly in favour of acquisition of technology substitutes financed through a certain amount of debt and an opening of the domestic market to an international marketplace of economic production; of economic and political ideas; and of international economic organisations. In order to gain the benefits of interdependence, national entities must be able to give up a certain degree of independence – and, for instance, be willing to accept and respond to shifting trends in the global economy.

3 TIME SEQUENCING OF REFORM TO BALANCE THE COMPETING REQUIREMENTS OF ECONOMIC EFFICIENCY AND POLITICAL ACCEPTABILITY

The integral nature of comprehensive reform provides insights into the potential for future progress: if comprehensive reform is to be successful, all the reforming nation must be committed to full implementation of all components of reform – that is, economic reform cannot be accomplished without political reform. While the early stages of reform will present the greatest chances for systemic breakdown or reform failure, attaining a threshold of reform in each of these components could result in synergistic outcomes, cumulative and reinforcing in either a negative or positive direction. Nikolai Bukharin, the ideologist of Lenin's Party when he wrote the *Economics of Transition* (1920) and as an adversary of Stalin when he argued for a more balanced economic development in 1928, gave some clues on transition.

But, in the main, Mikhail Gorbachev seems to be learning *en route*. The 'debates' centre on the following:

- Quality versus quantity.
- Industrial or agricultural and service sectors first.
- Resource allocation: guns, growth or butter.
- Political economics of price reform.
- Central control and democratic decentralisation.
- Interdependence or modified autarky.

Note

1. These 'debates' are discussed in more detail in Hardt, John P. and Heslin, Sheila, '*Perestroika*: A Sustainable Process for Change', with commentary by Academician Oleg Bogomolov, to appear in *Occasional Papers*, Group of Thirty.

Reference

Bukharin, Nikolai (1920) 'The Economics of the Transition Period' in Tarbuck, K. J. (ed) *The Politics and Economics of the Transition Period* (London: Routledge and Kegan Paul, 1979)

Comment

Hans Schilar
CENTRAL INSTITUTE OF ECONOMIC RESEARCH, GDR
ACADEMY OF SCIENCES, BERLIN, GDR

The question about the international consequences of economic reforms in the socialist countries is apt to stimulate initially the wishful answer that these very reforms might (1) contribute to increasing the economic power of the country concerned, (2) contribute to raising the competitiveness of the national economy in international economic relations and (3) contribute towards heightening economic security in Europe and throughout the world. Undoubtedly, this is not only an ideal answer of the reformers in the socialist countries, but also one by all realistically minded persons in western countries, watching this process with great attention. However, it is at present not yet clearly foreseeable when and to what extent the above mentioned effects will occur. Professors Bogomolov and Lavigne (chapters 13 and 14 in this volume) adopt a different approach to these questions. Bogomolov put the major weight on the problems of development of *perestroika* and derived from it the international consequences. Lavigne revealed the spectrum of the international consequences of economic reforms from a 'capitalist' point of view, as she pointed out. The word 'capitalist' is used with quotation marks. Indeed, a number of consequences of economic reforms are not separate, but common problems of both social systems. To this belongs first of all, as Bogomolov wrote, the process of reduction in atomic and conventional weapons which can release great economic potential.

It is self-evident that the answers given in both papers to the questions asked have frequently turned into questions again. Undoubtedly, this is at present due to the lack of clarity on what a reformed socialist economy should actually look like. Both authors are concerned with the problem of the economic opening up of the socialist countries and, in consequence, with the greater measure of competitiveness required. I support the idea of a greater economic opening of CMEA countries which, however, can be done successfully only on the basis of a greater competitiveness. This idea has already been repeatedly put forward. But greater competitiveness of the socialist countries is not only beneficial for these countries themselves. Lavigne is right in saying that there are 'feedback effects', that is, effects also in the interest of the western countries. But how is it possible to bring about this greater degree of competitiveness?

Clearly, joint ventures and other forms of investment are considered to be substantive roads leading to a definite technological and economic level, and they can actually qualify as such. However, a durable stable solution cannot be brought about from outside, but only from inside. For this reason I would like once again to take up the discussion on the question about the structure and the content of the economic mechanism, complying with modern claims, and to outline briefly my own standpoint.

It will not be difficult for me to understand that excessive centralisation in planning and management has to be eliminated. It is equally easy for me to conceive that the market forces in the socialist economy, which so far have not had any appropriate place, will have to be developed. Therefore I also understand that great expectations must lie with market forces because frustrations exist in the defective functioning of the traditional planned economy. It is *not* imaginable, however, that an economic mechanism can function effectively in the 1990s and beyond if planning, and specifically central planning, are allowed to play only a minor role. In support of the comments on planning made by Z. Sadowski and S. Chakravarty (chapters 4 and 11 in this volume) I would like to reaffirm that any thoughts and reflections on the mode of functioning of market forces in a socialist economy are likely to lead to realistic solutions only in connection with ideas on the role of planning.

Production at the end of the twentieth century is known to push further ahead to the concentration of economic potentials and to perspective planning. Planning to be carried out with a 'societal dimension' will also become a question of survival for the western countries. Thus the transition from the industrial society to the information society is apt to modify the orientation in time. It is therefore required that long-term plans will take the place of short-term profit thinking.

Analyses into the mode of functioning of capitalist groups of companies have shown that long-term research, production and market strategies are pursued which, according to their basic outlines, are often controlled and run across countries and continents. Markets are 'created', which means they are planned. All this is no temporary trend, but a phenomenon originally coupled with the modern forces of production. This means that the multinational combines will be required to pay still greater attention to capital concentration and planning.

A planned economy which is in the process of reform is not allowed of course to bypass the objective processes of the development of productive forces. The indispensable dismantling of overcentralisation cannot be regarded as calling into question the need for centralism in the economy. The same applies (with a different emphasis, however) to the market forces. Their insufficient existence and functioning must not result in an approach that expects total salvation from market forces. No doubt it is a feature of the present international discussion that only little is being said about the quality and the indispensable characteristics of centralism in a modern socialist economy. The definition of the place and function of the market in a socialist economy capable of meeting the present and future social, economic and scientific-technical challenges, is, in my view, feasible and practicable only in connection with a definition of the role and function of planning.

In all probability, the new quality of the economic mechanism has to be seen in the need for the 'coexistence' between central planning and market coordination because neither can alone, or mainly alone, effectively resolve the economic and social problems. And in this context the structure of this relationship appears to be determined by history and time, and is different from country to country.

Lavigne wrote: 'competition from outside is beneficial and effective only when there is competition inside'. Indeed, the creation of real situations of competition in the economy is a decisive problem.

With the establishment of the combines the GDR has created relatively big economic units and has thus promoted the development of sole manufacturers (monopolies) in a certain way (at present in industry there are 126 centrally-run combines with an average number of 20 000 employees per combine). The importance of foreign trade activities of the GDR economy (about half of the national income is affected by foreign trade) is apt to diminish the negative effects of sole manufacturers or monopolies. Most of the combines are faced with international competitive situations due to the high rate of exports. As an example, VEB Kombinat Polygraph 'Werner Lamberz' Leipzig, the sole manufacturer of printing machines, exports to 80 countries. About 50 per cent of the production of the combine is exported to western countries. On account of this continued confrontation with international markets there is the permanent guarantee that the inevitable comparison with economic optimal and maximal parameters is possible. As a matter of fact, the question of the creation of effective competitive conditions cannot be bypassed, but this question need not be answered in any case at a national level.

The new qualities required for the economic mechanism have, in my view, to include the following: an effective relationship and cooperation of centralism and enterprise autonomy; a high flexibility of planning; the orientation towards profit of management and the great independence of enterprises and combines in foreign trade.

In the next few years the comprehensive application of the principle of the self-generation of funds will be in the centre of GDR economic reform. At present there are experiments under way in 16 combines. From 1991 onwards all centrally-run combines of industry and construction will successively be managed according to this principle. With this, an important step is taken in the direction of the strengthening of the economic independence of the economic units. The application of this principle creates new conditions within the entire system of management since value and monetary indicators and parameters will increasingly be shifted into the focus of management. Economic processes of evaluation, notably price formation, are given a key function within the system of economic accountancy. And this all the more since a policy of the enforcement of the principle of self-generation oriented on the principle of performance will make it necessary that the funds generated by combines and enterprises are an expression of the achievements that are actually reached. This approach to price formation will primarily require more intensive consideration than so far the benefits enjoyed by the user of the product. The greater independence achieved due to the mode of functioning of self-generation is also bound to be coupled with changes in the system of planning and balancing.

At the end of her paper Lavigne dealt with the political, ideological and social effects caused by the reform movement in the east European countries and affecting the western world. Inflation, unemployment and social polarisation together with uncertainty are presently phenomena in several socialist countries which are on the road to reform. Conceivably, this should not have the effect of a model, neither in the east, nor in the west. Of course, these are phenomena resulting from a definite logic of economic reform. Without claiming that economic reforms can be carried out without any negative social consequences, I nevertheless think that in the first place the social sphere has to put restrictions on the concept of economic reforms. This was and is still one of foremost requirements for reforms in the GDR which safeguard the employment, social security and stability of prices for products of basic needs, tariffs and rents.

Index of Names

Subject Index